Notebooks in Cultural Analysis

/)

Notebooks in Cultural Analysis

An Annual Review

Norman F. Cantor, Editor
Nathalia King, Managing Editor

Advisory Editors: Harold Bloom, Bruce Mazlish, Robert Wohl

Duke University Press   Durham 1984

Notebooks in Cultural Analysis is published by Duke University Press.
It is available for sale in both hard cover (ISBN 0-8223-0617-4)
and paperback (ISBN 0-8223-0618-2). All orders and business
correspondence should be addressed to Duke University Press, 6697
College Station, Durham, North Carolina 27708.

Notebooks is edited at the Institute for Cultural Analysis, New York
University. All manuscripts should be addressed to Nathalia King,
Institute for Cultural Analysis, 113 University Place, New York, New
York 10003.

Contents

Introduction

Coming across the title of this review for the first time, many people have asked what was meant by "cultural analysis." To some those words seemed to imply the study of faraway cultures or distant times: topics that might be written about objectively, without reference to the self. A notebook, however, is designed for those who write as much about themselves as about the texts or cultures through which they make their ways. A notebook provides a record of observations, associations, and ideas that manifest themselves in a recognizable relation to the experience of passing time; it documents the many juxtapositions of the self with the other. This concept has facilitated the design of a book which, in spite of the variety of cultural texts under analysis, and unlike other journals, is intended to be read as a whole. Each essay offers an interpretation of the mutual influence between pattern and matter, a relation inherent to culture from its beginnings in the tilling of soil. But the further work of cultural analysis, that of recognizing the unwritten patterns in these pages, is left up to the reader.

Those following the vigorous debate of basic ideas and values in the humanities and the human sciences will acknowledge that it has made disciplinary boundaries increasingly less compelling. Contemporary intellectual thought has focused on issues that both confront and bridge the traditional isolation of the various academic fields. This publication provides a forum for the interdisciplinary discussion of those issues: origin, nomination, and representation; the role of the intellectual; the authority of discourse, whether fact or fiction.

This first volume also contains a theme somewhat less familiar but one which stands in an interesting relation to cultural analysis. It is that of cannibalism. The New Testament is seen to subsume the Old; Queen Gormlaith involuntarily partakes of one of her husbands; the French *physiologistes* have an awesome appetite for individuals. And there is the presence of Montaigne's essay on the subject, an essay in which he writes:

> I have a song composed by a prisoner which contains this challenge, that they should all come boldly and gather to dine off him, for they will be eating at the same time their own fathers and grandfathers, who have served to feed and nourish his body. 'These muscles,' he says, 'this flesh and these veins are your own, poor fools that you are. You do not recognize that the substance of your ancestors' limbs is still contained in them. Savor them well; you will find in them the taste of your own flesh.' An idea that certainly does not smack of barbarity.[1]

Both the prisoner's challenge and Montaigne's final comment seem appropriate to what follows.

Norman Cantor and Nathalia King

Notes

1. *Montaigne's Essays and Selected Writings*, trans. and ed. Donald M. Frame (New York: St. Martin's Press, 1963), p. 111.

Notebooks in Cultural Analysis

"Before Moses Was, I Am": The Original and the Belated Testaments / *Harold Bloom*

> " 'Your father Abraham rejoiced that he was to see my day; he saw it and was glad.' The Jews then said to him, 'You are not yet fifty years old, and have you seen Abraham?' Jesus said to them, 'Truly, truly, I say to you, before Abraham was, I am.' " (John 8:56–58)

This exchange from The Gospel According to St. John will be my text. In the Christian triumph over the Hebrew Bible, a triumph which produced that captive work, the Old Testament, there is no more heroic stroke than the transumptive trope of John's Jesus: "Before Abraham was, I am." Too much is carried by that figuration for any range of readings to convey, but one reading I shall give is the implied substitution: "Before Moses was, I am." To my reading, the author of the Gospel of John was and is a more dangerous enemy of the Hebrew Bible than even Paul, his nearest rival. But I can hardly go on until I explain what I intend to mean by "an enemy of the Hebrew Bible."

It is now altogether too late in Western history for pious or humane self-deceptions on the matter of the Christian appropriation of the Hebrew Bible. It is certainly much too late in Jewish history to be other than totally clear about the nature and effect of that Christian act of total usurpation. The best preliminary description I have found is by Jaroslav Pelikan:

> What the Christian tradition had done was to take over the Jewish Scriptures as its own, so that Justin could say to Trypho that the passages about Christ "are contained in your Scriptures, or rather not yours, but ours." As a matter of fact, some of the passages were contained only in "ours," that is, in the Christian Old Testament. So assured were Christian theologians in their possession of the Scriptures that they could accuse the Jews not merely of misunderstanding and misinterpreting them, but even of falsifying scriptural texts. When they were aware of differences between the Hebrew text of the Old Testament and the Septuagint, they capitalized on these to prove their accusation. . . . The growing ease with which appropriations and accusations alike could be made was in proportion to the completeness of the Christian victory over Jewish thought.
>
> Yet that victory was achieved largely by default. Not the superior force of Christian exegesis or learning or logic but the movement of Jewish history seems to have been largely responsible for it.

Pelikan's dispassionate judgment on this matter is beyond disputation. Though the Christians were to "save" the Old Testament from those like Marcion who would cast it out completely, that is precisely what they saved—*their* Old Testament. The New Testament is to a considerable extent a reading of that Old Testament and I would judge it a very mixed reading indeed. Some of it is a strong misreading, and much of it is a weak misreading, but I will concern myself here entirely with strong misreadings because only strong misreadings work so as to establish lasting enmities between texts. The author of the Gospel of John is an even stronger misreader than St. Paul, and I want to compare John's and Paul's strengths of what I call poetic misprision before I center upon John. But before commencing, I had better declare my own stance.

"Who is the interpreter, and what power does he seek to gain over the text?" That Nietzschean question haunts me always. I am an enemy of the New Testament. My enmity is lifelong and intensifies as I study its text more closely. But I have no right to assert that my own enmity carries the force of the normative Jewish tradition because I am not a representative of that tradition. From a normative Jewish perspective, let us say from the stance of the great Akiba, I am one of the *minim*, the Jewish Gnostic heretics. My own reading of the Hebrew Bible, even if I develop it into a strong misreading, is as unacceptable in its way to the normative tradition as all Christian readings necessarily are. I state this not to posture, but to make clear that I do not pretend to the authority of the normative tradition. In my view, the Judaism that moves in a continuous line from the Academy of Ezra through the Pharisees and on to the religion of my own parents is itself a very powerful misreading of the Hebrew Bible and so of the religion of the Yahwist, whatever we might take that religion to have been. But my subject here is not the text of the Yahwist.

What kind of authority can a literary critic, whose subject is the secular literature of the English language, bring to a reading of the New Testament, particularly to a reading that sees the New Testament as a text in conflict and confrontation with the Hebrew Bible? I cannot speak for other literary critics, as here too I am a sect or party of one, and have no authority other than whatever my ideas and my writings can assert for me. But the central concern of my own literary theory and *praxis*, for some fifteen years now, has been the crisis of confrontation and conflict between what I have called strong poems, or strong texts. I cannot say that my formulations in this area have met with a very amiable reception, even in the most secular of contexts, and so I do not expect an amiable response as I cross the line into the conflict of scriptures. Still, I have learned a great deal from the response to my work, a response that necessarily has become part of my subject. One lesson has been that there are no purely secular texts, because canonization of poems by the secular academies is not merely a displaced version of Jewish or Christian or Moslem canonization. It is precisely the thing itself, the investment of a text with unity, presence, form, and meaning, followed by the insistence that the canonized text possesses these attributes immutably, quite apart from the interpretive activities of the academies.

If so many partisans of Wordsworth or Whitman or Stevens find the offense of my work unbearable, then clearly I must expect a yet more pained response from the various custodians of the Hebrew Bible or the New Testament. I won't take more space here for unhappy anticipation or personal defense, yet I do want to make the modest observation that several years spent intensely in reading as widely as I can in biblical scholarship have not left me with the impression that much authentic *literary* criticism of biblical texts has been written. To make a clean sweep of it, little seems to me to have been added by recent overt intercessions by literary critics, culminating in Northrop Frye's *The Great Code*, a work in which the triumph of the New Testament over the Hebrew Bible is quite flatly complete. Frye's code, like Erich Auerbach's *figura*, which I have attacked elsewhere, is only another belated repetition of the Christian appropriation and usurpation of the Hebrew Bible.

But these matters I will argue elsewhere. I come back again to the grand proclamation of John's Jesus: "Before Abraham was, I am." What can an antithetical literary criticism (as I call my work) do with the sublime force of that assertion? Or how should that force be described? Is it not the New Testament's antithetical reply to one of the Hebrew Bible's most sublime moments, when Moses agonizingly stammers: "If I come to the people of Israel and say to them, 'The God of your fathers has sent me to you,' and they ask me, 'What is his name?' what shall I say to them?" God said to Moses, "I AM WHO I AM." This is the Revised Standard Version, and like every other version, it cannot handle Yahweh's awesome, untranslatable play upon his own name: *ehyeh asher ehyeh*. I expand upon a suggestion of Martin Buber's when I render this as "I will be present wherever and whenever I will be present." For that is the Hebrew Bible's vision of *olam* as "a time without boundaries," and of the relation of Yahweh to a dynamics of time that transcends spatial limitations.

The Hebrew vision of God certainly would seem to center with a peculiar intensity upon the text of Exodus 3:13–14. But the entire history of ancient Jewish exegesis hardly would lead anyone to believe that this crucial passage was of the slightest interest or importance to any of the great rabbinical commentators. The *Exodus Rabbah* offers mostly midrashim connecting the name of God to his potencies which would deliver Israel from Egypt. But *ehyeh asher ehyeh* as a phrase evidently did not have peculiar force for the great Pharisees. Indeed Jewish tradition does very little with the majestic proclamation until Maimonides gets to work upon it in *The Guide for the Perplexed*. One of my favorite books, Marmorstein's fascinating *The Old Rabbinic Doctrine of God*, has absolutely not a single reference to Exodus 3 in its exhaustive one-hundred-fifty-page section on "The Names of God." Either we must conclude that *ehyeh asher ehyeh* has very little significance for Akiba and his colleagues, which I think probably was the case, or we must resort to dubious theories of taboo, which have little to do with the strength of Akiba.

This puzzle becomes greater when the early rabbinical indifference to the striking *ehyeh asher ehyeh* text is contrasted to the Christian obsession with Exodus 3, which begins in the New Testament and becomes overwhelming in the Church Fathers, culminating in Augustine's endless preoccupation with that passage, since for Augustine it was the deepest clue to the metaphysical essence of God. Brevard Childs, in his commentary on Exodus, has outlined the history of this long episode in Christian exegesis. Respectfully, I dissent from his judgment that the ontological aspects of Christian interpretation here really do have any continuity whatsoever either with the biblical text or with rabbinical traditions. These "ontological overtones," as Childs himself has to note, stem rather from the Septuagint's rendering of *ehyeh asher ehyeh* as the very different ἐγώ εἰμι ὁ ὤν and from Philo's very Platonized paraphrase in his *Life of Moses*: "Tell them that I am He Who is, that they may learn the difference between what is and what is not." Though Childs insists that this cannot be dismissed as Greek thinking, it is nothing but that, and explains again why Philo was so crucial for Christian theology and so totally irrelevant to the continuity of normative Judaism.

The continued puzzle, then, is the total lack of early rabbinical interest in the *ehyeh asher ehyeh* text. I labor this point because I read John's greatest subversion of the Hebrew Bible as what I call his transumption of Yahweh's words to Moses in the extraordinary outburst of John's Jesus, "Before Abraham was, I am," which most deeply proclaims: "Before Moses was, I am." To me, this is the acutest manifestation of John's palpable ambivalence toward Moses, an ambivalence whose most perceptive student has been Wayne Meeks. John plays on and against the grand word-play on Yahweh and *ehyeh*. However when I assert even that, I go against the authority of the leading current scholarly commentary upon the Fourth Gospel, and so I must deal with this difficulty before I return to the Johannic ambivalence toward the Moses traditions. And only after examining John's agon with Moses will I feel free to speculate upon the early rabbinic indifference to God's substitution of *ehyeh asher ehyeh* for his proper name.

Both B. Lindars and C. K. Barrett in their standard commentaries on John insist that "Before Abraham was, I am" makes no allusion whatsoever to "I am that I am." A literary critic must begin by observing that New Testament scholarship manifests a very impoverished notion as to just what literary allusion is or can be. But then here is Barrett's flat reading of this assertion of Jesus: "The meaning here is: Before Abraham came into being, I eternally was, as now I am, and ever continue to be." Perhaps I should not chide devoted scholars like Lindars and Barrett for being inadequate interpreters of so extraordinary a trope, because the master interpreter of John, Rudolf Bultmann, seems to me even less capable of handling trope. Here is his reading of John 8:57–58:

> The Jews remain caught in the trammels of their own thought. How can Jesus, who is not yet 50 years old, have seen Abraham! Yet the world's conception of time and age is worthless, when it has to deal with God's revelation, as is its conception of life and death. "Before Abraham was, I am." The Revealer, unlike Abraham, does not belong to the ranks of historical personages. The ἐγώ which Jesus speaks as the Revealer is the "I" of the eternal Logos, which was in the beginning, the "I" of the eternal God himself. Yet the Jews cannot comprehend that the ἐγώ of eternity is to be heard in

an historical person, who is not yet 50 years old, who as a man is one of their equals, whose mother and father they knew. They cannot understand, because the notion of the Revealer's "pre-existence" can only be understood in faith.

In a note, Bultmann too denies any allusion to the "I am that I am" declaration of Yahweh. I find it ironical, nearly two thousand years after St. Paul accused the Jews of being literalizers, that the leading scholars of Christianity are hopeless literalizers, which of course the great rabbis never were. I cannot conceive of a weaker misreading of "Before Abraham was, I am" than Bultmann's retreat into "faith," a "faith" in the "pre-existence" of Jesus. If that is all John meant, then John was a weak poet indeed. But John is at his best here, and at his best he is a strong misreader and thus a strong writer. As for Bultmann's polemical point, I am content to repeat a few amiable remarks made by Rabbi David Kimhi almost eight hundred years ago:

> Tell them that there can be no father and son in the Divinity, for the Divinity is indivisible and is one in every aspect of unity unlike matter which is divisible.
> Tell them further that a father precedes a son in time and a son is born through the agency of a father. Now even though each of the terms "father" and "son" implies the other . . . he who is called the father must undoubtedly be prior in time. Therefore, with reference to this God whom you call Father, Son, and Holy Spirit, that part which you call Father must be prior to that which you call Son, for if they were always coexistent, they would have to be called twin brothers.

I have cited this partly because I enjoy it so much, but also because it raises the true issue between Moses and John, between Abraham and Jesus, which is the agonistic triple issue of priority, authority, and originality. As I read John's trope, it asserts not only the priority of Jesus over Abraham (and so necessarily over Moses), but also the priority, authority, and originality of John over Moses, or as we would say, of John as writer over the Yahwist and his revisionists as writers. That is where I am heading this account of the agon between the Yahwist and John, and so I turn now to some general observations upon the Fourth Gospel—observations by a literary critic, of course, and not by a qualified New Testament believer and/or scholar.

John's Gospel seems to me the most anxious in tone of all the gospels. Its anxiety is as much what I would call a literary anxiety as an existential or spiritual one. One sign of this anxiety is the palpable difference between the attitude of Jesus toward himself in the Fourth Gospel as compared to the other three. Scholarly consensus holds that John was written at the close of the first century, and so after the Synoptic Gospels. A century is certainly enough time for apocalyptic hope to have ebbed away and for an acute sense of belatedness to have developed in its place. John's Jesus has a certain obsession with his own glory and particularly with what that glory ought to be in a Jewish context. Rather like the Jesus of Gnosticism, John's Jesus is much given to saying "I am," and there are Gnostic touches throughout John, though their extent is disputable. Perhaps, as some scholars have surmised, there is an earlier, more Gnostic gospel buried in the Gospel of John. An interesting article by John Meagher of Toronto, back in 1969, even suggested that the original reading of John 1:14 was "And the Word became *pneuma* and dwelt among us," which is a Gnostic formulation, yet curiously more in the spirit and tone of much of the Fourth Gospel than is "And the Word became flesh."

The plain nastiness of the Gospel of John toward the Pharisees is in the end an anxiety as to the spiritual authority of the Pharisees and it may be augmented by John's Gnostic overtones. A Jewish reader with even the slightest sense of Jewish history feels threatened when reading John 18:28–19:16. I do not think that this feeling has anything to do with the supposed pathos or problematic literary power of the text. There is a peculiar wrongness about John's Jesus saying, "If my kingship were of this world, my servants would fight, that I might not be handed over to the Jews" (18:36); it implies that Jesus is no longer a Jew, but something else. This unhappy touch is another sign of the pervasive rhetoric of anxiety in the Fourth Gospel. John's vision seems to be of a small group—his own, presumably —which finds its analogue and asserted origin in the group around Jesus two generations before. In the general judgment of scholars, the original conclusion of the gospel was the parable of doubting Thomas, a manifest trope for a sect or coven undergoing a crisis of faith.

It is within that anxiety of frustrated expectations, perhaps even of recent expulsion from the Jewish world, that John's agon with Moses finds its context. Wayne Meeks has written very sensitively of the Fourth Gospel's ambivalence toward the Moses traditions, particularly those centered upon the image of Moses as prophet-king, a unique amalgam of the two roles that John seeks to extend and surpass in Jesus. My interest in John's handling of Moses is necessarily different in emphasis, for I am going to read a number of John's namings of Moses as being tropes more for the text than for the supposed substance of what the New Testament (following the Septuagint) insists upon calling the Law. I myself will call it not Torah, but ultimately J or the Yahwist, because that is where I locate the agon. Not theology, not faith, not truth is the issue, but literary power, the scandalous power of J's text, which by synecdoche stands for the Hebrew Bible as the strongest poem that I have ever read in any language I am able to read. John, and Paul before him, took on an impossible precursor and rival, and their apparent victory is merely an illusion. The aesthetic dignity of the Hebrew Bible, and of the Yahwist in particular as its uncanny original, is simply beyond the competitive range of the New Testament as a literary achievement, as it is beyond the range of the only surviving Gnostic texts that have any aesthetic value—a few fragments of Valentinus and the Gospel of Truth that Valentinus may have written. But I will return at the end of this discourse to the issue of rival aesthetic achievements. John's struggle with Moses is at last my direct concern.

There are so many contests with Moses throughout the New Testament that I cannot contrast John in this regard to all of the other texts, but I do want to compare him briefly with Paul, if only because I intend later to consider some aspects of Paul's own struggle with the Hebrew Bible. I think there is still nothing so pungent in all commentary upon Paul as the remarks made by Nietzsche in 1888, in *The Antichrist*:

> Paul is the incarnation of a type which is the reverse of that of the Savior; he is the genius in hatred, in the standpoint of hatred, and in the relentless logic of hatred. . . . What he wanted was power; with St. Paul the priest again aspired to power,—he could make use only of concepts, doctrines, symbols with which masses may be tyrannised over, and with which herds are formed.

Of course Nietzsche is extreme, but can he be refuted? Paul is so careless, hasty, and inattentive a reader of the Hebrew Bible that he very rarely gets any text right; in so gifted a person this kind of weak misunderstanding can come only from the dialectics of the power drive, of the will to power over a text, even when the text is as formidable as Torah. There is little agonistic cunning in Paul's misreadings of Torah; many indeed are plain howlers. The most celebrated is his weird exegesis of Exodus 34:29–35, where the text has Moses descending from Sinai, tablets in hand, his face shining with God's glory—a glory so great that Moses must veil his countenance after speaking to the people, and then unveil only when he returns to speak with God. Normative Jewish interpretation, surely known to Paul, was that the shining was the Torah restoration of the *zelem*, the true image of God that Adam had lost, and that the shining prevailed until the death of Moses. But here is II Corinthians 3:12–13:

> Since we have such a hope, we are very bold, not like Moses, who put a veil over his face so that the Israelites might not see the end of the fading splendor.

There isn't any way to save this, even by gently calling it a "parody" of the Hebrew text, as Wayne Meeks does. It isn't a transumption or lie against time, which is the Johannine mode; it is just a plain lie against the text. Nor is it uncharacteristic of Paul. Meeks very movingly calls Paul "the Christian Proteus," and Paul is certainly beyond my understanding. Proteus is an apt model for many other roles, but perhaps not for an interpreter of Mosaic text. Paul's reading of what he thought was the Law increasingly seems to me oddly Freudian, in that Paul identifies the Law with the human drive that Freud wanted to call Thanatos. Paul's peculiar confounding of the Law and death presumably keeps him from seeing Jesus as a transcending fulfillment of Moses. Instead, Paul contrasts himself to Moses, hardly to his own disadvantage. Thus, Romans 9:3:

> For I could wish that I myself were accursed and cut off from Christ for the sake of my brethren, my kinsmen by race.

It may seem at first an outburst of Jewish pride, of which I would grant the protean Paul an authentic share, but the Mosaic allusion changes its nature. All exegetes point to Exodus 32:32 as the precursor text. Moses offers himself to Yahweh as atonement for the people after the orgy of the golden calf: "But now, if thou wilt forgive their sin—and if not, blot me, I pray thee, out of thy book which thou hast written." How do the two offers of intercession compare? After all, the people *have* sinned, and Moses would choose oblivion to save them from the consequences of their disloyalty. The allusive force of Paul's offer is turned against both his own Jewish contemporaries and even against Moses himself. Even the Pharisees (for whom Paul, unlike John, has a lingering regard) are worshippers of the golden calf of death, since the Law *is* death. And all Moses supposedly offered was the loss of his own prophetic greatness, his place in the salvation history. But Paul, out of supposed love for his fellow Jews, offers to lose more than Moses did, because he insists he has more to lose. To be cut off from Christ is to die eternally, a greater sacrifice than the Mosaic offer to be as one who had never lived. This is what I would call the daemonic counter-Sublime of hyperbole, and its repressive force is enormous and very revelatory.

But I return again to John, whose revisionary warfare against Moses is subtler. Meeks has traced the general pattern, and so I follow him here, though of course he would dissent from the interpretation I am going to offer of this pattern of allusion. The allusions begin with John the Baptist chanting a typical Johannine metalepsis, in which the latecomer truly has priority ("John bore witness to him, and cried, 'This was he of whom I said: He who comes after me ranks before me, for he was before me'"), to which the author of the Fourth Gospel adds: "For the law was given through Moses; grace and truth came through Jesus Christ" (John 1:15, 17). Later, the first chapter proclaims: "We have found him of whom Moses in the law and also the prophets wrote, Jesus of Nazareth" (1:45). The third chapter daringly inverts a great Mosaic trope in a way still unnerving for any Jewish reader: "No one has ascended into heaven but he who descended from heaven, the Son of man. And as Moses lifted up the serpent in the wilderness, so must the Son of man be lifted up" (3:13–14). John's undoubted revisionary genius is very impressive here merely from a technical or rhetorical point of view. No heavenly revelations ever were made to Moses, whose function is reduced to a synecdoche, and indeed to its lesser half. To use one of my revisionary ratios, Jesus on the cross will be the *tessera* or antithetical completion of the Mosaic raising of the brazen serpent in the wilderness. Moses was only a part, but Jesus is the fulfilling whole. My avoidance of the language of typology, here and elsewhere, is quite deliberate and will be defended in my conclusion, where I will say a few unkind words about the Christian and now Auerbachian trope of *figura*.

The same ratio of antithetical completion is invoked when Jesus announces himself as the fulfiller of the sign of manna, as would be expected of the Messiah. But here the gratuitous ambivalence toward Moses is sharper: "Truly, truly, I say to you, it was not Moses who gave you the bread from heaven; my Father gives you the true bread from heaven. For the bread of God is that which comes down from heaven, and gives life to the world" (6:32–33). As the trope is developed, it becomes deliberately so shocking in a Jewish context that even the disciples are shocked, but I would point to one moment in the development as marking John's increasing violence against Moses and all the Jews: "Your fathers ate the manna in the wilderness, and they died. . . . I am the living bread . . . if any one eats of this bread, he will live for ever; and the bread which I shall give for the life of the world is my flesh" (6:49, 51). It is, after all, gratuitous to say that our fathers ate the manna and died; it is even misleading, since had they not eaten the manna, they would not have lived as long as they did. But John has modulated to a daemonic counter-Sublime and his hyperbole helps to establish a new, Christian sublimity in which Jews die and Christians live eternally.

Rather than multiply instances of John's revisionism, I want to conclude my specific remarks on the Fourth Gospel by examining in its full context the passage with which I began: "Before Abraham was, I am." I am more than a little unhappy with the sequence I will expound, because I find in it John at nearly his most unpleasant and indeed anti-Jewish, but the remarkable rhetorical strength of "Before Abraham was, I am" largely depends upon its contextualization, as John undoes the Jewish pride in being descended from Abraham. The sequence, extending through most of the eighth chapter, begins with Jesus sitting in the temple, surrounded both by Pharisees and by Jews who are in the process of becoming his believers. To those he has begun to persuade, Jesus now says what is certain to turn them away:

"If you continue in my word, you are truly my disciples, and you will know the truth, and the truth will make you free." They answered him, "We are descendants of Abraham, and have never been in bondage to any one. How is it that you say, 'You will be made free'?" (8:31–32)

It seems rather rhetorically weak that Jesus should then become aggressive, with a leap into murderous insinuations:

"I know that you are descendants of Abraham; yet you seek to kill me, because my word finds no place in you. I speak of what I have seen with my Father, and you do what you have heard from your father." (8:37–38)

As John's Jesus graciously is about to tell them, the Jews' father is the devil. They scarcely can be blamed for answering, "Abraham is our father," or for assuming that their accuser has a demon. I look at the foot of the page of the text I am using, *The New Oxford Annotated Bible, Revised Standard Version* (1977), and next to verse 48, on having a demon, the editors helpfully tell me, "*The Jews* turn to insult and calumny" (p. 1300). I reflect upon how wonderful a discipline such scholarship is and I mildly rejoin that by any dispassionate reading John's Jesus has made the initial "turn to insult and calumny." What matter, since the Jews are falling neatly into John's rhetorical trap? Jesus has promised that his believers "will never see death" and the astonished children of Abraham (or is it children of the devil?) protest:

"Abraham died, as did the prophets; and you say, 'If any one keeps my word, he will never taste death.' Are you greater than our father Abraham, who died?" (8:52–53)

Jesus responds by calling them liars, again surely rather gratuitously, and then by ensnaring them in John's subtlest tropological entrapment, which will bring me full circle to where I began:

> "Your father Abraham rejoiced that he was to see my day; he saw it and was glad." The Jews then said to him, "You are not yet fifty years old, and have you seen Abraham?" Jesus said to them, "Truly, truly, I say to you, before Abraham was, I am." (8:57–58)

It is certainly the most remarkable transumption in the New Testament, though I had better explain what I mean by transumption, which is a little exhausting for me, since I have been explaining the term endlessly in eight books published over the last nine years. Very briefly, transumption or metalepsis is the traditional term in rhetoric for the trope that works to make the late seem early and the early seem late. It lies against time, so as to accomplish what Nietzsche called the will's revenge against time, and against time's assertion, "It was." Uniquely among figures of speech, transumption works to undo or to reverse anterior tropes. It is therefore the particular figure that governs what we might call "interpretive allusion." Ultimately, it seeks to end-stop allusiveness by presenting its own formulation as the last word, which insists upon an ellipsis rather than a proliferation of further allusion.

When John's Jesus says, "Before Abraham was, I am," the ultimate allusion is not to Abraham but to Moses and to Yahweh's declaration made to Moses, "I am that I am." The transumption leaps over Abraham by saying also, "Before Moses was, I am," and by hinting ultimately: "I am that I am"—because I am one with my father Yahweh. The ambivalence and agonistic intensity of the Fourth Gospel achieves an apotheosis with this sublime introjection of Yahweh, which is simultaneously a projection or repudiation of Abraham and Moses. I am aware that I seem to be making John into a Gnostic Christian, but that is the transumptive force of his rhetoric, as opposed perhaps to his more overt dialectic. His Gospel, as it develops, does seem to me to become as Gnostic as it is Christian, and this is the kind of Gnosticism that indeed was a kind of intellectual or spiritual anti-Semitism. Obviously I believe that there are Gnosticisms and Gnosticisms, and some I find considerably more attractive than others. Just as obviously, the Gnostic elements in John, and even in St. Paul, seem to me very shadowed indeed.

Earlier in this discourse, I confessed my surprise at the normative rabbinical indifference, in ancient days, to Yahweh's sublime declaration, *ehyeh asher ehyeh*. If the great Rabbi Akiba ever speculated about that enigmatic phrase, he kept it to himself. I doubt that he made any such speculations, because I do not think that fearless sage was in the habit of hoarding them and I am not enough of a Kabbalist to think that Akiba harbored forbidden or esoteric knowledge. To the normative mind of the Judaism roughly contemporary with Jesus, there was evidently nothing remarkable in Yahweh's declining to give his name, and instead almost playfully asserting: "Tell them that I who will be when and where I will be am the one who has sent you." That is how Yahweh talked and how he was. But to the belated author of the Fourth Gospel, as to all our belated selves, "I am that I am" was and is a kind of *mysterium tremendum*, to use Rudolf Otto's language. That mystery John sought to transcend and transume with the formulation, "Before Abraham was, I am." Prior to the text of Exodus was the text that John was writing, in which the Jews were to be swept away into the universe of death, while Jesus led John on to the universe of life.

This transformation is an instance of just how the New Testament reduced the Hebrew Bible to that captive work, the Old Testament. Though the reduction is necessarily of great theological influence, it of course does not touch the Hebrew Bible. I have read the Hebrew Bible since I was a child and the New Testament since I first took a course in New Testament Greek as an undergraduate. Clearly I am not a dispassionate reader of the New Testament, though I do not read the Hebrew Bible as the normative Jewish tradition has read it, either. I come back to the issue of the interpreter's authority. When I read, I read as a literary critic, but my concerns have little in common with those of any other contemporary critic. Idealizations of any text, however canonical, or of the reading process itself are not much to my taste. Emerson said he read for the lustres. I follow him, but emphasize even more that the lustres arise out of strife, competition, defense, anxiety, and the author's constant need for survival *as an author*. I don't see how any authentic literary critic could judge John as anything better than a very flawed revisionist of the Yahwist, and Paul as something less than that, despite the peculiar pathos of his protean personality. In the aesthetic warfare between the Hebrew Bible and the New Testament, there is just no contest, and if you think otherwise, then bless you.

But surely the issue is not aesthetic, I will be reminded. Well, we are all trapped in history, and the historical triumph of Christianity is brute fact. I am not moved to say anything about it. But I am moved to reject the idealized modes of interpretation it has stimulated, from early typology on to the revival of *figura* by Erich Auerbach and the Blakean *Great Code* of Northrop Frye. No text, secular or religious, fulfills another text and all who insist otherwise merely homogenize literature. As for the relevance of the aesthetic to the issue of the conflict between sacred texts, I doubt finally that much else is relevant to a strong reader who is not dominated by extraliterary persuasions or convictions. Reading *The Book of Mormon*, for instance, is a difficult aesthetic experience and I would grant that not much in the New Testament subjects me to rigors of quite that range. But then John and Paul do not ask to be read against *The Book of Mormon*.

Can the New Testament be read as less polemically and destructively revisionary of the Hebrew Bible than it actually is? Not by me, anyway. But don't be too quick to shrug off a reading informed by an awareness of the ways of the antithetical, of the revisionary strategies devised by those latecomers who seek strength and who will sacrifice truth to get strength even as they proclaim the incarnation of the truth beyond death. Nietzsche is hardly the favorite sage of contemporary New Testament scholars, but perhaps he still has something vital to teach them.

What do Jews and Christians gain by refusing to see that the revisionary desperation of the New Testament has made it permanently impossible to identify the Hebrew Bible with the Christian Old Testament? Doubtless there are social and political benefits in idealizations of "dialogue," but there is nothing more. It is not a contribution to the life of the spirit or the intellect to tell lies to one another or to oneself in order to bring about more affection or cooperation between Christians and Jews. Paul is hopelessly equivocal on nearly every subject, but to my reading he is clearly not a Jewish anti-Semite; yet his misrepresentation of Torah was absolute. John is evidently a Jewish anti-Semite and the Fourth Gospel is pragmatically murderous as an anti-Jewish text. Yet it is theologically and emotionally central to Christianity. I give the last word to the sage called Radak in Jewish tradition, that David Kimhi whom I cited earlier. He quotes as proof-text Ezekiel 16:53: "I will turn their captivity, the captivity of Sodom and her daughters." And then Radak comments, rightly dismissing from his perspective all Christians as mere heretics from Judaism: "This verse is a reply to the Christian heretics who say that the future consolations have already been fulfilled. *Sodom is still overturned as it was and is still unsettled.*"

Anthropological Tales: Unprofessional Thoughts on the Mead/Freeman Controversy / *Dennis Porter*

Well into the eighteenth century there was in Europe a flourishing minor genre of fictitious travel literature that fed reader fantasy by purporting to offer authentic accounts of voyages to remote parts of the globe. It flourished alongside that more venerable tradition of consciously literary accounts of distant places which, from Thomas More to Jonathan Swift and Voltaire, combined social criticism with utopian hope. Unlike the fictions of the latter type, the lurid inventions of the minor genre caused its authors to be dismissed as travel liars.[1] Although Derek Freeman uses no such epithet in reference to Margaret Mead, his massive critique of her first book, *Coming of Age in Samoa*,[2] in his widely publicized *Margaret Mead and Samoa: The Making and Unmaking of an Anthropological Myth*,[3] in effect, accords it a fictitious status similar to those of her European predecessors. And the fact that she blends social criticism with a proto-utopian purpose does nothing to mitigate such a judgment. Derek Freeman does not, of course, claim that Margaret Mead never visited American Samoa or that she deliberately concocted a work of fantasy in the expectation of producing a best-seller. However, his unflattering judgment is that, for a number of causes he has no difficulty in identifying, Mead's book contains a description of Samoan life and culture which is as fanciful in its own way as those tales of monstrous races and fabulous creatures produced by fraudulent travelers down through the eighteenth century.

Freeman's study of the Mead work has occasioned such widespread critical commentary since its publication in early 1983 that the subject is in danger of becoming a bore. Yet in spite of all that has been written, some of the fundamental questions raised by Freeman's work have been overlooked. It is certainly a disappointing book but in spite of itself also an interesting one.

Much speculation has focused on the purpose and motives of writing in the nineteen-eighties a book debunking a work that appeared a half-century earlier during what might now be called the heroic age of modern anthropology. Reviewers of various kinds have tended to regard *Margaret Mead and Samoa: The Making and Unmaking of an Anthropological Myth* as an exercise in academic muckraking and have for the most part found Freeman's sweeping indictment of the former *doyenne* of modern American anthropology unwarranted. Whether or not they have any sympathy for Freeman's revisionist view of Samoa, reviewers have tried to weigh the evidence and decide who of the two is right, whose data the more complete, and whose research methods the more precise. Yet they have largely ignored more important questions about the relationship of the anthropological researcher to the object of his research and the truth value of anthropological modes of representation.

That Freeman's instincts were correct in submitting the Mead book to an up-to-date critical scrutiny cannot be doubted. Given the canonical stature of the work, its status as an anthropological best-seller, and its widespread use over several decades in educational institutions as a text book in general cultural courses as well as in departments of anthropology, there is every justification for analyzing its practice and seeking to understand the causes of its popularity. Yet Freeman's work is unsatisfactory, for a non-anthropologist at least, because it fails to consider problems that were central to the theory and practice of anthropology in the nineteen-twenties and are even more conspicuous in the eighties. As a result, his work is less important for what it says or does not say about Margaret Mead than for its status as a symptomatic text. Like *Coming of Age in Samoa*, *Margaret Mead and Samoa* is a text of its time, informative at least as much for what it does not know about itself as it is for its claims to knowledge. And from the perspective of the present, it is Freeman's work rather than Mead's which if anything appears the more naive. *Coming of Age in Samoa* is not without its problems from the point of view of modern critical thought but many of these problems reappear with far less justification fifty years later in Freeman's own book.

Freeman makes the blithe assumption that although Mead got things badly wrong, all that is needed to get things right is a minimum of methodological self-criticism. In Freeman's opinion, it is a question of restoring a lost balance in anthropological research between culture and biology. In order to avoid Mead's errors, one needs to divest oneself of the ideology of an exclusive cultural determinism and to acknowledge the equally important role played by biology in shaping collective human behavior.

What Freeman does with the nineteen-twenties classic can be briefly stated. The purpose of *Margaret Mead and Samoa* is effectively summed up in the subtitle, *The Making and Unmaking of an Anthropological Myth*. The book is divided into two parts to which is added a short coda. The first tells the story of the circumstances—ideological, institutional, personal—that determined the choice of the research topic, the approach to it, the research methods adopted, and the results produced. The second shows how Margaret Mead got it all wrong and why; it sets out to demonstrate systematically that for reasons related to her ideological stance, her inexperience, and her faulty research practices, Margaret Mead's conclusions about Samoan culture are a tissue of inaccuracies and misrepresentations. The short final section attempts to outline the foundations on which a properly scientific anthropology should be constructed, an anthropology that would be a synthesis of the insights into social behavior furnished by an understanding of biological as well as cultural determinants.

Freeman is obviously well read in the literature on Samoa and shows convincingly that Margaret Mead's account of the ease and harmony of life on her Western Samoan island is to say the least frequently at odds with the testimony of a great many other witnesses. But probably the most interesting part of Freeman's study for the non-specialist is the excursion into intellectual history in the first part. The author summarizes the important polemic which divided biological and cultural determinists from the late nineteenth century down through the nineteen-twenties. The significance of eugenics in the early part of this century, both inside the scientific community and in the culture at large, will probably come as a revelation to those who associate ideas on race improvement simply with Nazism. Freeman's discussion of eugenics helps to make clear why certain representatives of the intellectual and scientific community, perceiving the serious political implications of theories of race and selective breeding, reacted against such a discourse by discounting the influence of biology in the explication of apparent differences of behavior and achievement between peoples. Freeman illuminates the historical conjuncture and the institutional circumstances that made Margaret Mead's work possible. He succeeds in throwing light on those ideological, professional, and personal commitments which determined how important it was that Margaret Mead's findings be approximately what they turned out to be. Although Freeman never quite says so, the upshot of his investigations is that *Coming of Age in Samoa* is a political intervention, calculated to give liberal social theory a solid scientific foundation.

In his criticisms of Mead, Freeman limits himself for the most part to a systematic refutation of her views of Samoan culture in general and of the behavior of adolescent Samoan girls in particular. His major premise is that her errors derive from the doctrine of cultural determinism she assimilated from her mentors Franz Boas and Ruth Benedict. She was, so to speak, "in ideology," and therefore produced an ideologically distorted image of Samoan culture. Freeman, on the other hand, assumes that because he has a properly balanced view of the role of both biology and culture as determinants of human behavior, he is able to stand in the place of science and produce universally valid knowledge. And it is here that any thoughtful reader of Freeman's book must begin to have serious doubts. It is apparent that just as Freeman fails to turn a critical eye on his own activity as anthropologist, he also fails to raise certain crucial questions about Margaret Mead's text. On the evidence of *Margaret Mead and Samoa*, he seems to be completely out of touch with the hermeneutical tradition and the *Methodenstreit* in Germany over the differences between the natural and human sciences, including the criticism formulated by Gadamer in connection with the latter as "the methodological alienation of the knower from his own historicity." [4] And perhaps even more surprisingly, Freeman completely ignores Lévi-Strauss's formidable structuralist critique of the positivist tradition in anthropology[5] and Foucault's seminal work on the historical transformation of discourses or regimes of truth. Thus he is able to affirm, without discussion, his own faith in Karl Popper's positivist model of scientific inquiry virtually without modification as equally appropriate in the social sciences as in the natural sciences.[6] Finally, what is ignored in all of this, along with the historicity of the writer's own present, is the nature of writing itself. Freeman makes the naive assumption that one can write without taking critical responsibility for the discourse one employs and its relation to an intellectual heritage. Although he describes in some detail the general historical and institutional determinants that bore on Mead's early work, he seems to assume that he himself is not implicated in relations of signification and of power.

To read *Margaret Mead and Samoa* side by side with *Coming of Age in Samoa* is to realize that both works embody myths about themselves, about their status as texts, their methodological practices, and their purposes. It is the most significant features of these myths that I should like to try to identify in what follows. To begin with, it is important to reconsider critically *Coming of Age in Samoa* from a point of view that is overlooked by Freeman. It will then be possible to reflect on the assumptions on which Freeman's claims to the practice of a scientific anthropology rest. As a literary scholar, I make no claim to the expertise of the professional anthropologist. Yet as Freeman's study of Mead reminds us, anthropologists write books about our collective human behavior that concern us all. In our critical age when generic distinctions as well as disciplinary boundaries have quite properly become suspect, it should, therefore, come as no surprise if the temptation to read anthropological works differently has proved irresistible to this student of literature. Textuality is not a phenomenon reserved exclusively for the traditional category of the literary. Submitting a work of anthropology to the kind of close reading traditionally reserved for literary texts will, I hope, find its justification in its results.

What will be clear is that the institutional boundaries we erect between disciplines and the separation of genres which always begins with the separation between fiction and non-fiction are what Foucault calls strategies of exclusion.[7] In a familiar phrase D. H. Lawrence once enjoined readers to trust not the teller but the tale. Current orthodoxy in literary theory, on the other hand, requires that we trust neither. Telling is always overdetermined, always a matter of unconscious and conscious substitutions, displacements, condensations as well as of collective discursive practices and intertextual referrals. As a result, even the most stripped down scientific paper must also be seen as a "work of literature," intended at the very least to insinuate in its form its "scientificity."

Even a casual reader of *Coming of Age in Samoa* cannot but notice the puzzling heterogeneity of its various discourses, its various beginnings, and its postponed conclusions. Nevertheless it promotes the myth about itself that it is both a unitary and scientific text. This myth functions in relation to two concepts of special significance in modern literary theory, namely, representation and ideology. Representation has traditionally depended on the theory that language is neutral or transparent to an already given reality and on the belief in the anteriority and self-identity of the represented in relation to language. Traditional theory has assumed the quasi-magical power of the word to make the absent present. In the case of ideology, the view traditionally promulgated is that it constitutes the antithesis of scientific cognition. Whereas ideology was always implicated in history and was the expression of some form of false consciousness, science was able in one way or another to transcend historical circumstance and achieve a form of universally valid knowledge.

As far as representation is concerned, it has gone largely unrecognized, at least in the United States, that ethnographic works which are field studies of specific cultures are governed by conventional literary modes of representation just as much as realist novels or the travel journals of non-anthropologists. As a result of the influence of modern literary theory, the claims once made for realist representation in fiction have been radically revised. But there is not too much evidence of such critical scrutiny among professional anthropologists. In a public discussion among anthropologists of the Mead/Freeman controversy that I attended, it was assumed that if Margaret Mead employed a form of poetic language, dated even in her time, in certain sections of her book, this was a legitimate popularizing gesture and that such a discourse in no way invalidated the scientific language which characterized most of her book. The assumption was not simply that ordinary language may be used for the purposes of scientific description but also that the heavily coded language of parts of *Coming of Age in Samoa* could be discounted. Its rhetorical effects could be ignored along with its intertextual models, its metaphysics, and its ideology. And it is clear that that is how Mead's work views itself. The assumption made is that there exists an epistemic or scientific language which constitutes an objective way of recording the truths about alien societies. And this in turn depends on the view that the truthful representation of experience in verbal form is possible because language is founded on a system of precise equivalences between words and the things they "stand for." A theory of adequation is involved that amounts to, in effect, a repression of the means of representation. It is a theory that continues to view representation simply as mimesis, or as the restoration of a prior event, and not as productive of such events through its very structure.

Thus Margaret Mead's text is interesting not least because the whole apparatus of representation peculiar to the discipline of anthropology is exemplified there. A field study invariably involves a showing and a telling, descriptions of alien life and findings that are derived from them. A glance at the titles and table of contents of *Coming of Age in Samoa* suggests the institutional norms and the variety of determinants that gave rise to the complex weaving of the final textual artifact. The work reaches the reader with a formidable array of preliminaries announcing its beginning. The title page of the Modern Library edition with its long subtitle and its announcement of forewords and prefaces is particularly impressive. It is followed by an unusually cumbersome academic apparatus of acknowledgements, a table of contents, a preface by the author, a foreword by the most eminent American anthropologist of his day, Franz Boas, and an introduction that is itself followed by what is virtually a prologue before the anthropological narrative itself begins in chapter 2. The main body of the work is comprised of chapters 3 through 12. The descriptive material of these chapters is then followed by two further chapters which in a prescriptive way draw the lessons of the Samoan experience for the United States. Finally, the work shows as much reluctance to end as it did to begin, leading the reader through no fewer than five appendices containing a mixed bag of material, including the researcher's notes, summaries of the quantitative data used in the study, an account of the methodology employed, and a report on the impact on Samoan culture of its contacts with the West.

The significance of the disciplinary norms and practices that determined the cumbersomeness of the textual structure has in large measure to do with a certain ideology of science. It is a question, on the one hand, of a certain practice of writing and of the establishment, on the other, of a position of authority from which to comment on the material represented and address the reader. But from the very title itself, it is evident that linguistic choices are made for rhetorical reasons alien to the scientific purity which is part of the traditional ideological self-image of the social sciences. Given the social scientific experiment the book describes, one might have expected not *Coming of Age* but *Adolescence in Samoa*. Such a title would at least have had the virtue of introducing the crucial concept of developmental psychology that plays such a central role in the study and would have implied the contrastive term so frequently invoked there, "adolescence in America." The phrase is, however, less evocative than the somewhat archaic "coming of age" with its implication of rites of passage, especially when combined with the peculiarly charged proper name of Samoa and the operation of the play of assonance in what Jakobson called the poetic function of speech.

The subtitle is equally coded in its precision: *A Psychological Study of Primitive Youth for Western Civilization*. It manages to embody three important propositions. First, it defines its approach in the choice of the adjective "psychological," where "anthropological" might have been expected. Second, it specifies the object of its researches—"primitive youth." Third, it defines its audience with some panache—"Western civilization." The English prepositions "of" and "for" are worked hard. The fundamental opposition which the subtitle expresses, the hierarchical opposition on which anthropology itself was founded, is that of (Western) "civilization" and (non-Western) "primitivism." Thus it is clear that although the two categories derive their meaning from the polarity, "Western civilization" is the norm by means of which the other may be known and defined variously as "barbaric," "primitive," or "undeveloped." It is "Western civilization" that is the subject of and audience for knowledge and "non-Western primitivism" which is its passive object. The human sciences, as Foucault in particular has taught us, have traditionally involved the objectivization of the human for the purposes of division and control.[8]

In the chapters following Margaret Mead's 1952 preface and Boas' brief foreword, the assumption that a transcendental Western consciousness may survey and accurately describe an alien culture is pursued. Yet in seeking to affirm the authoritative position from which a survey might be conducted, Margaret Mead's doubts and hesitations appear in the curious instability both of the person of narration and of the tense structure. Given the by now commonplace distinction in modern narrative theory between story and discourse, between the events of a story and their disposition in the narrative, between the protagonist of the action and that of the narration, it is clear that in *Coming of Age in Samoa* authoritative claims for knowledge are articulated from a curiously shifting point of view.

The introduction is addressed to an educated lay public assumed to be relatively unfamiliar with the social science of anthropology. It begins by invoking the work of "the psychologist" and "the biologist" in order to suggest the role to be played in the investigation of human behavior by the newcomer on the established scientific scene, "the anthropologist." This collective singular has the effect of giving an instant, mythic authority to the figure of the anthropologist by placing him/her in the company of more established scientists. The strategy is also designed to emphasize the necessity of his/her appearance on the scientific scene. There follows a shift from the distinct disciplines of psychology and anthropology to that place where both meet in the interdisciplinary role of "the student of adolescence," and it is at this point that the author associates herself with her own scientific colleagues by using the first person plural pronoun "we" (". . . we wish to test . . ."). Finally, a page further on the first person singular appears for the first time ("So, in order to investigate the particular problem, I chose . . ."). The strategy of enunciation employed has involved a progression from the impersonally authoritative third person of "the anthropologist" to the narrator's association of herself with such impersonal authority ("we") and then to her sole usurpation of that position of authority. The young Mead's right to speak had previously been established for her in a foreword written by the founding father of modern American anthropology, Franz Boas himself—a paternal blessing which ensures a legitimate continuity.

From its opening pages, *Coming of Age in Samoa* reveals, then, that its narrative strategies and rhetorical effects are as conventionalized and as literary in their own way as those to be found in a realist novel. Moreover, the project of representation and its overdetermined character is suggested in a revealing sentence that appears on page twelve of the introduction:

> But I have tried to present to the reader the Samoan girl in her social setting, to describe the course of her life from birth until death, the problems she will have to solve, the values which will guide her in her solutions, the pains and pleasures of her human lot cast on a South Sea island.

The impersonal scientist whose pronouncements are backed by the prestige of the discipline discloses her own presence here in pronouncing herself the source of the enunciations that will follow. She also deliberately writes in her reader in order to implicate him/her in a communicative exchange that is guaranteed by this profession of the narrator's good faith. Note also that the first line of the sentence repeats the subtitle by indicating that the object of the exchange between Western author and Western reader will be "the Samoan girl," an object guaranteed to attract the libidinal investment of your average male reader, among others.

The most important word of this opening phrase is, however, the active verb in its infinitive form, "to present." It signals the possibility of an immediacy of experience to which the more common "represent" does not quite lay claim, and therefore, lays itself open even more obviously to the familiar Derridean critique. The faith expressed here is in that possibility of adequation between words and things referred to above. It assumes that the referential function of language may be engaged in the absence of all others for the purposes of cognition, that words them-selves do not live the systemic life of signs and are without those specific cultural histories which in part account for their polyvalence. The phrase "to describe the course of her life from birth to death" emphasizes by means of repetition the nature of the anthropological task, since "to describe" here is a synonym for "to present." It is also the word chosen by Boas to define the anthropologist's task in the first sentence of his foreword:

> Modern descriptions of primitive people give us a picture of their culture classified according to the varied aspects of human life.

The metaphoric character of such apparently straightforward language is evident in the choice of the word "picture." The paradox that surfaces here is that although the anthropologist is associated from the beginning of *Coming of Age in Samoa* with other scientists, his activity is defined in terms that suggest the artist. "To present," "to represent," "to paint a picture," are all tasks that the mimetic tradi-tion has set itself in both the literary and the visual arts. Nevertheless, neither in Mead's book nor in Freeman's lengthy critique of it is the question of the epis-temological foundations of such a view of representation ever raised. In particular, the textual strategies imposed by that special combination of descriptive showing and cognitive telling which characterize anthropological field studies remain un-examined.

Finally, one of the more remarkable aspects of Mead's sentence is the variety of conventional rhetorical figures it employs. Note, for example, the hidden metaphor of the river of life suggested by "course"; the traditional trope of the antithesis "pain/pleasure," which is reinforced by the use of alliteration; the choice of the relatively archaic phrase "human lot" to suggest tragic limits; the selection of the metaphoric and distinctly "poetic" word "cast" to reinforce the notion of destiny; and the traditional word order of well-written English in which two breath groups of words are linked to each other across a pause by means of the alliterative "t" (lot/cast). As a result, the long rhythmically controlled sentence ends with a falling cadence and the evocative phrase "cast on a South Sea island" in an emphatic position.[9]

This brief demonstration makes the point that one finds here, in the context of the statement of a social scientific task, a rhetoric of persuasion which obeys con-ventional aesthetic norms. The connotative force of the sentence overwhelms the denotative function in order that the metaphysics of "the human condition" may once again rear its stubborn head. The lesson of such sentences, and there are a great many of them throughout *Coming of Age in Samoa*, is that rhetoric is not intermittent and superficial but ubiquitous and profound. It is on the level of certain regularities of expression, more or less conscious word choices and figures of speech, that a given discursive practice may become visible or ideology reveal itself. If it is in the nature of language to be overlooked, it is because, like Poe's purloined letter, it is before our very eyes. Thus it is no eccentricity of genius that leads Lévi-Strauss to conclude there is no scientific metalanguage by means of which myth may be represented outside of myth itself.[10] The point is unconsciously acknowledged in *Coming of Age in Samoa* to the extent that, in attempting to represent Samoan social reality, Mead has recourse to a variety of representational styles that run the gamut from the mythopoeic to the precisely quantitative. Chapter 2, "A Day in Samoa," offers the most developed example of mythopoeic representation.

For Margaret Mead's apologists, this chapter poses the greatest difficulties. How is one to read it? Is it to be taken seriously for its truth value in representing how life was actually lived by the Samoans in the nineteen-twenties? Is it to be explained away as a form of popularizing "poetic" writing that allows itself to deviate from the letter of the truth in order to suggest the spirit of a place to a lay reader? Is it to be dismissed as an unfortunate effort at the writing of idyllic romance in an otherwise properly scientific work?

However one explains the language of chapter 2, it is something of a shock in a number of respects. The most important questions relate to its status in the work as a whole and the representational techniques it employs. It is "a picture" of Samoan life, but not necessarily of the type that Boas had in mind when he defined the anthropologist's task at the beginning of his foreword. Language is not used here for its denotative precision but for its familiar poetic and connotative effects. These pages are not something that Margaret Mead could have jotted down in her research notes, the product of observations made during the course of a single day. The passage is not "unmediated representation" but an artful composition; it represents a generalized or composite day that has the mythic characteristic of timelessness.

Read as a whole the chapter, in fact, embodies a recognizable literary topos, namely that of the infallibly good place or paradise. It is the realm in which there is an abundance of good things, ease of living, and a natural harmony between the earth and its creatures, including its human creatures. In a similar vein the whole chapter is a picture of noble savagery that, coming as it does immediately after the introduction, explains the purpose and importance of Mead's research, engages the reader's fantasy, and determines his/her attitude to what follows. The opening sentences of the first paragraph of chapter 2 are characteristic:

> The life of the day begins at dawn, or if the moon has shown until daylight, the shouts of the young men may be heard before dawn from the hillside. Uneasy in the night, populous with ghosts, they shout lustily to one another as they hasten with their work. As the dawn begins to fall among the soft brown roofs and the slender palm trees stand out against a colourless, gleaming sea, lovers slip home from trysts beneath the palm trees or in the shadow of beached canoes, that the light may find each sleeper in his appointed place. Cocks crow, negligently, and a shrill-voiced bird cries from the breadfruit trees. (p. 14)

This is a passage that bears all the hallmarks of a traditional kind of good writing. It is characterized by careful phrasing, rhythmic variety, and a number of familiar figures of speech, including metaphor ("the life of the day") and alliteration ("lovers *s*lip home from try*st*s"). However its most notable stylistic features are its choice of coded words ("palm trees," "canoes," and "breadfruit trees" have in our culture the value of the seductively primitive and the exotic); its fondness for evocative adjectives and adverbs ("soft brown roofs," "slender palm trees," "shrill-voiced bird," "lustily," "negligently"); a heavily connotated verb ("lovers slip home"); and an archaic word associated with romance ("tryst"). That such writing allows its cognitive function to be invaded by associations generated by the play of the particular signifiers chosen appears most clearly in that figure which embodies the transference of a quality to something other in the text than that to which it is ostensibly attached. Thus the "lust" of the young men is not in their shouting but in their love-making, and the "negligence" is not, in fact, an attribute of the cock's crow but of a whole way of life characterized by uncompetitive ease. Finally, it should be noted that in attributing "unease" to the young men, Margaret Mead adopts the position of the omniscient narrator of traditional realist fiction. Yet it is typical of her discourse here and throughout that it systematically overlooks the conventions and tropes it employs.

The chapter ends with the sentence: "Sometimes sleep will not descend upon the village until long past midnight; then at last there is only the mellow thunder of the reef and the whisper of lovers, as the village rests until dawn"(p. 19). Is it the noise of the reef that is "mellow" or the observer taking notes in the bungalow? Would another observer attribute the same quality to the same noise or substitute instead a different adjective—"monotonous," for example? Does she, in fact, hear the lovers "whispering" or is that noun chosen to suggest surreptitious pleasure? In short, is this chapter fact or is it fiction? To which, it seems to me, the only possible answer is fiction. It is, moreover, fiction of that special kind we call myth.

The passage invokes in its content such familiar elemental oppositional forces of myth as the day and night, the moon and, by anticipation in the dawn, the sun itself. Typically, it concerns itself with the collective life of the community. Here there are no names, no individuals, just categories of people such as infants, youths, adults, males, females, village elders. Categories of activities are catalogued in a similar way. Furthermore, in its whole mode of enunciation, it adopts the impersonal authoritative style of mythic discourse. To the question, "Who is speaking?," it furnishes no answer, deliberately eliding those pronouns which disclose the presence of a personal narrator along with those deictic marks which speak to the when, where, and how of enunciation. Finally, the narrative tense it employs is the present. But it is not the historical present of certain forms of narration, which is the equivalent of the preterite, but one that is distinctly archaic in English. It is a present of habitual action which is associated chiefly with the ahistorical time and endless repetitions of myth or romance.

To be fair to Margaret Mead, it should be acknowledged that in the context of the book taken as a whole, chapter 2 does appear to be relatively anomalous. The representational techniques employed there are associated in a more systematic and obvious way with various kinds of literary narrative than other sections of her work. Yet the more closely one examines the texture of Mead's writing throughout

Coming of Age in Samoa, the more one becomes aware of its stylistic heterogeneity not only between chapters, which might be assumed to be devoted in turn to popularizing narration or scientific description or pure quantitative analysis, but also frequently within chapters. There is, it must seem to us now, considerable innocence in, for example, the shift of register that occurs in chapter 5, entitled "The Girl and her Age Group." This chapter is written mainly in the mode of generalizing summary followed by detailed descriptions of behavior patterns typical of the body of the work, but every now and then a passage such as the following appears:

> On moonlight nights they [groups of prepubescent girls] scoured the villages alternately attacking or fleeing from the gangs of small boys, peeking through drawn shutters, catching land crabs, ambushing wandering lovers, or sneaking up to watch a birth or a miscarriage in some distant house. . . . They were veritable groups of little outlaws escaping from the exactions of routine tasks. (p. 62)

The prose here is no way distinguishable from that of the fiction of youthful adventure familiar, say, from the tradition of *Tom Sawyer*. The reader is invited to look fondly on the mischievous pranks of the Samoan girls through the choice of a consciously literary style that embodies an attitude of tenderness toward that which it represents.

The significance of such a passage is that it shows no such radical break as one might at first sight suppose between the mythic romance of chapter 2 and the following chapters whose dominant mode seems to be neutral scientific description. The shift in the pronoun of enunciation from the first person of the end of the introduction to the impersonal third person of chapter 2 is largely stabilized in the body of the text through the use of the third person of the scientific observer. Yet to read the work in the nineteen-eighties is to realize that if *Coming of Age in Samoa* is so readable and has remained so popular for so long, it has in large measure to do with qualities in the writing which cast doubt on the reliability of its truth value as science. Would another anthropologist have seen and reported on seeing groups of adolescent girls "scouring," "peeking," and "sneaking up"? If not, does Margaret Mead's (re)presentation of Samoa amount to anything more than a travel journal like Robert Louis Stevenson's? In such a context, do the quantitative data of the appendices amount to anything more than a further rhetorical flourish designed to reinforce the work's truth claims by connoting "scientificity"?

A close reading of *Coming of Age in Samoa* serves to remind us once again that description is always a form of representation and that representation, no matter how scientific the context, is always literary, a question of textuality. Margaret Mead's work also suggests that the human sciences, in spite of the claims often made for them, are also ideological discourses. Derek Freeman's attack on Mead's book makes this clear in one important respect. As noted above, in what are the most interesting sections of his work, he demonstrates that her anthropology was conducted under the banner of an emergent cultural determinism that diagnosed biological determinism as dangerous for political and intellectual reasons. Yet Freeman assumes that if the scientific validity of Mead's findings is undermined by a *parti pris* held as a matter of faith, anthropology itself may emerge strengthened from the kind of self-criticism he engages in to reestablish its claim to produce scientific knowledge. This naively unproblematic view of the issues seems to be unaware of much of the debate of recent decades in Germany, France, and England that has focused on the relation of science to ideology. Thus here as elsewhere, although Freeman touches on important questions, he does not go very far toward resolving them.

Coming of Age in Samoa raises the problem of ideology in the social sciences in two important respects. In the first place, it embodies statements about the methods and purposes of anthropology that deserve greater critical attention than Freeman is able to give them. In the second place, it expresses an ideological content that amounts to a profession of faith in liberal humanism and in anthropology itself as the humanistic science par excellence. Such a faith is succinctly expressed in a sentence from Mead's introduction:

> Each primitive people has selected one set of human gifts, one set of values, and fashioned for themselves an art, a social organization, a religion, which is their unique contribution to the history of the human spirit. (p. 13)

The metaphysics of this hardly needs emphasizing. It is there in a discourse which makes free use of the adjective "human" and which chooses words such as "gifts" and "contributions" to suggest both a benevolent creation and a teleological order. Even more obviously, it is there in the notion of the "unicity" ("one set of human gifts . . . ," "their unique contribution . . .") and, therefore, necessity of each people's role. Finally, the category of "the human spirit," a typical substitution in a post-religious age for "the holy spirit," goes unacknowledged in the text. The view of the world and its peoples expressed in the passage is dependent on a universalist humanist faith summarized in the phrase, "the family of man." It implies a benevolent cosmic order and a conscious shaping process as well as a submerged Judeo–Christian faith in the equality of all souls before God that is transferred here to the world's peoples before history.

The presence of universal categories is evident in the above quotation and it is clear elsewhere in the introduction that similar categories structure Mead's descriptions of Samoan culture throughout. The purpose of her research project is summed up in two questions:

> Are the disturbances which vex our adolescents due to the nature of adolescence itself or to the civilisation? Under different conditions does adolescence present a different picture? (p. 11)

The fundamental category here is that of adolescence, a category derived from developmental psychology and one that determines the structure of the whole book. It is opposed throughout to childhood, on the one hand, and adulthood, on the other, and is thus assumed to have a stable identity within the culture and to remain a fixed category across cultures. Further, the personal adjective "our" is an indication of the point of view from which anthropological research is traditionally conducted.

Both Boas's foreword and Mead's introduction justify the anthropologist's task and self-consciously address a lay public in order to emphasize the scientific character of his/her work and its social value. The struggle undertaken by anthropology, as Boas makes clear from the beginning, is against ethnocentricity. The task of its comparative method is to distinguish what is universal in human behavior from what is culture-bound. Thus the Boasian model implies a common core of universal human behavior attributable to "human nature" along with a huge variety of different behaviors that can be explained in terms of different cultural patterns and that are, therefore, susceptible to modification. Anthropology is introduced by Boas as the skeptical science and investigations like those of Margaret Mead's are designed to show that "much of what we ascribe to human nature is no more than a reaction to the restraints put upon us by our civilization." The category of "human nature" is not questioned as such but there is the recognition that it is in need of redefinition. In this last sentence one may also detect the libertarian hypothesis that Western intellectuals from Rousseau to Marcuse have been living off in one form or another for the past three hundred years, a hypothesis that characterizes the whole of Mead's book. That hers is the discourse of liberal meliorism is evident from the first page of the introduction in the references to "the fulminations of the pulpit, the loudly voiced laments of the conservative philosopher" and to "the cautious reactionary" and "the radical propagandist."

Margaret Mead's liberal faith also finds expression in her choice of research project and in her way of conceiving her task. Her explicit concern is with a specific and important problem of contemporary American society, namely the rebelliousness and stresses of adolescence, and she sets out to find out if such a condition is universal or culture specific. The assumption made is that a single negative instance, a single example of a culture in which adolescence was lived through without apparent difficulty, would suffice to prove that the problems of America's adolescents are to be explained by the culture and not by human nature. *Coming of Age in Samoa* leads one to conclude that either an adolescence without stress is the norm rather than the exception or that Margaret Mead was remarkably lucky in finding upon her first attempt a culture demonstrating the opposite of what apparently obtained in American adolescence. Freeman does not, in fact, point out that Mead's biggest incentive to find a culture characterized by a non-turbulent adolescence must have been that to have discovered the opposite would have been a waste of her time. Since she was not conducting a broad ethnographic study but focused on a single issue, to find yet another culture in which adolescents were subject to stress and rebellion would have left the question open to further research in other cultures until a negative instance was finally encountered. To have made the findings she did was, on the other hand, to assert at one stroke both the importance of anthropology in comparison with biology and psychology and to provide a scientific foundation for the cause of broad educational reform and social change in the United States. It was to show triumphantly that since certain kinds of experiments on people were excluded by the nature of things, anthropology could take over where psychology had left off by testing hypotheses in the field. The claim of anthropology to produce knowledge and to contribute like other sciences to the improvement of society at large was effectively established. The promise held out by Mead's book is that societal problems may be analyzed objectively without reference to religious faith or political ideology and that social policy may be reformed in the light of such findings. The goal is universal betterment, a future that is different, more rationally organized, and therefore happier than the past. In short, *Coming of Age in Samoa* was in its time an important political intervention whose remarkable influence came to be exercised particularly through the various ideological apparatuses of the educational system.

The example of Margaret Mead's classic makes clear that modern anthropology in the United States is linked to a broader social purpose. Yet its scientific purity is compromised by the fact that it is a science *for* something. Therefore, like the social sciences in general, it may be said to be "in ideology" in two separate senses. First, it consciously takes up an interventionist social role; its findings are expected to issue one way or another in changed social practices. Second, no sciences, including anthropology, can escape the ideology embodied in its self-image as science. Every science has an object of study, has practices and purposes, research methods and principles, that must be satisfied by the production of truths, the place it occupies within science as a whole and its relations to other sciences, and, finally, its relations to society at large and to the species as a whole.

As far as Margaret Mead's anthropology is concerned, the most revealing section of *Coming of Age in Samoa* in this respect is relegated to appendix 2. It bears the straightforward title "The Methods of this Study" and, as one might expect, its purpose is to outline the general problems inherent in anthropological field work and the particular solutions adopted by Margaret Mead in Samoa. Placing such a discussion at the end of the book is a reminder of the heterogeneity of Mead's work. In a study addressed to a purely scientific audience, research methods would either be taken for granted or, if a justification were needed, would probably appear at the beginning of a work. A lay audience, on the other hand, is much more likely to find such a debate relatively tedious and prefer to turn directly to the subject matter proper. The fact that the discussion of research methods is not omitted altogether, but placed in an appendix, suggests the kind of compromise already encountered in other aspects of the work's composition. Such a position suggests that there is no need to read it but its mere presence serves as a sign of the "scientificity" that lends authority to the work's judgments. Its purpose is obviously to justify Mead's conclusions: if the investigative methods employed are shown to be appropriate given the circumstances, then the findings are presumably valid.

In fact, Margaret Mead's appendix on methodology is not a very strenuous piece of writing. Working with inherited concepts whose hold over her thinking is not acknowledged, she is forced into a number of contortions in justifying her approach. In a straightforward way the appendix gives expression to the difficulties and doubts experienced by the young researcher, to certain apparently unresolvable problems and the various ad hoc solutions she adopted. She begins by stating her regret that, because of the kind of questions ethnographic studies raise, it is impossible to produce "a single and unified picture of the adolescent girl in Samoa." And the reasons she gives for this inevitably open up the now hackneyed question of "presence." Thus she concludes that in order to study "the adolescent girl in present-day Samoa," the anthropologist must take account of "traditional observances and attitudes" because "the present environment and the girl's reaction to it" contain features of the past. What she regrets is "this double necessity of describing not only the present environment and the girl's reaction to it, but also of interpolating occasionally some description of the more rigid cultural milieu of her mother's girlhood" (p. 259). And the cause of her regret is that it "mars to some extent the unity of the study." The problem Mead encounters is, of course, one that has become familiar in the structuralist guise of the dichotomy between synchrony and diachrony, structure and event. And the frustration she expresses derives from the impossibility of ever isolating a present that is complete in itself, uncontaminated by traces of the past.

Her second important point involves her choice of a "detailed intensive investigation" over "a more diffused and general study," of "detailed observations and the individual cases" over "merely external observations" (p. 259). The relative imprecision of the language here is in itself disturbing. The criteria by which this opposition of research methods is established are by no means obvious. And the reader's doubts are likely to be increased when he reaches the conclusion that in any case "the student of the more intangible and psychological aspects of human behavior is forced to illuminate rather than demonstrate a thesis" (p. 260). If a case cannot be "demonstrated," the claim to have "illuminated" it makes no sense at all. This odd antithesis alone suggests the methodological doubts Margaret Mead apparently harbored concerning her project.

A third disclaimer in the appendix focuses on the role of the observer in anthropological research and here Mead raises a perennial problem: "The conclusions are also subject to the limitations of the personal equation. They are the judgments of an individual upon a mass of data" (p. 261). The concession made is particularly damaging because it acknowledges that what she somewhat euphemistically calls "the personal equation" is always determinative in the last instance. To contrast so pointedly "one individual" with "the mass of data" is to acknowledge the relative arbitrariness of the findings. Moreover, Mead's defense that the results obtained are in some sense commensurable because the observer remained stable throughout the months of research—"the personal equation was held absolutely constant"—is in itself problematic and does little to overcome the fundamental objection that the results obtained have to be virtually taken on trust. The point Mead makes here suggests particularly well the inappropriateness of the Popperian model of scientific investigation invoked by Freeman. Mead, in effect, concedes that her experiment is neither repeatable nor falsifiable.

In going on to discuss the "particular methods used," Mead once again acknowledges the irreducible nature of the observer's role. She states how, using the Samoan language throughout, she gathered her material "in orthodox fashion" through interviews with carefully chosen informants, how she checked the information obtained with other Samoans, how she accumulated a great deal of objective data on age and family circumstances, and how she administered questionnaires and intelligence tests. Yet she acknowledges that in the end the quantitative data was useful only in supplementing "months of observation of the individuals and of groups." Her conclusions were largely based on the latter: "This information cannot be reduced to tables or to statistical statements." Finally, in cases where individual behavior presented special difficulties she asserts that "the investigation was pursued until I felt that I understood the girl's motivation . . ." (p. 264). Anyone expecting to find a tough-minded, scientific methodology based largely on quantitative data is likely to be particularly disturbed by the emphasis given in this sentence to the verb "felt." In making judgments in such cases the whole onus is placed on the researcher's correct "feeling."

In the most systematic account of the methodology adopted in her research, then, Margaret Mead acknowledges that the accuracy of the description given of an alien culture, and the judgments made, depend on the powers of the observer. In short, although she herself does not attempt to explain what these powers consist of, her own general statements and her practice suggest that they amount to some kind of combination of skill, intuition, and experience. Given the state of her discipline in the nineteen-twenties and her own relative youth, it is not surprising that she does not go so far as to recognize that an art of interpretation is involved. Yet that is, in effect, the conclusion to which her scattered remarks point. Understandably the word hermeneutics does not appear in her book, but one finds something like that being practiced there. One can only conclude that the kind of anthropology of which *Coming of Age in Samoa* is a classic example is an unselfconscious form of hermeneutics masquerading as a hard science. The hesitations and confusions that are apparent in Mead's discourse, in the heterogeneity of its registers and contradictory discursive practices, derive, then, from a disciplinary blindness. Moreover if Derek Freeman makes no comment on such blindness fifty years later in over three hundred and fifty pages of commentary, it is because he apparently still shares it.

The effect of Margaret Mead's methodological appendix is to demonstrate in spite of itself that the anthropologist is a *bricoleur* or "handyman" in the sense that Lévi-Strauss has given to the term.[11] In his celebrated discussion of mythic thought, Lévi-Strauss contrasted the latter's approach to problem solving with that of the engineer. His point was that whereas the engineer dealt with a given problem in the light of a body of specialized theory and a set of interlocking concepts specifically designed for the task in hand, the *bricoleur* practices a kind of concrete thought and constructs solutions out of the heterogeneous material that happens to be available. In deconstructing Lévi-Strauss's hierarchical opposition in his turn, Derrida extended the notion of *bricolage* to all forms of thought by demonstrating that in spite of appearances to the contrary, the engineer too is a *bricoleur*.[12] Lévi-Strauss's concept of the engineer is a myth or a "theological idea": "A subject who would be the absolute origin of his own discourse and would supposedly construct it 'out of nothing' would be the creator of the 'verbe', the 'verbe' itself."[13] As far as anthropology is concerned, it is clear that Margaret Mead is unable to invoke an object of knowledge, a body of theory, a set of concepts and research procedures, or a mode of description that definitively separates her field of inquiry from other forms of knowledge or that give rise to findings universally acknowledged to be independent of an observer. Thus in spite of her intermittent use of a scientific discourse in *Coming of Age in Samoa*, there is *a priori* no reason why we should attribute a greater degree of truth to her account of Samoan life than we might to a travel journal or a realist novel on the same subject. And the same is true of Derek Freeman's diametrically opposite conclusions about Samoa.

An analysis of the Mead book from the point of view of certain concerns of contemporary literary theory is interesting for its own sake. It is even more compelling as a corrective to Freeman's account of the earlier work. To turn to Freeman's book after rereading *Coming of Age in Samoa* is to be particularly aware that the historical conditions of understanding and the dimension of discourse are completely overlooked by the Australian anthropologist. It is a lack that is particularly serious because it leads him not only to ignore the issues touched on above relating to representation and ideology at the level of discursive practice, but also to ignore entirely the question of his own hermeneutic situation and his own discourse.

The burden of Freeman's charge against Mead is that her ideological conditioning was such that she uncritically rewrote in *Coming of Age in Samoa* the Western myth of the South Sea islands that goes back to Bougainville and was reinforced in more recent times by writers such as Robert Louis Stevenson and Rupert Brooke— he would have done well to add Gauguin. Thus in his view it was no accident that Mead chose to carry out her research on adolescence in Samoa since, on the basis of various travelers' accounts of the South Seas, there was more than some likelihood she would find the stress-free adolescence that she was looking for. It is Freeman's contention that her views of Samoan culture are systematically and radically wrong. The longest section of his book amounts to a point by point refutation of Mead's findings concerning such questions as rank consciousness, levels of cooperation, aggressive behavior, modes of punishment, child rearing, sexual morals in general, and female virginity in particular. Thus he comments at different points in his book on her "fanciful account of Samoan sexual behavior" (p. 108); that contrary to her claims of the non-competitive character of Samoan culture, the Samoans are "an intensely competitive people" (p. 146); that far from being amiable and peaceful they are "unusually bellicose" (p. 156); that she "almost wholly misconstrues the nature and significance of religion in both ancient and twentieth century Samoa" (p. 170); that her comments on the lack of punishment are "inaccurate and misleading" (p. 191); that her views of the relatively trouble-free relations between children and parents "is markedly at variance with the facts of Samoan existence" (p. 201); that far from living in a stress-free society "Samoans as children, adolescents, and adults, live within an authority system the stresses of which regularly result in psychological disturbances ranging from compulsive behaviors and *musu* states to hysterical illnesses and suicide" (p. 225); that contrary to Mead's view that premarital sex was tolerated and widespread in the culture, "the cult of female virginity is probably carried to a greater extreme than in any other culture known to anthropology" (p. 250). By the time he has finished, Mead's Samoan myth has apparently been decisively "unmade."

For the non-specialist, more interesting than Freeman's emphatic, detailed refutations of Mead's findings are the explanations he comes up with in order to account for such systematic aberration. As was suggested above, they are basically of two fundamental types. The first type concerns the general intellectual and institutional milieu in which Mead was trained and carried out her research; the second relates to more specific disabilities in the researcher herself and her approach to the cultural object of her project. The latter explanations are of little general interest, since they involve a series of *ad feminam* charges, which may or may not be without foundation, but that in any case only concern the professional competence of the young Margaret Mead. Thus Freeman comments on her general unpreparedness, her inadequate training for the task, her immaturity in the profession, her lack of background in biology, her inadequate knowledge of the Samoan language, her isolation from the day-to-day living situation of Samoans in the dispensary of the American physician, the narrowness of her focus on the adolescent girls, and the latter's general unreliability as informants.

Much more fundamental not only to the Mead book, but also to anthropological field work in general, are the explanations of the first type that Freeman comes up with for Mead's seriously flawed picture of Samoan society, namely the unfortunate role played by her intellectual and institutional milieu. As previously noted, Freeman attributes her failures to the fact that Margaret Mead was "in ideology." Her research was conducted within the Boasian paradigm, that is to say according to the doctrine of "the explanation of human behavior in purely cultural terms" (p. 48) or what Freeman calls cultural determinism. By proclaiming in the second decade of the twentieth century "the complete independence of cultural anthropology," the leading figures in American anthropology such as Boas himself, Robert Lowie, and Alfred Kroeber were in Freeman's view overreacting in opposition to the biological determinism championed in particular by the eugenicists. Freeman claims that in the mid-nineteen-twenties, cultural anthropology had become "an ideology, that in an actively unscientific way, sought to exclude biology from the explanation of human behavior" (p. 282). As a student of Boas, therefore, Margaret Mead was wholly predisposed to find the kind of tension-free cultural environment she describes in *Coming of Age in Samoa* long before she ever set foot in American Samoa. Freeman even claims that Mead's field work in Samoa was designed by her mentor himself to put to the empirical test the hypotheses of cultural determinism. As a result, he finds that "her eristic approach to anthropological inquiry is fundamentally at variance with the methods and values of science . . ." (p. 282).

Freeman's discussion of the shortcomings of Mead's work and the reasons he adduces for them suggest that many of her findings are to be taken with more than a grain of salt. What he does not apparently realize, however, is that many of the weaknesses he attributes to Mead's work, relating to a system of belief and to research procedures as well as to the use of evidence, apply with almost equal force to his own analyses and to anthropological research in general. It is above all Freeman's claim to stand "in science" and to be able to produce a knowledge, as opposed to an ideology of Samoa, its truth and not its myth, that is particularly open to challenge in the light of modern critical theory. One is reminded of Althusser's ironic comment that "one of the effects of ideology is the practical *denegation* of the ideological character of ideology by ideology: ideology never says, 'I am ideological.'"[14]

In Freeman's eyes the cultural determinist school of anthropology, and Margaret Mead along with it, were seriously in error in neglecting the important biological determinants of human behavior. Their hypothesis that human nature is an infinitely malleable material, producing a great variety of behaviors as the result of different cultural patterning, leads them to ignore certain universal givens and, as a result, to overestimate the possibilities for social improvement. Thus, in rejecting Mead's claim that Samoan adolescents lead lives characterized by casualness and ease, Freeman claims that she ignores "a dark side of their lives" and that this dark side is "something they share with all human societies" (p. 278). And a similar claim about the universality of human behavior is made in connection with Mead's finding that the child/mother bond in Samoa is not particularly strong: "The primary bond between child and mother is very much a part of the biology of Samoans, as it is of all humans" (p. 203) — an assertion of human universality that he does little to substantiate in his text.

Coming of Age in Samoa is, then, for Freeman a classic case of the triumph of ideology over science, since it shows how "the deeply held beliefs of those involved may lead them unwittingly into error" (p. 292). The lessons he draws from Mead's book are important but misguided ones: "A crucial issue that arises from this historic case for the discipline of anthropology . . . is the extent to which other ethnographic doctrines may have been distorted by doctrinal convictions, as well as the methodological question of how such distortion can be avoided" (p. 296). And the answer he finds to his quest for an anthropological science pure of politics is in the model of scientificity promoted by Karl Popper. Following Popper, he asserts that in order for a scientific theory to be accepted in terms of correspondence with the truth of phenomena, it must be potentially falsifiable; it must be subjected to "the critical method of error elimination" — "rational criticism entails the testing of any particular statement in terms of its correspondence with the facts." Thus Mead's proposition that American Samoa is a negative instance "is fully open to testing against the relevant empirical evidence" (p. xii). He has no difficulty with the notion that fifty years after the fact Mead's findings still remain open "to an empirically based examination of their truth or falsity" (p. 114). And it is precisely this process that he claims to have carried out in his own researches into Samoan culture. His strategy for avoiding misrepresentation as a result of ideological distortion is to subject propositions "to indefatigable rational criticism," a phrase that has more of the quality of a moral exhortation than of a fail-safe guide in the conduct of research. It is no more useful than lecturing an alcoholic on the evils of liquor.

A further difficulty is that the question as to what constitutes an anthropological fact, how it is to be recognized and recorded, and the relative importance to be attributed to it in a given ethnographic description, is not even raised as a potential problem by Freeman. In accordance with a certain naive positivism, facts are assumed to offer themselves to any unbiased observer as self-evident entities prior to any body of theory or discursive order that summons them into view. Nor does Freeman have anything to say in justification of the assumption that he finds an extraordinary continuity in Samoan culture over a period of some one hundred and fifty years. Anyone who used the account of travelers to Victorian England in order to draw inferences about collective behavior in the Britain of the post-1960s would not be taken very seriously, but that is what Freeman does as part of his attack on the reliability of Mead's findings. Finally, Freeman does not seem to acknowledge any more than Mead that there is any problem in reading the sign systems of alien cultures. How does rebelliousness or its antithesis manifest itself in Samoa? It seems highly unlikely that it looks like rebelliousness in the West, but neither writer has anything specific to say on how they learned to read Samoan behavior as a semiotic system.

Perhaps most disappointing of all in *Margaret Mead and Samoa* is Freeman's outline of what a genuine science of anthropology should look like. In accusing both the cultural and the biological determinists of having allowed ideological commitments to blind them to the necessity of taking into account both cultural and biological determinants in their descriptions of human behavior, Freeman advocates the kind of synthesis that is associated with E. O. Wilson's well-known work, *Sociobiology: The New Synthesis.*[15] Yet what such a synthesis would amount to in anthropology is by no means clear either from Freeman's theoretical pronouncements or from his practice in *Margaret Mead and Samoa*. The blandness of his assertions and the lack of precision given in his outline of this new science are unlikely to awaken much confidence in his approach.

The very title of the important chapter here—"Toward a More Scientific Anthropology"—induces skepticism. Isn't that comparative itself a giveaway? Isn't science always a matter of either/or? Freeman goes on to note that "in the etiology of adolescence . . . both nature and nurture are always involved," that "human nature" is not "a tabula rasa" (p. 296), that anthropology must abandon "the paradigm fashioned by Kroeber and other Boas students, and must give full cognizance to biology, as well as to culture, in the explanation of human behavior and in situations" (p. 297).

In brief, in spite of the lessons he draws from the making, if not the unmaking, of the Meadian myth of Samoa, Freeman continues to believe in an anthropological science that will possess the most important attributes of those physical sciences from which Popper derived his model of the scientific approach to the establishment of truth. There is nothing in Mead's work or in his own professional experience that leads him to discard the image of the anthropologist as engineer. *Bricolage* apparently does not appeal to him even though both the book he debunks and his own work massively engage in it. Perhaps most surprising is that although he borrows the notion of the scientific paradigm from Kuhn in order to comment negatively on Mead's work[16]—he refers frequently to "the Boasian paradigm"— he remains blind to that concept's implications in his own case. The problematic light cast by Kuhn's work in the history of science on the traditional notion of scientific truths and scientific development is overlooked, as is the potential contradiction between Popper's and Kuhn's views of these matters. Freeman still clings to the heroic view of the history of science, which tells the linear tale of continuity and progress and recognizes no discontinuity or period epistemes.[17] Thus nowhere in his book does he worry about the limits of the paradigm within which he himself is functioning or reflect on the historical conditions which motivate current modes of conceptualization in his own discipline. And in his struggle to assert the validity of his own findings over those of Margaret Mead—a struggle that seems to derive less from an anxiety of influence than a rage to desecrate—he shows himself equally blind to the fact that it was just as important for his doctrine of cultural/biological synthesis to find stress in Samoan adolescence as it was for Mead to find transition to adulthood characterized by harmony and ease. In proclaiming the universality of certain human behaviors, including the ubiquity of a so-called darker side, Freeman shows himself to be just as much "in ideology" as Mead herself. But then how could he not be?

In the end neither Mead's nor Freeman's book suggests why we should trust the professional anthropologist's account of foreign places and foreign peoples any more, or less, than we do those of travelers with less scientific pretensions. In both cases, all we have is "travel literature" and the emphasis in that phrase needs to fall equally on noun and adjective. Whether he or she is an anthropologist or not, a travel writer is always, as Sartre taught us long ago, in situation, always arriving from somewhere else at a particular historical moment in the relations between peoples for a reason, even if that reason is an apparently innocent study of a given population in the light of the current regime of truth in an academic discipline. The naiveté of Freeman's attack on Margaret Mead is such that it forces one to restate the banalities that the present is not a privileged position, that there is no "truth" of Western Samoa that is not the "truth" of an observer from a given social formation at a given historical moment, whose consciousness and discursive practice are always imbricated in a system of relations of signification and power.

This is not the place or the time to attempt to be specific about the undeclared sociopolitical doctrines that found Freeman's own kind of anthropology. Yet if one suggests, as Freeman does, that behind the cultural determinism which guided Mead's anthropological research stands the ideology of the energetic liberal reform-ism of the 1920s, then it is just as reasonable to assume that beneath Freeman's bio-cultural synthesis lurks an anti-utopian belief in limits and a neoconservative pragmatism that is in tune with our chastened post-colonial age. Mead's and Freeman's contradictory findings are, in short, motivated as much as anything by two different sets of hopes. Where Mead's fellow travelers were Bernard Shaw and André Gide, Freeman's are V. S. Naipaul and Paul Theroux.

There is a final irony in the fact that in order to emphasize the universality of certain features of human behavior, Freeman himself should have recourse to myth and to the philosopher whose genealogies have probably done most in modern times to undermine our faith in the truths and continuities of science, Friedrich Nietzsche.[18] To find authority, as Freeman does in his conclusion, for a scientifically based anthropology in the supposed coexistence of the Apollonian and the Dionysian in all human existence is, in effect, to acknowledge the limits of a scientific metalanguage in anthropology. It is to embrace Lévi-Strauss's view that the most appropriate linguistic mode to adopt in commenting on myth is itself mythic. There is less risk for all concerned if we recognize that what our travelers bring back are never the truths of alien cultures but only our own provisional and more or less generous fictions.[19]

Notes

1. See Percy G. Adams, *Travelers and Travel Liars, 1660–1800* (Berkeley: University of California Press, 1962).

2. Margaret Mead, *Coming of Age in Samoa: A Psychological Study of Primitive Youth for Western Civilization* (New York: William Morrow and Co., 1928). Page references in this article are to the Modern Library Edition of 1953.

3. Derek Freeman, *Margaret Mead and Samoa: The Making and Unmaking of an Anthropological Myth* (Cambridge and London: Harvard University Press, 1983).

4. Hans-Georg Gadamer, *Philosophical Hermeneutics* (Berkeley, Los Angeles, London: University of California Press, 1976), p. xiv.

5. *Tristes Tropiques* is obviously the paradigmatic text here.

6. Karl Popper, *The Logic of Scientific Discovery* (New York: Basic Books, 1959).

7. See for example "Discourse on Language" in *The Archaeology of Knowledge* (New York: Harper, 1972).

8. For a recent summary of Michel Foucault's project, see his afterword, "The Subject and Power," to H. L. Dreyfus and P. Rabinow, *Michel Foucault: Beyond Structuralism and Hermeneutics* (Chicago and London: University of Chicago Press, 1982).

9. In the earlier part of this century "castaway books" set on tropical islands from the Caribbean to the South Pacific had a wide readership and not only among the young. Probably the best known were *Treasure Island, Coral Island,* and *The Swiss Family Robinson.*

10. See the Overture of *The Raw and the Cooked* (New York: Harper and Row, 1969).

11. Claude Lévi-Strauss, "The Science of the Concrete" in *The Savage Mind* (Chicago: University of Chicago Press, 1966), pp. 16–22.

12. "If one calls *bricolage* the necessity of borrowing one's concepts from the text of a heritage which is more or less coherent or ruined, it must be said that every discourse is *bricoleur.*" "Structure, Sign, and Play in the Discourse of the Human Sciences" in *The Languages of Criticism and the*

Sciences of Man, ed. Richard Macksey and Eugenio Donato (Baltimore and London: Johns Hopkins University Press, 1970), p. 255.

13. *Ibid.*, p. 256.

14. Louis Althusser, "Ideology and Ideological State Apparatuses" in *Lenin and Philosophy* (New York and London: Monthly Review Press, 1971), p. 175. In an article that draws on the German hermeneutical tradition and the critical hermeneutics of Habermas in the effort to define the relations between science and ideology, Paul Ricoeur echoes Althusser's comment when he notes that "the man of suspicion" all too easily assumes that "ideology is the thought of my adversary, the thought of the *other*. *He* does not know it, but *I* do." "Science and Ideology" in *Hermeneutics and the Human Sciences* (Cambridge: Cambridge University Press, 1981), p. 224.

15. E. O. Wilson, *Sociobiology: The New Synthesis* (Cambridge and London: Harvard University Press, 1975).

16. Thomas S. Kuhn, *The Structure of Scientific Revolutions* (Chicago: The University of Chicago Press, 1970).

17. See the fascinating debate between Noam Chomsky and Michel Foucault on this question, "Human Nature: Justice versus Power" in *Reflexive Water: The Basic Concerns of Mankind*, ed. Fons Elder (London: Souvenir Press, 1974).

18. "I fight all the tartuffery of scientific manners (Wissenschaftlichkeit)." *The Will to Power* (New York: Vintage Books, 1968), p. 229.

19. Richard Rorty reaches a similar conclusion in the course of attempting to define the common ground between American pragmatism and French post-structuralism. He accuses positivism of only having gone halfway in the development of a culture without God, since it "preserved a God in the notion of a portion of culture where we touch something not ourselves, where we found truth naked, relative to no description." Unlike positivism, pragmatism, he claims, "does not erect Science as an idol to fill the place once held by God. It views science as one genre of literature—or, put the other way round, literature and the arts as inquiries, on the same footing as scientific inquiries." *Consequences of Pragmatism* (Minneapolis: University of Minnesota Press, 1982), p. xiii.

Sartre's Concept of the Intellectual: A Foucauldian Critique / *Mark Poster*

The immediate postwar period (1944–47) is generally recognized as a time of great expectations of social progress, even of revolution. With fascism defeated and the right in general discredited, Western Europe looked forward to a period of democratic rebuilding and renewal. In France, perhaps more than elsewhere, these hopes were supported by a substantial left-wing majority in government. Leftist intellectuals, who participated to varying degrees in the Resistance movement, shared the sanguine spirit of the time. In particular the existentialists—Sartre, Merleau-Ponty, and de Beauvoir—were strongly taken by the mood of optimism, a fact that might surprise those who view their philosophy as one of despair, anguish, and melancholy. In 1944 the existentialists were fully convinced that they could make important contributions to the movement toward social freedom.[1] The widespread success of existentialist thought in these years served to convince Sartre and his friends that their ideas might have a prominent role in shaping the political future of France and Europe.

In fact things did not turn out as expected either for France or for the existentialists. Sartre quickly became embroiled in controversies with his erstwhile allies and friends, the communists. In the press and on the radio existentialism became subject to scandal and smear tactics.[2] Liberals like Camus and Aron also became estranged from the existentialists.It did not take long before the alliances forged during the struggle against fascism dissolved into bitter and enduring enmities. To make matters worse, those who were devoted to existentialism were often not the sort of people Sartre aspired to impress. Although opinions evolved quickly during these years, it was a time more conducive to frantic activity and frustrated hopes than to solid advances.

One of the central problems for Sartre and his group during the mid-1940s was to define the work of intellectuals. The events of the war years had so drastically transformed the lives of philosophers, novelists, and scholars that they could not easily return to the quiet study, the contemplation of eternal questions of being, or the crafting of an artistic object that spoke only to itself. Nor was it easy, as Julien Benda had a generation earlier,[3] to claim privileged status for intellectuals, one which allowed them to stand back from the world and speak down to it as a teacher to his pupils, condemning this and praising that according to the dictates of reason. On the other hand, engagement in the world also contained its share of snares and false promises. Many intellectuals had rushed into the Communist Party, assured of a direct connection with the progressive social forces. But many of them soon found that the tools of the critical intellect were useless in a shop that produced justifications for pragmatic action rather than theories to guide it. Thus the situation for the existentialists was not unambiguous: on the right, outmoded notions of purity and transcendence; on the left, compromising subservience to opportunistic political parties. Yet one had to choose. So the existentialists opted to forge a new kind of weapon out of the materials of intellectual life, one that would preserve the virtues of reflection and literature while engaging fully in the whirl of history.

Looking back at the predicament of the existentialists and the conclusions they drew about the role of intellectuals, one can distinguish not only the innovative figure of engagement but also certain deeply rooted continuities with the past. Michel Foucault's recent criticisms of earlier generations of intellectuals enable us to consider afresh the posture of the existentialists and to elaborate a more nuanced analysis of the limitations of their notion of intellectual life. In this paper I will adopt the vantage point outlined by Foucault to reexamine the definition of the intellectual put forward by the existentialists during the years from 1944 to 1947. In particular I will hold the Foucauldian lens up to the major work on the topic of intellectuals: Sartre's *What is Literature?*

From the 1950s to the present France has, it can be argued, experienced three distinct periods of intellectual activity. Until the early 1960s, discussion was dominated by a developing synthesis of Marxism and existentialism which I have termed "existential Marxism." In the mid-1960s, structuralism came to the fore. Both of these intellectual currents were characterized by a strong totalizing impulse, a tendency toward systemization, and by the profoundly held assumption that reason was adequate to the comprehension of reality. In the 1970s a third period, that of post-structuralism, emerged which reversed the earlier trends quite drastically. In the hands of Jacques Derrida and Michel Foucault, the most arresting post-structuralists, the potential scope and claims of reason were sharply curtailed. Derrida attacked what he called "The Western Philosophical Tradition" for its logocentrism, the assertion of the immediacy of reality to thought, and the assumption of the ability of reason to represent reality.[4] In a similar but separate vein, Foucault argued, notably in *Les mots et les choses*, that the limits of discourse were determined by underlying epistemological constraints which were outside and beneath the ken of their authors.[5] In both instances post-structuralism drew attention to the impasses and errors incurred when the inevitable limitations of the scope of reason were transgressed.

In recent essays and interviews Foucault has expanded his critique of reason to include the role of the intellectuals. He has been extremely critical of the traditional pretension of the intellectual, the claim that he or she alone can represent the universal. With Voltaire and Sartre in mind, Foucault characterized the intellectual as follows: "For a long time the 'left' intellectual spoke and was acknowledged to have the right of speaking in the capacity of master of truth and justice."[6] Armed with the lance of reason and the sword of the written word the intellectual presented himself as a crusader for universality, a grasp of which would enable him alone to win the battle of progress. The difficulties that ensue from this "universal intellectual," Foucault contends, are all too evident in the history of Marxism. The proletariat, a historically constituted, finite social group, initially has universality attributed to it only to have it promptly stolen by the intellectual who now claims the consciousness of this universality. The theorist or party leader can speak for the proletariat in the name of a universality that is somehow lost amidst the grime of the process of production. In this way the intellectual's assertion of universality easily becomes an alibi for grasping power; knowledge and power are locked in a *mésalliance* which can be traced back to Plato's philosopher-king.

Foucault discerns a trend, however, beginning after World War II, that rejects the universal intellectual in favor of a figure he terms "the specific intellectual." With Robert Oppenheimer representing the point of transition, the specific intellectual no longer claims *to speak for* another group or to give voice to an oppressed consciousness. The role of the specific intellectual is rather to facilitate, for a subordinate social group, its ability to speak for itself. The specific intellectual represents nothing and no one; he or she enables the oppressed to name themselves and write their own *cahiers de doléances*. In addition, the specific intellectual is not "the man of justice" who floats above society, alert to its inequities, ready to denounce the atrocities of capitalism and put them in a universal perspective. Instead the specific intellectual is rooted in a particular institution. From his position in, and knowledge of, that institution he may speak about its structure of domination without claiming for himself more than is his due.

In outlining the distinction between universal and specific intellectuals, Foucault does not analyse the social conditions which bring the latter on the scene. He does not mention changes in the structure of the capitalist mode of production which spread intellectual functions throughout society, in the factory, the government bureau, the welfare agency, the hospital, even the military. Despite this limitation, I believe that Foucault's distinction is an important one and that it can serve to identify difficulties in the existentialist definition of the intellectual in the immediate post-war years.

In 1947 Sartre wrote a series of articles which appeared in *Les Temps modernes* and were later collected and published as *What is Literature?*. In light of the recent devastating war and the current hopes for large-scale social change, Sartre reconsidered the nature of writing and the role of the intellectual in history. It was apparent to Sartre that one could no longer ignore history, that one could no longer write and think in a philosophical and aesthetic vacuum. Because the intellectual had been engulfed by the activities of war, it was now essential that he conceive of writing as action. "Thus the prose writer is a man who has chosen a certain method of secondary action which we may call action by disclosure."[7] The intellectual who committed himself to writing as a form of action in the world was *engagé*, a term that became the catchword for a generation of intellectuals throughout the West.

The notion that intellectuals do not simply interpret the world but act upon it and change it is associated with the writings of Karl Marx, specifically with the eleventh thesis on Feuerbach. Sartre, however, held that the notion of the engaged writer derived equally from his own brand of existentialism. In *What is Literature?* he couched his argument in the philosophical phrases not of Marx but of *Being and Nothingness*. Writing is a form of doing and "doing reveals being. Each gesture traces out new forms on the earth. Each technique, each tool, is a way that opens upon the world; things have as many aspects as there are ways of using them. We are no longer with those who want to possess the world, but with those who want to change it" (p. 165). The existentialist writer must therefore "plunge things into action" and develop a form of literature that has as its singular aim that of "making history," eschewing the literature of *exis* (passivity) for that of *praxis*.

Although the engaged writer was a child of existentialism, Sartre was not satisfied with his writings of the thirties. The contemplative musings of Roquentin in *Nausea* were rejected as a model for the protagonist in *Paths of Freedom*. The purely philosophical stance taken by Sartre in *The Transcendence of the Ego*, *L'Imaginaire*, and *Being and Nothingness* was rejected thereafter in favor of more politically motivated writing such as one finds in *Critique of Dialectical Reason*. Furthermore, after 1947, Sartre sought an appropriate form of political action. A consistent political thread runs through Sartre's activities from the *Rassemblement Démocratique Révolutionnaire* of 1948, through the years of fellow traveling with the Communist Party, down to May 1968 and the support he gave to Maoists by selling their newspapers in the street. In each case Sartre was attempting to fulfill the program of *What is Literature?*, or as he later put it, to transform a leftist intellectual into an intellectual leftist. The success or wisdom of Sartre's politics may be debated, but one cannot doubt the consistency of the effort.

Sartre also relied on the philosophical positions of *Being and Nothingness* in outlining the character of the engaged intellectual's contribution to history. Freedom was the central concept in defining the role of the writer. For Sartre human beings were free because consciousness is a lack, an opening to the world that no object can determine. This freedom gave human beings the opportunity to make themselves and, more particularly, was the basis for the intellectual's opportunity to have an effect on the world. The writer of literature transcended the given and in so doing challenged it. He held up against the given a world of facticity, containing possibilities that the reader could recognize and yet that could awaken his sense of freedom. "Literature," Sartre argued, "is the work of a total freedom addressing plenary freedoms and thus in its own way manifests the totality of the human condition as a free product of a creative activity. . . . Every day we must take sides; in our life as a writer, in our articles, in our books. Let it always be by preserving as our guiding principle the rights of total freedom as an effective synthesis of formal and material freedoms. Let this freedom manifest itself in our novels, our essays, and our plays. And if our characters do not yet enjoy it, if they live in our time, let us at least be able to show what it costs them not to have it" (p. 192). Anything but an aesthetic activity, literature was to be the gadfly of existential freedom, urging the reader, perhaps against his will, to recognize oppression, envisage authenticity, and struggle for revolution.

Although Sartre viewed literature as an appeal to the freedom of the reader, he was realistic enough to discern that many obstacles stood between the author's freedom as embodied in a work of fiction and the reader's freedom. The chief obstacle in 1947, according to Sartre, was the class nature of society. The realization of the freedom projected in literature was only possible in a classless society. In such a world, one where toil and oppression were not disproportionately imposed on one group at the expense of another, the fortunate writer would find that his subject matter was closely related to the perspectives of the whole society. Although literature, according to Sartre, always dwelled upon man as a being-in-the-world, the actual reading public was a far more restricted group than the general public or than society at large. This disparity had been the condition for a possible confusion in which "the interests and cares of man" are taken to be "those of a small and favored group" (pp. 105–6).

It is, of course, debatable whether "man in the world" is the only subject of literature. Many would argue, for example, that language is the only subject of literature. Still, Sartre's position is clear: in a class society the writer identifies only with certain groups, capturing the totality from the vantage point of those groups. A bourgeois writer writes from a bourgeois perspective, depicting workers only as the bourgeois sees him. That is clear enough in a monarchist like Balzac, a bourgeois like Flaubert, and a democrat like Zola. The consequence of this partiality is that the relation of freedom to freedom is broken as ideology betrays the voice of freedom. In a classless society, on the contrary, the writer defends the interests of all. Under these circumstances, Sartre insists,

> The writer will renew [the world] as is, the raw, sweaty, smelly, everyday world, in order to submit it to freedoms on the foundation of a freedom. Literature in this classless society would thus be the world aware of itself, suspended in a free act, and offering itself to the free judgment of all men, the reflective self-awareness of a classless society. It is by means of the book that the members of this society would be able to get their bearings, to see themselves and see their situation. (p. 107)

Sartre's understanding or vision of the writer in a classless society conforms to the definition of the universal intellectual as Foucault has sketched it. The writer speaks for everyone. The writer is the great representative of humanity's freedom. The voice of the writer, and his alone it would seem, can utter the words of freedom. His pen can transcribe in the book the needs and aspirations of every individual. His imagination can invent the figures that confront everyone with his potential for freedom, his aspiration to authenticity. Thus Sartre perpetuates, at least in his dream of the perfect writer in the perfect world, the prejudice against partiality, the critique of factions, and the doctrines of natural rights and universal reason, stances originating in the Enlightenment and culminating in Hegel's identification of truth with totality.

Surveying the situation in 1947, Sartre recognized clearly enough that the social conditions of writing were not those of the existentialist or Marxist utopia. Society was indeed divided into classes, sharply restricting the public available to the writer.

The question that confronted the engaged writer, therefore, was how to acknowl-edge the prevailing social conditions and still allow space for his own influence. Sartre attempted a dialectical formulation of the problem in which the writer and the public entered into a reciprocal interaction that was effective but not completely determining.

> One cannot write without a public and without a myth—without a *certain* public which historical circumstances have made, without a *certain* myth of literature which depends to a very great extent upon the demand of this public. In a word, the author is in a situation, like all other men. But his writings, like every human project, simultaneously enclose, specify, and sur-pass this situation. . . . (p. 101)

The writer was thus faced with the obstacle of an unfree situation, which was, paradoxically, a condition for the exercise of his freedom.

On the more concrete level of the particular circumstances of the postwar period in France, Sartre was compelled to acknowledge that things were bleak indeed. The situation might be necessary for freedom, but Sartre's situation, as he understood it, did not offer much prospect for the realization of the literature of praxis. The first harsh condition imposed by the situation of class society on the writer was, Sartre stoically pronounced, that the writer was bourgeois and his public was not. After a short sketch of the history of literature since the nineteenth century, Sartre was forced to admit the bourgeois nature of literary production. "That's what we are. In other respects, saints, heroes, mystics, adventurers, angels, enchanters, execu-tioners, victims, as you like. But, first of all, bourgeois" (p. 113).

Just as the writer was bourgeois, so were the readers, a second unwanted feature of the situation in 1947. No sophisticated statistical analysis of book sales was required to demonstrate that the people who bought Sartre's books, who sub-scribed to *Les Temps modernes*, who followed the arguments of the intellectuals in the periodicals were very much the same people who had a dominant position in the relations of production. Although this fact was true for writers in general, it seemed particularly valid with respect to Sartre. Postwar existentialism simply did not appeal to what Sartre considered the progressive social forces. What was worse, perhaps, was the charge by Communist intellectuals that those marginal groups who might turn to the Party were drifting away from it toward existentialism. The young bourgeois, who rejected the life of his parents and was open, at least poten-tially, to the appeal of the cause of Marxism, was instead devouring the message of the existentialists and choosing individualist solutions. Sartre was more than a little perturbed by these accusations, but he had no effective answer to them. All he could do was to point to his own experience in World War II. The individualist project of authenticity—the message of his earlier writings— was inappropriate to the situation:

> Our life as an individual which had seemed to depend upon our efforts, our virtues, and our faults, on our good and bad luck, on the good and bad will

of a very small number of people, seemed governed down to its minutest details by obscure and collective forces, and its most private circumstances seemed to reflect the state of the whole world. All at once we felt ourselves abruptly situated. (p. 147)

Though the force of circumstances was compelling enough to Sartre and his friends, the younger generation scandalously preferred to ignore it.

When Sartre analyzed the situation of the writer in 1947 more closely, he came upon still greater obstacles. There was still the proletariat to appeal to: "We turn toward the working class which today, like the bourgeoisie in 1780, might constitute for the writer a revolutionary public" (p. 174). Even if this rather simplistic analogy between 1947 and 1789 were appropriate, there was no reason to suspect that the working class would listen to Sartre. But he persisted. The existentialist rejected the Communist Party's heroic myth of the proletariat while accepting its importance in history. Therefore the conclusion was inevitable: ". . . it must be said without hesitation that the fate of literature is bound up with that of the working class" (p. 175). So much the worse because the distressing reality was that the working class, or so Sartre thought, was sequestered under the ever-watchful gaze of the Party. A bourgeois intellectual, associated in the eyes of the Party with the demimonde of Paris, could never break through the curtain of propaganda with which the Communists enshrouded him. With frustration and pathos Sartre wrote, "Unhappily, these men, to whom we *must* speak, are separated from us by an iron curtain in our own country; they will not hear a word that we shall say to them. The majority of the proletariat, straight-jacketed by a single party . . . forms a closed society without doors or windows. There is only one way of access, a very narrow one, the Communist Party" (p. 175).

In this situation Sartre was faced with an unpalatable choice: join the Party and gain access to the workers, but surrender all independence, or remain outside the Party and write for the bourgeoisie. Since the first alternative was impossible, he took his chances with the second. As a result, Sartre, perhaps the most famous writer of his day, had "readers but no public." Incredible as it sounds, the existentialist writer insisted that he had no audience, at least none he was willing to recognize as his own. But this predicament only strengthened Sartre's will. The challenge of the situation evoked a still greater determination to overcome the obstacles. In a sense proving his own thesis that the situation could be overcome by freedom, Sartre resolved to create his own public where none existed. Picturing himself as the underdog David in a death struggle with Goliath, Sartre wrote, "Our engagement must begin the moment we are repulsed and excommunicated by the Churches, when the art of writing, wedged in between different propagandas, seems to have lost its characteristic effectiveness" (p. 184). At this dramatic moment in his literary career, when all odds seemed against him, Sartre developed a strategy for combat in which there were certain assumptions concerning the nature of the intellectual, assumptions which betray the revolutionary posture he wished to adopt and which are central to the conclusions of this paper.

In *What is Literature?* Sartre outlined a program, consisting of three main proposals, by which he would fulfill the image of the engaged writer in the situation of 1947. The first task was the realistic assessment of the audience, those groups which could not be reached (workers, peasants, Christians) and those which potentially could be reached. It is worth noting that Sartre did not mention those groups that he had already reached, an omission that lends support to his detractors who denounced the followers of existentialism as social trash. Sartre's "virtual readers," the group he would now win over were certain uncommitted sections of the petty bourgeoisie—teachers and "those popular factions which have not joined up with communism" (p. 185). The appeal to the petty bourgeoisie as a potential source of radicalism is more astute than it might appear. Within Marxist circles a debate has flourished for some time concerning the role of the petty bourgeoisie in social revolution which clearly suggests the wisdom of addressing their concerns.[8] The first step in Sartre's program was eminently logical.

Next Sartre searched for a means to reach his virtual reader. In addition to the book, which Sartre thought only reached the bourgeoisie, he would turn to the mass media—radio, newspapers, and films. It was not a question of popularization, Sartre insisted, but of communicating to people in ways that could be heard. The mass media had opened new avenues for the exchange of ideas and it did not matter that they were not often used for this purpose. At age forty-two, Sartre was still sensitive enough to his surroundings to realize the importance of the mass media. He had recognized that the committed intellectual could, in the mid-twentieth century, escape from the traditional confines of politico–philosophical discourse. From the 1940s until his death Sartre made numerous efforts to employ the new media, including television, in order to spread his ideas. Doubtless he also enjoyed the attention the media gave him, becoming something of an intellectual star. It is surprising that he was seemingly oblivious to the dangers inherent in electronic publicity. Just as he regarded language as nothing more than a tool for the expression of conscious thoughts and feelings, so too he ignored the alienating effects of the media, the ways in which the structure of the media inserts its own meanings into communication regardless of the motives of the person being broadcast or televised.

The crucial question for Sartre remained: how to transform a disparate audience into a public, "an organic unity of readers, listeners, and spectators?" (p. 187). Only as a public, Sartre thought, could his audience change from passivity and isolation to collective solidarity and political effectiveness. The argument Sartre presented for creating a public reveals, I think, his limitations as a universal intellectual. At the outset Sartre betrays his allegiance to the typical myth of the intellectual: ". . . the man who reads . . . ," he claims, "puts himself at the peak of his freedom" (p. 187). (One has to assume that included here are also listening and watching.) Sartre has retreated to the Enlightenment distinction between thought and action. In the act of quiet reflection one is free; out in the world, one is subject to determining forces. Reading is a transcendental act that is beyond the constraining pressures of the Newtonian world of nature. Sartre writes, "Thus, by his very exigence, the reader attains that chorus of good wills which Kant has called the City of Ends . . ." (p. 187). The reading audience is a community of free subjects bound together by the strongest and most sublime spiritual ties. Still this community of free readers is not a public, not a force of historical change. In order for that to occur, two further conditions must be met: first, the reader must have an intuition of solidarity with others, and second, the community of good wills must become a real community (". . . these abstract good wills [must] establish real relations among themselves when actual events take place . . ."; p. 188).

Even if we grant Sartre the dubious claim about the freedom of the reader, we cannot go along with his next step: the assertion that the author can transform the spiritual community into a real one. For it is here that Sartre states explicitly, more explicitly than I have seen elsewhere, the fundamental assumption of the universal intellectual. "It is up to us," he writes, "to convert the city of ends into a concrete and open society—and this by the very content of our words" (p. 190). There is no ambiguity, no embarrassment, no hesitation in Sartre's maneuver: the writer creates the public, the intellectual fashions the revolutionary mass; ideas, in short, shape reality. The action the intellectual takes represents nothing less than a royal command to the audience. Sartre proclaims himself philosopher-king without the need to hold office. The most sanctified value of Western civilization is announced without a shred of recognition of its historic limitations: knowledge is power.

The obvious contradiction of Sartre's position goes unperceived: he wants free readers to create a free world; he condemns the Communist Party and the Church as external forces aborting freedom; yet he places himself in the same position with respect to his readers as they have to theirs. Sartre acts upon his readers the same way they act on their followers.

> If we start with the moral exigence which the aesthetic feeling envelops without meaning to do so, we are starting on the right foot. We must *historicize* the reader's good will, that is, by the formal agency of our work, we must, if possible, provoke his intention of treating men, in every case, as an absolute end and, by the *subject* of our writing, direct his intention upon his neighbors, that is, upon the oppressed of the world. (p. 190)

Sartre would play the role of God vis-à-vis his readers, determining their thoughts, changing their wills, yet allowing them to be free, indeed forcing them to create a free world. Quite an act of metaphysical acrobatics.

The phrases Sartre employs to speak of his relation to his public manifest the power of the intellectual: the reader "will be led by the hand until he is made to see that" (p. 191); "we must remind them"; "let us show them"; "let us point out"; "let us teach them" (p. 202). For one sensitive to the least nuances of language Sartre pays little heed to the manner in which he addresses free subjects. In one respect he can bemoan the fact that ". . . we are living in the age of mystifications" (p. 197), that language has become seriously corrupted. "Our first duty as a writer," he insists, "is thus to re-establish language in its dignity. After all, we think with words" (p. 197). The writer must not flinch, in an age of lies and duplicities, of cover-ups and alibis, to call things by their names, to speak the truth in all its plainness whatever the consequences may be. Yet in another respect Sartre imagines that he can establish a revolutionary public through decree, that he can hold up the banner of freedom by the force of his words.

The apparent contradiction in Sartre's position is explained by the assumption he holds about the nature of the intellectual. Although he maintains that all individuals are ontologically or potentially free, he writes as though only the intellectual were in fact free. Sartre takes it for granted that the truth is available to him alone and yet that this truth applies to all. Only on this basis is it possible for him to maintain that he knows the needs of his audience better than they themselves. "Our job is to reveal to the public its own needs . . ." (p. 186), a statement whose arrogance requires no elaboration. As is typical of the universal intellectual, Sartre does not even find it necessary to justify the privileged position of the intellectual. The arrogation of truth to the writer comes naturally and is not open to argument. Perhaps there is a remnant of patriarchy here: just as the father knows the needs of the child better than the child, so the intellectual knows best the needs of the public.

In the end it is a matter of whose voice will be heard. Sartre thinks that his voice can stand in place of his audience, can represent them. "Our job as a writer is to represent the world and to bear witness to it" (p. 199). The intellectual thus stands in the place of the audience, thinking and speaking for them. One can argue about whether this system is Leninist or bourgeois, democratic centralist or parliamentary. The Sartrean intellectual is Leninist in that the voice that speaks the truth or holds the proper theoretical position naturally assumes the mantle of power. But he is bourgeois in that he has won his audience in the marketplace of ideas, through a competition with others which is a kind of election.

The analysis of the concept of the intellectual in *What is Literature?* leads to the conclusion that Sartre's assumptions about the writer do indeed fit into the category of the universal intellectual as outlined by Foucault. The dangers inherent in such a definition of the writer are severe and work against the ideological ambitions of the engaged intellectual. Sartre, of course, did not presume to speak for the whole of society, just for the petty bourgeoisie, or an important section of it. Yet he laid the basis for his relation to that audience in the utopia of a classless society in which the intellectual would finally become universal. That utopia crept back into his sociologically realistic analysis of the situation in 1947 in the sense that Sartre's relation to his limited audience was couched in the same representational form that it would take in the classless world. In 1947 Sartre estimated that he could command only the voices of one group, while in the future he might speak for everyone.

The difficulty in this position, as Foucault sees it, is twofold: first, there is no justification, epistemological or otherwise, for the representationality of the intellectual; second, in this arrangement, since the popular forces never get the opportunity to speak, one never knows if the intellectual is indeed correct in his pronouncements or not. With regard to the first problem, a politically retrograde notion of truth is fostered: there is one truth and it is controlled by those who best manipulate logic and language.[9] With regard to the second problem, the masses are led to rely on the propositions of an external voice that can easily misrepresent them. Worse yet, the masses do not develop, in this form of intellectual practice, the habit of speaking for themselves, of developing discourses that relate to their practice. The absolute separation of discourse and practice is maintained, or better, a specialization of functions is established by which discourse emerges at one point in the field of forces and practice at another, a non-synchronous politics whose faults are well exemplified in both the bourgeois and the Communist camps.

Foucault, like Sartre, connects knowledge and power, intellect and will, but in a manner that undercuts the Sartrean "universal intellectual" in favor of the "specific intellectual." He does this by shifting the level of analysis to situations in daily life in which the intellectual function is closely bound in practice to the audience. He seeks those places in society where discourse is implicated in action: the hospital staff with its doctors; the welfare agency with its social service workers; the military with its scientific and technical cadres; the prison with its criminologists and legal experts. In these instances discourse and practice are mingled, each is constrained by the other. The intellect does not act upon the will as from outside but is always already formed by it. In Foucault there is no privileged place of freedom where knowledge becomes a general power. The specific intellectual cannot fabricate an "open society," to use Sartre's words, but only expose the pattern of domination inherent in a particular institution.

Foucault's critique of the universal intellectual has much to say for itself. It undermines, in a Nietzschean fashion, the traditional Western assumptions about truth, writing, and the philosopher. It opens up the question of the relation of theory to practice in a manner that has not been seen since the days of Marx. Foucault decenters and multiplies the locus of theory or discourse, upsetting an easy reconciliation with politics or the class struggle. At neither end of the dichotomy between theory and practice is there a simple resolution. The intellectual is not the universal theorist; the proletariat is not the universal revolutionary force. At the same time, there is a *practice* in the theory of the intellectuals and there is a *theory* in the practice of progressive social forces. Foucault's position is certainly a refreshing reformulation of issues that have long remained stagnant and uncompelling.

Nevertheless there are dangers in Foucault's position, the most obvious of which is the credence it seems to lend to a problematic form of pluralism. If the intellectual is proscribed from theorizing the totality, consigned instead to the boundaries of local institutions, political protest, it would appear, must also remain confined to individual issues, local affairs, interest group pressures. General social transformation has apparently been abandoned in favor of a guerrilla warfare of structural reforms. If the dangers of representing the totality are so great that no one may speak for society, there arises the implication that everyone has something to say about their limited circumstances. If there is no general Truth and no general Politics, then all particular truth and all particular politics are sanctioned. Foucault, of course, does not maintain this position or even concede validity to it. Yet he has not clarified his position on pluralism, lending it a sort of silent approval.

Pluralism can also be closely related to anarchism. The critique of the general intellectual goes arm in arm with a rejection of general politics. On many occasions Foucault has spoken against the traditional assumption that power emanates from the central state. In its place he has argued for a multi-centered view of power, one in which power is dispersed throughout the social field in the smallest corners of everyday life. When power is conceived this way, the struggle against domination takes on a new pattern. The goal becomes one of counteracting nefarious forms of domination on all fronts and political life becomes a generalized assault on "the micro-physics of power." Such a view of politics goes along with the notion of the specific intellectual, but it also suggests an anarchist position in which society is ruled at once by no one and by everyone. The difficulty that must be faced, however, is that if domination is everywhere in daily life, the struggle against it seems hopeless.[10] Nothing prevents new forms of domination from replacing old ones, the new ills perhaps exceeding the old.

The second danger in Foucault's position is a logical one. The universal intellectual can only be criticized by a stance that itself is at some level universal. Foucault legislates in favor of the specific intellectual, the writer organically connected with an institution and group. Yet the negation he posits is itself universal. Anyone who maintains the stance of the universal is subject to the representational fallacy. But to attack this "anyone" requires a universal statement. Foucault himself represents the totality when he denounces totalizing positions. Only by stepping beyond the limits of the specific intellectual can Foucault proclaim his universal theory in its favor. In sum, Foucault's statements about the universal intellectual are themselves universal and his theory of the specific intellectual is a *general* theory of the intellectual. I do not think there is any way around this aporia, but it cannot be dismissed as a logical oddity without material effects.

By denying that general theory is possible, or that a general theory is truly revolutionary, Foucault is implicitly totalizing the situation. Taking a position against totalization, he incurs a totalizing statement. Foucault needed to develop an epistemology and sociology of the intellectual which would account for the position of the critique of the universal intellectual. The question that needs to be raised, which Foucault has not raised, is: under what conditions might the universal intellectual be rejected in favor of the specific intellectual? One cannot avoid the problems of the universal intellectual simply by negating that figure.

Foucault's difficulty with this issue can be clarified in relation to his peculiar refusal to present his own authorial voice in personal terms. At the moment of his greatest recognition as an author, the occasion of his Inaugural Lecture ("The Discourse on Language") at the highly prestigious College de France, Foucault would have preferred to disappear and remain nameless, disappropriating his own voice:

> I would really like to have slipped imperceptibly into this lecture, as into all the others I shall be delivering, perhaps over the years ahead. . . . At the moment of speaking, I would like to have perceived a nameless voice, long preceding me, leaving me merely to enmesh myself in it, taking up its cadence,

and to lodge myself, when no one was looking, in its interstices as if it had paused an instant, in suspense, to beckon to me.[11]

Foucault desires an inaudible beginning to his discourse in order to avoid a certain "anxiety" that surrounds words. Since discourse and power are closely interlinked, words are the source of "conflicts, triumphs, injuries, dominations and enslavements." To begin a discourse is thus to enter into a political world.

Perhaps the constraints on the specific intellectual also provide an explanation for Foucault's reluctance to appear on the mass media. Unlike Sartre, who eagerly participated in radio and television shows, Foucault avoided such publicity whenever possible. He is far more aware than Sartre was of the profound effects of the media. When he wanted to assist prisoners in their protests against conditions in the jails in the early 1970s, he calculated his appearance at demonstrations outside prisons so that the media would be attracted to the location and therefore publicize the prisoners' demands. But he refused himself to speak in front of the cameras; only the prisoners must be heard; their voices, not that of the intellectual, must pronounce the list of complaints.

The same urge for anonymity is found in the opening pages of *The Archeology of Knowledge*, Foucault's major statement on methodology in the human sciences. Written shortly before the "Discourse on Language," the *Archeology* does not fully develop the relation between discourse and power. Consequently discourse can be depicted as a means by which the intellectual conceals himself from the powers that be. Foucault, addressing his reader directly, states:

> What, do you imagine that I would take so much trouble and so much pleasure in writing, do you think that I would keep so persistently to my task, if I were not preparing—with a rather shaky hand—a labyrinth into which I can venture, in which I can move my discourse, opening up underground passages, forcing it to go far from itself, finding overhangs that reduce and deform its itinerary, in which I can lose myself and appear at last to eyes that I will never have to meet again. I am no doubt not the only one who writes in order to have no face. Do not ask who I am and do not ask me to remain the same: leave it to our bureaucrats and our police to see that our papers are in order.[12]

Faceless or voiceless, Foucault preferred, it would seem, not to be noticed.

Although Foucault's impulse toward anonymity is the same in both cases, the more recent position creates a greater difficulty for his notion of the specific intellectual. Once a close relation between knowledge and power is posited, as it is in the "Discourse on Language," the urge to aural oblivion, to impersonality, erases particularity in favor of universality. The specific intellectual after all is characterized by his personal relation to his audience: he is not a distant representative but a close participant. By contrast Sartre, the universal intellectual, the "voice of reason," appears to his audience only in the silence of reading, an impersonal, distant voice, a transcendental presence who brings the good news of freedom to the oppressed and confused masses. The critique of the Sartrean intellectual cannot be made in a nameless discourse that merely reproduces universality in another form. Instead the specific intellectual would fully have to accept the burden of his own discourse/practice. Through the particularity of voice the specific intellectual would avoid the pretense to universality that Foucault objects to but embraces as a cloaked disguise.

It is clear that much remains to be done in clarifying the implications of Foucault's critique of the universal intellectual. Nonetheless, it does afford a perspective by which one can view the limitations of the existentialist concept of the writer. The conclusion is inevitable that the postwar existentialists were far less revolutionary in their theory of the writer than they thought. Their search for the third way, one beyond Marxism and liberalism, was less successful than they thought. The engaged writer was a true alternative neither to the party theorist nor to the olympian mandarin.

Notes

1. See, for example, Jean-Paul Sartre, "A Propos de l'existentialisme, mise au point," *Action* 17 (1944), p. 11.

2. For an account of the trials and hopes of the existentialists during this period, see Simone de Beauvoir, *Force of Circumstance*, trans. Richard Howard (New York: G. P. Putnam's Sons, 1964). Also useful are Michel-Antoine Burnier, *Choice of Action*, trans. Bernard Murchland (New York: Vintage, 1968); David Caute, *Communism and the French Intellectuals: 1914–1960* (New York: Macmillan, 1964); Mark Poster, *Existential Marxism in Postwar France* (Princeton: Princeton University Press, 1976); B. D. Graham, *The French Socialists and Tripartisme: 1944–1947* (Toronto: Toronto University Press, 1965), for the general political situation.

3. Julien Benda, *La Trahison des clercs* (Paris: Grasset, 1927).

4. Jacques Derrida, *Of Grammatology*, trans. Gayatri Spivak (Baltimore: Johns Hopkins University Press, 1974).

5. Michel Foucault, *Les mots et les choses*, trans. as *The Order of Things: An Archaeology of the Human Sciences* (New York: Pantheon, 1970).

6. Michel Foucault, "Truth and Power," trans. in *Working Papers*, ed. Meaghan Morris, Paul Patton (Sydney: Feral Publications, 1979), p. 41. This piece is also available in Michel Foucault, *Power/Knowledge: Selected Interviews and Other Writings*, ed. Colin Gordon (New York: Pantheon, 1980).

7. Jean-Paul Sartre, *What is Literature?*, trans. Bernard Frechtman (New York: Washington Square Press, 1966), p. 14. Subsequent page references in the text are to this edition.

8. See, for example, Jonathan Wiener, "Marxism and the Petty Bourgeoisie: A Reply to Arno Mayer," *Journal of Modern History* 48 (1976), pp. 666–71.

9. See David Carroll, "The Subject of Archeology or the Sovereignty of the Episteme," *Modern Language Notes* 93 (1978), pp. 695, 722.

10. Jean Baudrillard, *Oublier Foucault* (Paris: Editions Galilée, 1977).

11. Michel Foucault, "The Discourse on Language," in *The Archaeology of Knowledge*, trans. A. M. Sheridan Smith (New York: Pantheon, 1972), p. 215.

12. Michel Foucault, *The Archaeology of Knowledge*, p. 17.

The Lion and the Fox: Politics and Autobiography in the Renaissance / *Marc E. Blanchard*

In chapter XVIII of Machiavelli's *The Prince* there is a reference to the centaur Chiron:

> You must, therefore, know that there are two means of fighting, one according to the laws, the other with force; the first way is proper to man, the second to beast; but because the first, in many cases, is not sufficient, it becomes necessary to have recourse to the second. Thereafter, a prince must know how to use wisely the nature of the beast and the man. This policy was taught to Princes allegorically by the ancient writers, who describe how Achilles and many of the ancient princes were given to Chiron the centaur to be raised and taught under his discipline. This can only mean that, having a half-beast and a half-man as a teacher, a Prince must know how to employ the nature of the one and the other; and the one without the other cannot endure. Since, then, a Prince must know how to make use of the nature of the beast, he should use from among the beasts the fox and the lion; for the lion cannot defend itself from traps and the fox cannot protect itself from wolves. It is, therefore, necessary to be a fox in order to recognize the traps and a lion in order to frighten the wolves. Those who play only the part of the lion do not understand matters.[1]

As the text suggests, Machiavelli did not invent this fable of the lion and the fox. It is a classical *topos* used by Plutarch among others and is also part of a broad centauric mythology.[2] That Machiavelli uses the paradigm of the lion and the fox as a rhetorical *topos* to discuss modes of political appearance is not unimportant: it indicates that problems of power and politics are initially problems of language and representation. The purpose of this paper is to explore some of the aspects of this representation in Machiavelli and Montaigne.

In Machiavelli's text centauric education implies that the recognition of a man-beast dialectic is central to politics. It also implies a downplaying of morals, insofar as animals have no morals, only instincts and needs. Perhaps this downplaying of morals is meant as an attack against the tradition of a man-measured world, where man is the lord of creation and rules over the animals. Three quarters of a century later, in the *Apologie de Raymond Sebond*, Montaigne would write against those who arrogantly assume that man is different from, and better than, animals.

> When I play with my cat, who knows if I am not a pastime to her more than she is to me?[3]

Machiavelli takes no position on the question of whether we are like beasts. For him the bestial scenario is simply a part of the political stage: "This policy was taught to Princes allegorically by the ancient writers . . . those who *play* only the part of the lion do not understand matters." For Montaigne, however, it is only the ability to *play* a role which distinguishes men from animals.

> But apropos of judging men, it is a wonder that, ourselves excepted, nothing is evaluated except by its own qualities. We praise a horse because it is vigorous and skillful . . . not for his harness; a greyhound for its speed, not for its collar, a bird for his wing, not his jesses and bells. Why do we not likewise judge a man by what is his own? (I, 42:189)

In an area of human relations where acting is of the essence (Montaigne: "I do not want to deprive deceit of its proper place; that would be misunderstanding the world" [III, 1:604]), the assumption that man can play the part of any animal, the fox or the lion, is a byproduct of what Isaiah Berlin refers to as the end of medieval and Renaissance monism, a view of the world in which all conducts are regulated by a single natural principle, be it reason or the divine creator.[4] Until the Renaissance, man is seen as acting out only his part in the whole system of creation. He does not have to appear other than he is. His conduct is prescribed, his existence fulfills God's will, without which he couldn't even begin to think of himself as existing inside or outside the body politic. With Machiavelli there is no longer such an agreement regarding the unity or the identity of the acting subject. Before the Italian and the French Renaissance, the metaphor of theater is frequent in descriptions of the various postures and professions of man in a world whose functional variety is a testimony to the power of God Almighty. During the Renaissance, while the feeling subsists from the Humanists to Shakespeare that the theater of man (*theatrum mundi*) continues to be the source of all anthropological knowledge and a model for all mimesis ("all the world's a stage"), there is a suspicion that these theatrics are not in simple accord with man's status on earth or his place in the world to come, but that they stand for man's relation to his *private* life.

This is made quite clear at the outset of both *The Prince* and the *Essays*. In the dedication to Lorenzo which opens his book, Machiavelli expresses the hope that the work will win him the much-needed favor of his prince, and he also reminds Lorenzo that by reason of certain rules of perspective, only someone who is not a prince can actually appreciate what makes a good prince.

> For just as those who paint landscapes place themselves in low position in the plain in order to consider the nature of mountains and the high places and place themselves high atop mountains in order to study the plains, in like manner, to know well the nature of the people, one must be a prince, and to know well the nature of the princes, one must be of the people. (p. 78)

Machiavelli suggests that the reverse of this comparison is also true. Just as only one of the people can see the prince as he stands out on his mountain above the valley, only the prince can see one who is his putative subject and appreciate the whole picture in which the subject is incorporated.

> And if your Magnificence will turn your eyes at some time from the summit of your high position towards these lowlands, you will realize to what degree I unjustly suffer a great and continuous malevolence of fortune. (p. 79)

Both Alberti and Leonardo had already stated that the object of vision can only be seen rationally through a mathematical reconstruction of the relation of viewer and viewed. Yet this reconstruction of vision, while putting man in a position in which he can understand how to construct representation and to encompass the physical world, leaves in abeyance his own status in relation to his environment. In spite of this skillful reconstruction, which establishes that the object to be seen is identical to the object of vision, the person looking in the looking glass is, like Machiavelli who never caught Lorenzo's attention, forever ignored. Or to put it another way, the question introduced by Machiavelli's perspective is one that Alberti had not been able to answer: by looking at the prince, whom do I see? Do I see the prince or do I see myself?

Montaigne opens his *Essays* with an advice to the reader, in which he also defines himself, however precariously and contradictorily, as an object of closer vision. It is for the next of kin and friends that he has written the *Essays*.

> I have dedicated it to the private convenience of my relatives and friends, so that when they have lost me (as soon they must), they may recover here some features of my habits and temperament, and by this means keep the knowledge they have had of me more complete and alive. (p. 2)

In this sense the character in the book would only be an image of the real Montaigne in his *natural form*. Yet the reader is also advised that in his book Montaigne did not paint his whole picture because in trying to do that he would have acted against the moral order.

> Had I been placed among those nations which are said to live still in the sweet freedom of nature's first laws, I assure you I should very gladly have portrayed myself here entire and wholly naked. (p. 2)

Montaigne suggests that in composing his book he has followed the manner of baroque painters who fill the sides of their paintings with all sorts of shapes, patches, and bodies: "fantastic paintings whose only charm lies in their variety and strangeness," designed to contrast with the main subject unified and highly integrated in the foreground. His work then is nothing but a concatenation of "grotesque and monstrous bodies," while the central theme of his enquiry, the true picture of self always escapes him (1, 28:135). While Machiavelli asserts the necessity of abiding by the rules of perspective to ensure a satisfactory communication between writer and reader (the man of the lower classes having a correct perspective on the prince on the mountain, and the prince in return being in a position to evaluate correctly the situation of his subject in the valley), Montaigne suggests that the reader keep in mind the rules of family perspective (domestic and private) before he ventures to pass judgment on the work. Only following this stipulation will he know who the author Montaigne really is. Yet even with this stipulation the enterprise appears problematic and Montaigne eventually suggests that his reader not waste his time with the *Essays*. "Thus, reader, I am myself the matter of my book; you would be unreasonable to spend your leisure on so frivolous and vain a subject" (p. 2).

The images projected in both Machiavelli's and Montaigne's books remain curiously aloof, requiring the constant and meticulous gaze of the spectator and escaping all other previously known contexts of reference. Montaigne's self-image is but a *grotesque* and Machiavelli's prince is a monstrous mixture of lion and fox. In both cases, because of an effect of perspective, it is difficult to isolate the reference beneath the art form. What is the difference between the figure in the painting or the hero in the book and the real man who serves as model for the painter or the writer? And is not this difference difficult to describe precisely because of the unexamined notion of model and mimesis? Must the model be fully imitable and thus run the risk of becoming indistinguishable from the imitation, or must it forever remain beyond the reach of the imitator? Just as Machiavelli's new prince leaves us uncertain whether he is himself or someone else, whether he plays the two parts of the fox and the lion or whether he appears in the single character of the centaur, so Montaigne's portrait leaves us in the lurch, unsure of what to believe.

> Nature reveals this confusion to us; painters hold that the movements and wrinkles of the face that serve for weeping serve also for laughing. In truth, before one or the other is completely expressed, watch the progress of the painting: you are in doubt toward which one it is going. And the extremity of laughter is mingled with tears. (II, 20:511)

Because political action is predicated on the determination of how it is going to be received, its course is always dependent on a general agreement between all concerned: between the prince who rules and the people who are willing to be ruled. If the prince appears to be an integral part of the city he governs, it is because he is on everybody's mind. Every one of his actions is subject to public scrutiny: "A prince must be very careful not to let anything slip from his lips which is not full of the five qualities mentioned above: he should appear to be all mercy and all faithfulness, all integrity, all kindness, all religion" (XVIII:135). The result of this extraordinary attention, however, is that the prince is merely an object for others: he is what and how they see him. Conversely, for the prince, subjects are only what they appear to be interested in (mercy, faithfulness). They may not have any real interest in the prince's actual virtue, but they insist that he appear to be virtuous and he is only too happy to oblige. Elsewhere Machiavelli states that as long as the prince refrains from damaging the honor of his subjects and from stealing their wives, he will have a better chance of remaining in power (XIX:136). The prince's omnipotence is thus the result of a tacit agreement between the prince and the people—a contract in which both parties commit themselves to maintaining the other's image. The result is a book totally concerned with the *eidos*, the representation of persons and things, especially in the later and more famous chapters in *The Prince* (XV–XXV), devoted not to princely *praxis*, but to the image of a prince concerned less with what he does than with how he appears in the eyes of his subjects. In Machiavelli's view, if the prince has few advisers and no friends, he is not lonely so much because he has to mistrust anyone and everyone, but because his remaining at a proper distance is the necessary condition to his citizens' proper focus on him as the image of the body politic.

Such a contract of intersubjectivity raises two questions. First, if it is based on appearances only, isn't this intersubjectivity problematic? Second, given the moral and religious tradition in the political theory of his time, how does Machiavelli manage to make the appearance of the prince the central tenet of his unorthodox policies?

In attempting to drive a wedge between the ideals of morality and those of politics, Machiavelli creates a void in which politics and morality are no longer aligned but serve as a cover for each other. They work well together, but their complementarity is only fictive, the mask of an interiority which can never be known as interiority. The feelings of the prince or the people matter little throughout, except in the case of honoring women. Even in that case it could be argued that women and honor crystallize for every male in Machiavelli's time those individual feelings which, while private and intimate, are to a large extent determined by the reactions of others. They represent that which a subject can lose even if it is never really his: the image that others have of him. Subjects are bound to a moral stand to which they know the prince pays only lip service. In other words, it can be said that the state established by the prince is a *simulacrum* made possible by a conjunction of appearances. It is very much a fiction, perhaps not the work of art that Burckhardt wanted it to be, but rather a place where the discourse of politics is being proffered under the assumption that it only provides a screen for a series of actions too subversive to be articulated.

Let us now look at Montaigne's view of the relation between self and other. While Machiavelli's text functions mainly by maxims or syllogisms through which a political intersubjectivity can be set up as a work of art, Montaigne examines the conditions under which intersubjectivity is at all possible. He is less interested in *exempla* from ancient history than in the reality reflected by his own experience.

> However that may be, I mean to say, and whatever these absurdities may be, I have had no intention of concealing them, any more than I would a bald and graying portrait of myself, in which the painter had drawn not a perfect face, but mine. (I, 26:108)

This quote offers a counterpoint to Machiavelli's remark that in the best of all possible worlds one would wish to act honestly, but that in this world of ours the politician has no choice but to embrace deception. It is to the principle of this deception that Montaigne objects. He claims that if social intercourse is based on self-knowledge (i.e., the better a man knows himself the better he will be able to know others), the acquisition of self-knowledge will in turn affect social inter-course. People who have developed a sense of self-knowledge and self-worth will not stoop to "covering [themselves] with other men's armor until they don't show even their finger-tips" (I, 26:108). Contingencies of politics being what they are, it is clear for Montaigne that this acquisition of self-knowledge and of the proper institution leads to abandoning all hope of participating in the political life — mostly because a courtier cannot be expected to exercise his free judgment while he remains under permanent obligation to curry favor from his master. This promo-tion of self-knowledge and the ensuing abandonment of politics in Montaigne is not surprising since Montaigne begins his *Essay* on education by declaring his opposition to almost all forms of academic teaching.[6]

It is exactly here that one can notice a cleavage between Montaigne's personal institution and Machiavelli's political institution. For Montaigne public life, even though it may exclude political life, includes social discourse (*conférer*) and all those forms of social activity which enable the self to define itself. For Machiavelli political life includes only the kind of self-knowledge which is derived from the knowledge of others. For Montaigne public life is not concerned with the reception of the self among others but with the inclusion of others within the circle of self. For Machiavelli political life implies a form of otherness determined by the form one chooses to give to one's actions.

In the process of reducing the world of antiquity to his own, Montaigne finds that the diversity of the *exempla* keeps him from being able to chart a consistent course of action. Plutarch contributes to this uncertainty by offering an encyclo-pedia of these *exempla* in his *Moralia* and a series of double standards in the *Lives*. Moreover, in the composition of the *Lives*, he often mixes considerations of his heroes' private lives with reflections on the conduct of war or politics.[7] This is exactly the kind of lively chaos Montaigne enjoys. He says:

> The life of Caesar has no more to show us than our own; an emperor's or an ordinary man's, it is still a life subject to all human accidents. Let us only listen: we tell ourselves all we most need. (III, 13:822)

What this example of Caesar shows — and Montaigne is referring more to Plutarch's "Julius Caesar" in the *Lives* than to Caesar's own commentary — is that a con-sideration of the historic *exempla* of antiquity automatically brings, in the effort to understand them, a reflection upon oneself. This reflection allows a moment of suspense as Montaigne withdraws into himself. This operation is the reverse of Machiavelli's. While Machiavelli uses Chiron as a paradigm for covering up the relevant with the irrelevant, for disguising what one really wants with what others want in order better to achieve one's goals, Montaigne preaches a strategy of unmasking: "The young of bears and dogs show their natural inclination, but men, plunging headlong into certain habits, opinions, and laws, easily change or disguise themselves" (I, 26:109). He also states his interest in deconstructing, through a critique of those who cover themselves "with other men's armor," Aristotle's doc-trine of imitation that "tragedy is an imitation of personages better than the ordinary man."[8] Through this critique Montaigne hopes to bring about, not the picture of a prince as he is seen by his subjects, but the possibility he has never had, to see himself. It is the primacy of self-reflection in what constitutes the essayist's moral imperative and what Hugo Friedrich saw as the first lineaments of a *moral science* preempting any consideration of political action that characterizes the Montaignian moment at the end of the sixteenth century. The short-circuiting of politics by the quest for a personal ethics is not simply the product of an anti-Machiavellian strand of the post-Renaissance (Montaigne had read Machiavelli mostly through Bodin and Gentillet);[9] nor should the moral experiment of the *Essays* be seen in the perspective of a return to a Thomist view of the human city on earth. What is at stake here is a deconstruction of the duplicity inherent in all policies based on mutually exclusive relations between self and other and where conventional morality is simply an idealized image of those relations. Montaigne seeks to destroy this image and to examine the possibility of a moral knowledge and of a moral self underlying or preempting the existence of all actions, political or otherwise.

There is, however, in the *Essays* one area of comparison between self and other not mediated by a reading of ancient historians and thus not wholly explicable by a model reference to Plutarch, the encounter of Montaigne with the cannibals— *others*, if there ever were. The distance between Montaigne and the cannibals is not only cultural (instead of Plutarch he must now read travel books), but also geographic and linguistic. He experiences many of the problems which he has had in his apprenticeship of Latin, French, and Greek. In "Of Cannibals" Montaigne tells how he came to meet three Brazilians, no longer through the books of historians and explorers like Léry, Thevet, and Gomara, but through the mediation of an interpreter (*un truchement*) whose linguistic ability and general intelligence he had reason to think suspect. As Montaigne starts to recount his experience he routinely inserts this modern episode into the framework of authority of the ancient historians. His essay actually begins with an anecdote of Pyrrhus' first encounter with the Romans borrowed from Plutarch, in which the king expresses his amazement at the Romans not being the barbarians he expected them to be ("I do not know what barbarians these are for so the Greeks called all foreign nations" [1, 31:150]). However this reference to Plutarch does not solve Montaigne's problem with the *truchement* — more than a passing inconvenience in that it affects Montaigne's capacity to communicate with the cannibals and to experience their otherness. The whole episode can be seen as illustrating the difficulty in translating one culture into another, the alien into the familiar, other into self. Solving this problem would advance the understanding of the historical process, as historians are usually incapable of communicating to their readers the specifics of a situation, of setting in clear relief the otherness of the experience they have had. Montaigne quips: "We ought to have topographers who would give us an exact account of the places where they have been" (1, 31:152). Understandably the experience of the imperfect *truchement* impels Montaigne to look for his own representation of the mental space of the cannibals. It is then that he decides to explore the possibility of being himself another or a part of the other and of doing away with the mediation of a *truchement.* He does so twice: first, in the essay on the cannibals, and second, in the essay "Of Coaches."

Montaigne discusses the cannibalistic operation where the cannibal eats his enemy.[10] Because the enemy is a cannibal too, eating one's enemy becomes a dual operation in which a person, by ingesting another who may already have eaten a parent or a friend, reclaims that which is legitimately his. Montaigne dwells on the process, dismissing the negative literature on cannibalism.[11] He also ignores the religious controversy looming in the background of a discussion of the cannibals: whether it is proper for man to eat his kin, eat of man, as the model of the Eucharist.

The cannibal feast demonstrates a working through, a *Durcharbeitung* of the sign in the constitution of primitive identity. The body of the cannibal enemy is voided of its life but also of that which makes it totally other. By eating their enemy, the cannibals manage, in an operation more complex than the imitation of the Machiavellian beast, not only to regain from others what is rightfully theirs, but also to acquire and to absorb the enemy's awesome courage and steadfastness. However, because this operation encompasses both similarity and difference and exposes the amphibology of all interpretive mechanisms, the enemies, by reasserting, on the point of death, the power which had made it possible for them to assert their own difference in the first place, refuse to participate in the exchange of signs with their captors: "They defy them, insult them, reproach them with their cowardice and the number of battles they have lost to the prisoners' own people" (I, 31:157).

Ultimately this whole operation, while functional on a purely semiotic level, becomes problematic in the moral context of European culture where similarity and difference are articulated on the basis of an unalterable distance between the one and the other. To help himself Montaigne resorts to irony. Only thus can he hope to grasp the validity of the cannibals' experience: if they are savages to us, we must be savages to them.[12] Only a perfect *truchement* could have proven this reversibility by demonstrating how one culture can be translated in the terms of another. But such perfect *truchement* would have been no *truchement* at all. It would have represented the possibility of a totally reciprocal understanding between two cultures. Thus Montaigne is left with the tools of his own *inventio*. It is the writer's business to suggest ways in which the other, the *barbaron*, can be approached and manipulated through an "ingenious mixture on the part of nature."

> If our faces were not similar, we could not distinguish man from beast; if they were not dissimilar, we could not distinguish man from man. All things hold together by some similarity; every example is lame, and the comparison that is drawn from experience is always faulty and imperfect; however, we fasten together our comparisons by some corner. (III, 13:819)

Montaigne's rhetoric can now help us reestablish the foundations upon which Machiavelli's Chiron had been hastily conceived. To conceive of the beast and the man in one single body is only possible as a metaphor condensing what in real life, in the competition between people and people, between a people and an individual, between individuals, is an endless process of displacement and distortion. This displacement cannot be taken for granted nor does it constitute a purely aesthetic effect.

In his patient reconstruction of the chronology of the *Essays*, Michel Butor has noted the possible link between essay XXVIII "Of Friendship," essay XXIX which serves as an introduction to the sonnets of La Boétie, essay XXX "Of Moderation," and essay XXXI "Of Cannibals." [13] Villey notes in his introduction to essay XXX that it is one of the first essays to discuss the notion of art—not only art proper, but also in its primitive form, the semiotics of arts and communication—and that in the essay on the cannibals (XXXI), Montaigne advances the notion of a return to nature.[14] Butor, anxious to reestablish the general plan of the *Essays* on the basis of a sequence between the relationship Montaigne had with La Boétie and that he had with his father, does not take into consideration the possibility that the essay on the cannibals might also be related to the one on friendship (XXVIII). In a more profound, philosophical sense, the composition of the *Essays* might depend less on the artistic model of an *encadrement manièriste* than on the natural form of the relation between self and other as experienced by the cannibals. If this were the case, any discussion of representation in the *Essays* should shift from the consideration of Montaigne as a commentator on ancient historians mediating his experience through that of legitimate authors or *truchement* to that of a Montaigne-autobiographer seeking, albeit in an almost impossible task, to mediate his own experience through the writing of the *Essays*. For that he only needs the cooperation of his reader.

The essay "Of Friendship" (XXVIII) leads Montaigne to the point at which, unable to describe the symbiosis of mind and heart between himself and La Boétie other than by piling similarity upon similarity, he attempts to define this experience beyond words.

> Beyond all my understanding, beyond what I can say about this in particular, there was I know not what inexplicable and fateful force that was the mediator of this union . . . it is I know not what quintessence of all this mixture, which having seized my whole will, led it to plunge and lose itself in mine . . . I say lose, in truth, for neither of us reserved anything for himself, nor was anything either his or mine. (I, 28:139)

The friendship between La Boétie and Montaigne becomes an ideal experiment in which the two participants decide to "hate and banish from between them these words of separation and distinction" (I, 26:141). The paradox of a friendship beyond words is movingly expressed in the dream of a confusion between words, those of Montaigne and La Boétie echoed by the famous: "Because it was he, because it was I" (I, 28:139). In the end, the positive resolution of the problem of self and other is the responsibility of the essayist, the writer. No longer preoccupied with the selection of the proper *topoi* for his *inventio* as at the beginning of the *Essays*, Montaigne dedicates himself to solving the problem of how to transcend the limits of language in defining and communicating experience. It is only through an experiment in writing about himself that he can hope to give himself the full-fledged subjective experience of what remains for Machiavelli a purely objective model, a *simulacrum*. He will now write the history of his own traveling between the regions of self and other, and it is in the full display of this metonymical relation to himself that Montaigne now wishes to understand his own play with representation: "It is very easy to demonstrate that great authors, when they write about causes, adduce not only those they think are true but also those they do not believe in, provided they have some originality and beauty" (III, 6:685).

The essay "Of Coaches" gives a symbolic account of this traveling. From the discussion of means of transportation Montaigne drifts to a discussion of luxury and ostentation in those means of transportation, which then leads him back to a discussion of the respective stages of civilization of the Spaniards and the Indians during the conquest of America. The device for this ongoing drift is Montaigne's ongoing description of his relation to his own body: his paradoxical inability to travel comfortably by the means of drifting par excellence, the water coach. Eventually, at the end of the essay, Montaigne acknowledges this drifting: "Let us fall back to our coaches" (III, 6:698).

Montaigne scholarship is generally agreed that the text "Of Coaches," like that "Of Cannibals," represents one of the first instances of European self-examination and autocriticism in the face of the invasion of the new world. But beyond a critique of colonialism based on a meditation upon the "Machiavellian" tricks of the Spaniards ("take away the ruses and tricks that they used to deceive them" [III, 6:694]), Montaigne is also famous for his inquiry into stages of historical progress: on the one hand, the Indians were at a stage in their development in which they were satisfied with a primitive economy; on the other hand, the evolution of our own economy has alienated us further and further from the ideal state of nature. The question for Montaigne is no longer the ethical one of whether the tricks and ruses used by the Spaniards should be allowed in the realm of politics, but rather the proto-anthropological and sociological ones concerning man's place in the realm of politics. It is only because of the tremendous difference in development between Spanish and Indian cultures that the Spaniards and the Portuguese were so easily able to subdue the whole of America. The Europeans were able to terrify the Indians who saw them as monsters, perhaps even as centaurs:

> Mounted on great unknown monsters, opposed to men who had never seen not only a horse, but any sort of animal trained to carry and endure a man or any other burden; men equipped with a hard and shiny skin and a sharp and glittering weapon, against men who, for the miracle of a mirror or a knife, would exchange a great treasure in gold and pearls . . . people taken by surprise, under color of friendship and good faith, by curiosity to see strange and unknown things: eliminate this disparity, I say, and you take from the conquerors the whole basis of so many victories. (III, 6:694)

Montaigne muses that it was the dissimilarity in the Indians' and Spaniards' development that was instrumental in the latter's victory over the former. Furthermore, if America had been conquered by Alexander or Caesar, the Indians would have fared much better, because the two great men would have wanted to make good use of the latter's honesty and disingenuity.

In this context, the return to the theme of the primitive in "Of Coaches" broadens the perspective on the relation between the use of deceit in the conduct of policy and the struggle between prince and subject in "Of Cannibals." There Montaigne had already noted that the relationship of the primitive chieftain to his tribe is not one of domination but one of emulation.

> When I asked him what profit he gained from his superior position among his people (for he was a captain, and our sailors called him a king), he told me that it was to march foremost in war. (I, 31:159)

This was only in line with other traits of cannibal culture in which differences are reduced to repetitions, a reduction symbolized by the act of ingesting the other as an attribute of the same. There also, the reader was squarely confronted with the problem of how to integrate the *barbaron* into his own culture and how to solve the more pressing problem of working out a mediation between cultures. In "Of Coaches" the absence of mediation is more radically underlined by the Indian chief who states that he is not about to exchange his religion for that of the Spaniards, having used his own for so long, and that he prefers taking advice from friends— which the Spaniards do not appear to be (III, 6:697). In the end, the Conquistadores themselves are punished for their contempt of the otherness of the Indians by their own insatiable greed. They end up eating one another: "they devoured one another" in "intestine wars" (III, 6:697). Having easily outfoxed the Indians, they end up playing lion to one another, thus proving, perhaps, that the mythical alliance of fox and lion cannot overcome its inherent contradiction, and that it leads, instead, to self-annihilation. This is where Chiron's lesson ceases to be productive. The two parts, the human and the beastly cannot work together. In this failure lies the end of politics. La Boétie had already said it in his *Discours de la servitude volontaire*:

> Therefore isn't it a shame that upon seeing so many obvious examples, and seeing that the danger is so imminent, no one dares appear wise at the expense of someone else? And that among so many people so willingly courting tyrants there is none who is well-advised and courageous enough to tell them, as the fox in the tale: "I wouldn't mind visiting you in your lair, yet I see enough tracks of animals which go towards you forward and none that go back the other direction?" [15]

Montaigne perceives this at the end "Of Coaches" when, in stopping the coach, he also stops the drift of his narrative: he recounts how the king of Peru, finally encircled, was thrown off his coach and taken prisoner on the ground.

At the end of a meditation on the writing of self and other in Machiavelli and Montaigne the question arises of a disparity, or at least an evolution, between genres. Machiavelli wrote a political treatise. Montaigne wrote what is currently considered to be one of the first autobiographies. Can one legitimately compare two works belonging to such diverse genres? Another way to phrase this question would be to ask why Machiavelli did not write an autobiography and Montaigne did not write a political treatise. We already know that Montaigne liked to take his distance from politics and that Machiavelli was loath to mix personal considerations with theoretical matters. Machiavelli's address to Lorenzo, however, shows that he intended his own personal condition to become visible just as the prince's political itinerary did. Indeed, the dedication is a clear instance of the belief that all knowledge, including self-knowledge, is actually the product of knowledge of the other: *The Prince* is dedicated to one who will "liberate not only Italy from the *Barbarians*" [the others] but also Machiavelli himself from the shackles of poverty (pp. 162, 79). Montaigne, on the other hand, believes the knowledge of self to be a precondition to the knowledge of the other. Moreover he understands this proposition as precluding the possibility of giving others responsibility for one's own life. In the *Essays* the other, the reader, is only the facilitator of Montaigne's own search for self, and the plural can take over from the singular: "Let us fall back to our coaches." In *The Prince* Machiavelli remains, to this day, a lonely voice. Chiron taught music and the art of war, but he never taught his pupils grammar, syntax, or the art of reading.

Ultimately an answer to the question of the relationship between self and other begs the practical question of the state and the existence of the state as mediating and authenticating this relationship in modern society. Both Machiavelli and Montaigne believed in the influence of Fortuna on human affairs, and while the former writes about seizing the political *kairos*, the opportunity of Fortuna, the other goes on recording the effects of Fortuna on his writing, thus mastering her only after the event (*après coup*). For both, however, Fortuna remains the obstacle to the achievement of personal freedom. Cassirer, in his book on *The Myth of the State*, insists that Machiavelli was, like Bodin, influenced by an astrological culture very prevalent in the sixteenth century and that he was therefore naturally inclined to resort to Fortuna to explain problems that could not be solved scientifically, i.e., since man's history is cyclical, men always have the same motives and therefore a science of history is possible.[16] However, the fact that in certain situations the Machiavellian man chooses to deal with Fortuna directly, rather than to go through a lengthy process of observation and induction, means that Machiavelli's concept of the state is to a large extent a byproduct of the political violence of the prince.

> Fortuna is a woman, and it is necessary, in order to keep her down, to beat her and to struggle with her. And it is seen that she more often allows herself to be taken over by men who are impetuous than by those who make cold advances; and then, being a woman, she is always the friend of young men, for they are less cautious, more aggressive, and they command her with more audacity. (XXV: 162)

Montaigne, who pays only lip service to the political imperative ("The goodness and capacity of the governor should free us absolutely and fully from worrying about his government" [III, 13:821]), seeks to mitigate the conflict between Fortuna and reason by suggesting in "Of Friendship" a distinction between complete and incomplete associations (*confédérations*).

> There is nothing to which nature seems to have inclined us more than to society. And Aristotle says that good legislators have had more care for friendship than for justice. For in general, all associations that are forged and nourished by pleasure or profit, by public or private needs, are the less beautiful and noble, and the less friendships, in so far as they mix into friendship another cause and object and reward than friendship itself. . . . In the relationships which bind us only by one small part, we need look out only for the imperfections that particularly concern that part. The religion of my doctor or my lawyer cannot matter. (I, 28:136, 142)

This full association of friendship becomes the model for a society based on common consent and nourished by a free and engrossing exchange between self and others. However, it remains for someone else in the sixteenth century to ask the question of whether a society can indeed operate on common consent and, if that is the case, how men can agree to surrender their freedom to a prince who then becomes the guarantor of the body politic. In the *Discours de la servitude volontaire* it is again La Boétie who poses the question of the state, in a perspective which will finally put an end to the game of mimesis between self and others[17] and lead ultimately to pose the rational question of the nature and function of the social contract. Before this can happen, however, the centaur under whose auspices we began our inquiry must go. Let me then return to Montaigne, who, by reminding us of Chiron's death, helps in effect to bring my paper to an end.

> Chiron refused immortality when informed of its conditions by the very god of time and duration, his father Saturn. Imagine honestly how much less bearable and more painful to man would be an everlasting life than the life I have given him. If you did not have death, you would curse me incessantly for having deprived you of it. I have deliberately mixed it with a little bitterness to keep you, seeing the convenience of it, from embracing it too greedily and intemperately. To lodge you in that moderate state that I ask of you, of neither fleeing life nor fleeing back from death, I have tempered both of them between sweetness and bitterness. (I, 20:67)

Notes

1. Niccolo Machiavelli, *The Prince*, chapter XVIII in *The Portable Machiavelli*, trans. Peter Bondanella, Mark Musa (Harmondsworth: Penguin, 1979), pp. 133–34. Subsequent page references given in the text are to this edition.

2. Chiron is half-beast, half-human. He is also mortal and immortal, being the offspring of Kronos and Polyra (Kronos had disguised himself as a horse to seduce Polyra). That Chiron teaches morals to Achilles who, in the *Iliad*, comes down on his enemies like a bird of prey (*Iliad*, XXI:252; XXII:139), is just a local, edited version of a more common centauric rite. Dumézil, *Le Problème*

des centaures, Etude de mythologie comparée indo-européene (Paris: Musée Guimet, 1929), pp. 4–53, tells us that from the time of the Little Mysteries at Eleusis and the Lupercalia in Rome to the beginning of the twentieth century, bands of roving peasants cavorted around the countryside teaching and threatening people, especially women, at the time of the equinox. They were dressed as horse-men, complete with artificial tail and detachable hindlegs, playing at being centaurs.

3. Michel de Montaigne, *The Complete Essays*, trans. Donald Frame (Stanford: Stanford University Press, 1965), II, 12:330–31. Subsequent page references given in the text are to this edition.

4. Isaiah Berlin, "The Originality of Machiavelli," in *Studies on Machiavelli*, ed. Myron P. Gilmore (Firenze: Sansoni, 1972), pp. 149–206.

5. Leon Battista Alberti, *Della Pittura*, edizione critica a cura di Luigi Malle (Firenze: Sansoni, 1950), pp. 55–75. Leonardo da Vinci, *Treatise on Painting*, trans. P. MacMahon (Princeton: Princeton University Press, 1956), pp. 119–201.

6. "For to sum up, I know that there is such a thing as medicine, jurisprudence, four parts in mathematics, and roughly what they aim at. . . . But as for plunging deeper, or gnawing my nails over the study of Aristotle, monarch of modern learning, or stubbornly pursuing some part of knowledge, I have never done it." (I, 26:107)

7. See, for instance, in the life of *Pericles*, Plutarch's incidental comments about Pericles' relationship with Aspasia at the time of the Athenian expedition against Samos. *Plutarch's Lives*, trans. B. Perrin (Harmondsworth: Penguin, 1914), III:9.

8. *Introduction to Aristotle*, ed. R. McKeon (New York: Random House, 1965), p. 644.

9. Whether Montaigne actually read Machiavelli is still debated. See Pierre Villey, *Les Sources et l'évolution des Essais de Montaigne* (Paris: Plon-Nourrit, 1953), 1:191; Alexandre Nicolai, "Le Machiavélisme de Montaigne," *Bulletin de la Société des Amis de Montaigne* 5–6, pp. 25–45 and 6–7, pp. 2–8; Marcel Tetel, "Montaigne and Machiavelli: Ethics, Politics and Humanism," *Rivista di Letteratura Moderne e Comparate* 29 (1976), pp. 165–81.

10. For the cultural context of this encounter, see André Thevet, *La Cosmographie Universelle* in Suzanne Lussagnet, *Les Français en Amérique* (Paris: P.U.F., 1953), II:270–84; Jean de Léry, *Histoire d'un voyage fait en la terre du Brézil* (Paris: A. Lemerre, 1880), II:43–58.

11. See, for instance, Léry, *Histoire d'un voyage* (otherwise quite fair), p. 52.

12. "Truly here are real savages by our standards; for either they must be thoroughly so, or we must be . . ." in Montaigne, *Essays*, I, 31:158.

13. Pierre Villey in *Les Essais de Michel de Montaigne, édition conforme au texte de l'exemplaire de Bordeaux, rééditée sous la direction et avec une préface de V. L. Saulnier* (Lausanne: Guilde du Livre, 1965), pp. 183–802; Michel Butor, *Essais sur les Essais* (Paris: Gallimard, 1968), pp. 62–79.

14. Villey, *Les Essais de Michel de Montaigne*, p. 197.

15. Etienne de la Boétie, *Le discours de la servitude volontaire*, (texte établi par P. Léonard) and *La Boétie et la question du politique par P. Clastres et C. Lefort* (Paris: Payot, 1976), p. 161.

16. Ernst Cassirer, *The Myth of the State* (New Haven: Yale University Press, 1946), pp. 145ff. Let me also remark that, Machiavelli notwithstanding, the problem of the *state* and more specifically, of the reinterpretation of the Machiavellian text, are essentially twentieth century problems. On this, see Leonid M. Batkin, "Machiavelli: Experience and Speculation," *Diogenes* 107 (1979), pp. 24–28.

17. See Claude Lefort, "Le nom d'Un," *Le discours de la servitude volontaire*, pp. 247–307.

Gormlaith ind Rígain: The History and the Legend / *Sarah Sanderlin*

In 1627 Conell Mageoghagan, a gentleman-antiquary from Lismoyne, County Westmeath in Ireland, compiled from many older sources a work which has since been called the Annals of Clonmacnois (AClon).[1] The title is a little misleading as the work includes literary and semi-historical material in the framework of a series of yearly entries relating to Ireland from the fifth through the fourteenth centuries. The extent of non-annalistic material is AClon's most striking feature. Most of these additions take the form of prose narratives and, where the antecedent was also in prose, the English translations are very close to the Irish or Latin of the original. When the antecedent was in verse, Mageoghagan paraphrased.

The little narratives are self-contained and may even contradict the account given immediately before in the annalistic series. For example Brian Boru's well-known domination of the Vikings in the late tenth and early eleventh centuries duly appears in AClon (from the twelfth-century O Brien panegyric *Cogadh Gaedhel re Gallaibh*, the War of the Gael with the Gall).[2] But the list of events leading up to the account clearly shows that it was his rival, Máelsechlainn Mór (†1022), who dominated the Vikings, even to the point of exacting tribute from them. By contrast, Brian comes out as an ambitious and unscrupulous war leader/king, making and breaking alliances of every sort (including marriage) with the various groups of Vikings—his only aim being to unseat Máelsechlainn and become High King of Ireland.

Mageoghagan's use of non-annalistic material raises questions about the extent to which early Irish history can be derived from widely differing sources. Historians today draw upon, among other sources, legal tracts, hagiographies, genealogies, and sagas to supplement the record in the major sets of Irish annals (which are voluminous). They can do this only by exercising caution and by analysing each source thoroughly. No one now would be inclined to augment an account of Columcille's early life (sixth century) with extracts from a fifteenth-century version of his Life. Even less likely would be a character study based partly on a few annal entries, partly on several poetic laments, and mostly on a dubious story of insult and revenge.

In the seventeenth century, however, these practices were acceptable. Considering the inevitably dry nature of annalistic entries (battles, deaths, natural phenomena), I should think such augmentations were quite desirable, perhaps especially so in AClon. Mageoghagan wrote for a particular reader, Terence Coghlan, who must have enjoyed the interludes. Coghlan was a close neighbor of Mageoghagan's in County Westmeath and was a younger member of the same section of Gaelic Irish landed society. AClon, therefore, was written (in English) for a young friend, not for a patron. So Mageoghagan, who evidently had no particular instructions for the contents of AClon, introduced extracts from *Cogadh Gaedhel re Gallaibh*, from the Irish Life of Columcille in the Book of Lismore,[3] and, in the case we shall follow here, from a combination of literary elements surrounding Gormlaith, daughter of Flann mac Maílsechlainn (High King of Ireland, †916) and wife to Cormac mac Cuilennáin, king of Munster (†908), Cerball mac Muirecán, king of Leinster (†909), and Niall Glúndub mac Áeda, High King of Ireland (†919).

Before discussing the trials of Gormlaith—historical and literary—we ought briefly to look at some characteristics of the Irish annals, the backbone of early Irish history. It is generally accepted that the early annalists tended to use whatever chronological material they could find when filling in gaps in the chronicle before their own times. Many entries before ca. 750 are not entirely historically reliable for that reason. It is also well known (and evident to the most casual, untrained reader) that the seventeenth-century compilers of annals usually incorporated substantial amounts of non-annalistic material. We have seen that AClon is a blend of sources; what is not immediately apparent is that this practice is not unique to seventeenth-century antiquaries. Earlier annalists such as those writing in the tenth century or at least of tenth-century events might also insert extracts from a saga.

There is a saga-like connected series of entries in the Annals of Ulster (AU)[4] from 912 (=913) to 920 (=921) concerning Niall Glúndub mac Áeda (coincidentally the third of Gormlaith's husbands) and the Vikings. The series recounts Niall's hostings to Dál nAraide in the North and to Mide in the Midlands and against the Vikings. A connected entry describes a fight between Ragnall, king of the Vikings at that time, and Scotland. Niall and Ragnall met in the Battle of Dublin (s.a. 918 = A.D. 919; Niall was killed) which, however, is not part of the series. I suspect there was already a longish entry about this famous battle in the Annals of Ulster so that no further detail was required. The final entry from this hypothetical saga comes at 920 (=921) when Gotfrith succeeded Ragnall as king of the Dublin Vikings. He plundered Armagh, even then the monastic city of Niall's family and the all but primatial see of Ireland. Muirchertach, son of Niall Glúndub and his successor as king of the Northern Uí Néill, promptly defeated Gotfrith, exacting a sort of revenge for his father's death. Not only are these entries connected, there are small pieces of detail which are not usually associated with annalistic entries. For example we are told how Oengus mac Flainn meic Maílsechlainn of Mide (Gormlaith's full- or half-brother) came upon a large body from Niall's main force collecting corn and firewood while on a December hosting in Mide.

None of these entries is found in any set of annals independent of AU. The whole series, perhaps including the Battle of Dublin, might be called Caithréim Néill Glúnduib ("The Victory of Niall Glúndub"). Considered as a series and compared with the same years in the two independent sets of annals, it is a strikingly obvious addition to the Annals of Ulster. When this addition was made is unknown at present. Its inclusion in AU is not likely to have been contemporary with the events it describes for several technical reasons. The final manuscript of

AU is late fifteenth century; the saga could have been incorporated at any time before then.

Several times I have referred to a set of annals as being "independent." This seems to imply the existence of dependent annals. Actually the relationships between the various annals are extremely complicated. My highly cursory discussion will unfortunately rather beg the question but it will be useful to establish a background for the historical elements of Gormlaith's story before we consider the story itself.

The annalistic foundation for all the surviving sets of annals (we are concerned only with the annals which cover the pre-Norman years, i.e., 432–1172) is a Chronicle of Ireland (Chron. Ir.) which first took shape around 550 A.D. Initially it is likely that this Chronicle consisted of Irish events interlined in a copy of the 549 edition of the Chronicle of Marcellinus Comes.[5] After repeated copyings, Chron. Ir. became almost exclusively a record of Irish affairs. In the course of some two centuries the annalists incorporated smaller house chronicles from various monasteries (notably from Iona), material from some of the English forerunners of the Anglo-Saxon Chronicle, and information found in a variety of other historical sources.

Most of the records were in some way datable although there are hints of sagas involving, for example, Muirchertach mac Erca († ca. 534), because his activities are unusually well represented in the annals. In the case of any saga or hagiographic material, the annalist was inclined to split up the narrative so that the events could be slotted into what he hoped were the correct years. We have already seen the AU annalist doing this with the hypothetical Niall Glúndub saga and the Chron. Ir. annalist treated his Muirchertach mac Erca material in the same way. Incidentally this latter source was probably not the Middle Irish "Aided [Violent Death of] Muirchertaig meic Earca"[6] except for the sequence detailing the Otherworldly manner of his death. Dividing the narrative like this was not to be Mageoghagan's custom in AClon.

By 750 the Irish annals are generally reliable and contemporary with the events they record. They were probably kept at Armagh, for they usually betray a Northern and Patrician bias in their choice of facts. Another set of annals had by this time been copied from Chron. Ir. and was being kept in Munster, possibly at the monastery of Emly, Armagh's rival for supremacy just as the Eóganachta of Munster were rivals of the Uí Néill branches in secular matters. It is quite possible that a third set was kept in Clonmacnois, chief monastery of the powerful Southern Uí Néill in the Midlands. This set did not survive intact since at some time toward the end of the tenth century it was amalgamated with the more comprehensive Chron. Ir. There are signs that the Clonmacnois Chronicle was fragmentary in any event.

The locations of the extant sets of annals coincide to some degree with the political centers. While there may be a connection between early secular powers and the survival of annals, it is more likely that the connection is fortuitous. There is no reason to suppose that every strong king or major dynasty encouraged the writing of annals—the information in those annals does not necessarily support such a theory. On the other hand the coincidence is interesting and it is useful to consider the political situation very briefly.

The descendents of Niall Noígiallach (Niall of the Nine Hostages, fl. early or mid-fifth century) formed two main groups: the Northern Uí Néill or Cenél nEógain, located in the present-day province of Ulster, and the Southern Uí Néill or Clann Cholmáin in and around present-day County Westmeath. The Uí Néill were relative newcomers and their dynastic name, which means the "descendents of Niall," was then (in the fifth century) an unusual formula. Much older as a dynasty were the Eóganachta of Munster. Even in the mid-eighth century, however, the Eóganachta were weakening. Too many sub-families could and did claim the Eóganacht kingship. In the tenth century the upstart kings of the Dál Cais (in northwest Munster near Killaloe), Cennétig (†951) and his sons Mathgamain (†976) and Brian (Boru, †1014), set about establishing a new dynasty in Munster so that first Mathgamain and then his younger brother took the kingship away from the Eóganachta.

There were other groups and families in Ireland, notably in Laigen (the modern province of Leinster, more or less) and Osraige (now County Ossory, roughly), but the three listed above are most central to the history of the Irish annals and to the history of Gormlaith.

The extant sets of annals are descended from one of the three sets at Armagh, Clonmacnois, and Emly. The Munster Annals of Inisfallen[7] is the oldest as far as manuscript age goes; the northern Annals of Ulster are considered the most authoritative over all (this is the kind of generalization that is almost immediately shown to be inadequate). The Clonmacnois group, only indirectly descended from the eighth-century annals, combined the northern and midlands sets in the middle of the tenth century. They are the fourteenth-century Annals of Tigernach;[8] the seventeenth-century Annals of Clonmacnois and Chronicum Scotorum (Chron. Scot.);[9] and the Annals of the Four Masters,[10] also seventeenth century but a combination of the annalistic text which AClon represents and the Annals of Ulster.

The survival of these annals and the circumstances of their composition differ. The Annals of Inisfallen was kept in a monastery and is a true monastic chronicle. The Annals of Tigernach appears to have been an exercise in annalistic composition; for example, it incorporates Latin extracts from Bede's *Ecclesiastical History* but has no hesitation in incorporating large lacunae as well. The largest, from the 770's to the 970's, occurs with no indication that the manuscript or the original was defective. With the Annals of Ulster we begin to see the effects of antiquarianism. This text was copied, probably from an older "working" set, for a patron of the Gaelic Irish aristocracy. The copyist seems also to have compared his text with a Clonmacnois version for he has interlined certain entries evidently omitted in the original. Later another hand did the same with another Clonmacnois set. The Annals of Clonmacnois, as we have seen, was written for a young friend who later was to act (along with Conell Mageoghagan) as a patron for the Four Masters. Chron. Scot. was the work of Dubhaltach Mac Firbisigh, perhaps for James Ware, the Anglo-Irish antiquary who employed him as a copyist. It is certain from his short preface that Mac Firbisigh was writing for someone. Finally, the Annals of the Four Masters was also compiled for a patron. Royal Irish Academy Stowe Manuscript C.iii.3 is thought to be the presentation copy and was written by all the compilers in turn. There is another set of annals, also by Mac Firbisigh, now called *Fragmentary Annals* (formerly *Three Fragments of Irish Annals*),[11] which includes considerable incidental material of the sort we will consider shortly. All the annals include scraps of poetry and other items not strictly historical. The smallest amount of this extraneous information is in the Annals of Inisfallen; the greatest is in AClon and the Three Fragments.

To summarize: In the first half of the tenth century there were annals being kept at Armagh (represented by AU), Emly (represented by the Annals of Inisfallen), and Clonmacnois (represented, after the late tenth-century collation with the Armagh annals, by AClon and Chron. Scot.). There were also the anomalous Fragmentary Annals, representing a late Ossory tradition. To these we must add the Annals of the Four Masters, representing both AU and the AClon text. These are our main sources. There were kings of the Northern Uí Néill and kings of the Southern Uí Néill (Clann Cholmáin) who alternated the title (no longer a historian's fiction) of High King of Ireland, i.e., High King of everything they could control except Munster. There was a weakening dynasty in Munster and a growing threat from the Dál Cais. There were kings in Osraige and Laigen who were powerful, though not of the strength of either branch of the Uí Néill. Finally there were Vikings, who are immaterial to our particular story; their impact has generally been extremely overrated.

The treatment of Gormlaith by her contemporaries and by historians has not been kind. In fact she has become rather notorious, largely through Mageoghagan's descriptions in the Annals of Clonmacnois. Had the nineteenth-century editor of AClon not seen fit to censor his text (without proper indications), it is likely that she would have been even less sympathetically regarded. Two aspects of her character appear in the various legends surrounding her. Both versions, not entirely contradictory, are in AClon. In addition there is a version which may be deduced from the annalistic entries themselves—entries which are not likely to have been influenced by her subsequent reputation in poetry. In AClon, therefore, we can conveniently examine the processes of compiling a set of annals from a variety of sources.

Gormlaith was married three times, probably for the sake of diplomacy each time. Her first husband was Cormac mac Cuilennáin, bishop-king of Munster. Cormac had a reputation for celibacy (indeed, extreme asceticism) which later native historians found difficult to reconcile with this marriage; it was generally assumed to have been unconsummated. It has been suggested[12] that in making Cormac king of Munster, the Eóganachta were settling for a compromise candidate who would not disrupt a shaky peace among the sub-families. He turned out to be one of the last notable kings the Eóganachta produced. In 908 he was defeated by a combined force of the Laigen and the Uí Néill (including Cormac's father-in-law,

Flann mac Maílsechlainn) in the Battle of Belach Mugna (or the battle of Mag Ailbe). Gormlaith was part of the spoils of victory; she was married to Cerball mac Muirecán, King of Leinster.

Cerball, who the Three Fragments say was Cormac's foster-brother, died the following year. AU, Chron. Scot., and the Four Masters, representing the common tradition, all say he was killed *dolore*—through pain. AClon, however, says that he died "deceitfully" (*dolose*—the *s* and *r* in Irish miniscule are very similar), which agrees with a note in the Leinster king list in the twelfth-century Book of Leinster:[13] *a gáe fein ros marb a laim a gillai fein* (his own spear killed him in the hand of his own servant). Mageoghagan, in a rare foreshadowing of his later discussion of the coarse joke Cerball played on Gormlaith, names the murderer in an extension of his entry:

> Cearvall Kinge of Leinster was deceitfully killed, itt is thought that hee was soe killed by Mortagh O'Neale [Muirchertach mac Néill Glúnduib]. (BL MS, fol. 75ʳ; TCD MS, p. 90)

No other set of annals blames Muirchertach for the killing; quite likely Mageoghagan had in mind his later story which I shall give in full in due course.

Gormlaith's last husband (following the historical sources) was Niall Glúndub, the man who succeeded her father as High King in 916. As before this has the appearance of a marriage alliance, this time between Clann Cholmáin and Cenél nEógain, the rival families for the High Kingship. This marriage lasted only until 919; Gormlaith survived him by nearly thirty years.

After the death of Niall, tradition has it that Gormlaith fell upon hard times. It is true that by the time she died, Gormlaith had outlived those of her family who could have aided her. Her sisters Murgél and Lilgach had died some twenty years earlier (the former in old age). Both were buried at Clonmacnois, but there is no indication that Gormlaith was. Her brother Donnchad, High King after Niall Glúndub, died in 945; her stepson, the powerful Muirchertach mac Néill, died in 943. Consequently it is not difficult to picture a woman who was abandoned by her family and perhaps by her successive husbands' families (her marriage to Cerball had already alienated Munster), and who was not buried in the ancestral ground.

This account of Gormlaith's husbands and fate is derived from the entries in the Irish annals, including AClon. It is almost certainly the version which Mageoghagan had before him when translating AClon's basic annalistic text. But Mageoghagan, called by one of his contemporaries an "industrious collecting Bee," also had some or all of the early Modern Irish poems which are attributed to Gormlaith.[14] We can see this in his expansions of two simple entries such as are still found in Chron. Scot.:

> [Chron. Scot. 915=916] Níall Glundup, mac Aodha, regnare incipit.

> [AClon 905] Neale Glunduffe was kinge three yeares and was maryed to ye Ladie Gormphley daughter to kinge fflann, who was a very faire, vertuous and learned damozell, was first married to Cormack O'Cuilleannann k. of

Mounster; Secondly to kinge Neale, by whom shee had issue a sonne, called Prince Donell, who was drowned, vpon whose death shee made many pittyfull and learned dittyes in Irish. And lastly shee was marryed to Kearvell mc Moregann kinge of Leinster; after all which royall marriadges shee begged from doore to doore forsaken of all her freinds and Allies, and glad to be relieved by her inferiours. (Arm. MS, fol 42ʳ)

[Chron. Scot. 947=948] Gormflaith *ingen* [daughter of] Flainn mic Maoilechlainn, in penitentia extensa, obiit.

[AClon 943] Gormphley daughter of k. Flann mc Moyleseachlin and Queene of Ireland died of a longe and grievous wound; which happened in this manner; she dreamed that shee saw k. Neale Glunduffe, wherevpon shee gott vpp and satt in her bed to behold him, whom hee for anger would forsake and leave her chamber, and as hee was departeing in that angry motion (as shee thought) shee gave a snatch after him, thinkeinge to take him by the mantle to keepe him with her, and fell vpon one of the bedstickes of her bed, that it pierced her breast even to her very heart, which received noe cure vntill shee died thereof. (Arm. MS, fol. 44ᵛ)

Mageoghagan's additions cover four subjects which I shall consider in this order: (a) her marriages (their order is significant); (b) her son Domnall mac Néill; (c) her life after Niall's death; (d) the manner of her death. All four of these elements are found in the Gormlaith poems.

The order of husbands, which gives Cerball after Niall, is as likely to have been suggested as much by the longer joke and revenge story I shall be discussing last as by a hint in a poem. It should be noted that the Gormlaith collection is also rather vague about the order of the first two husbands. The Niall-Cerball order is suggested in Poem VII, §§6–7:

> Diongmhála damh mac í Néill—
> ionmhain rí féta fírréidh,
> rob ionchuir é, ceann a cceann,
> is inghean airdrigh Éireand.
>
> Fada damhsa da éis sin
> a ttigh mic Muireagain mhir;
> fann mo threóir, anbhfann atú,
> ní fedaimsi a bheith a chrú.

["The son of Niall's descendent was a match for me—beloved the gentle gallant knight, he was the equal, point by point, of the daughter of the high-king of Ireland. Long have I been thereafter in the house of the son of vigorous Muiregán; feeble is my strength, I am weak, I cannot abide with them."]

Compare the order in Poem XI, §§9–10:

> Trí chéad bó [is] dá chéad each
> tug damhsa Cearball cloidhmheach;

> tug Cormac [i]s nír bheart ghann
> dá oiread a ttug Cearbhall.
>
> Créd fa cceilfinn ar mo rí[gh]
> a bhfuarus uadha do mhaoín?
> Oiread sin uile fa thrí
> fuarus ó Niall a n-aonmhí.

["Three hundred cows and two hundred horses Cerball of the sword gave me; Cormac—it was no mean act—gave twice as many as Cerball. Why should I hide from my king the wealth I have got from him? All that thrice over I got from Niall in one month."]

It is, therefore, highly likely that Mageoghagan was made certain of the Niall-Cerball order by his other literary source and did not need to search the poems for confirmation. On the other hand, AClon gives the historical order elsewhere (coinciding with that given in the other sets) and one is left with the feeling that Conell Mageoghagan did not always read his own annals. The entry about Cerball's death from his own spear in the hand of his own servant occurs in AClon some years before Niall's obituary. Despite the foreshadowing, which may or may not be present, Mageoghagan put Cerball's death too soon for Muirchertach's revenge of his father's disgrace to make sense. In other words, where historical fact (represented by an annal) is irreconcilable with literary accounts (represented by a poem or a prose narrative), Mageoghagan gives both, with no attempt at reconciliation.

The lamented death of Prince Donell (Domnall mac Néill Glúnduib), about which Gormlaith made so many mournful poems, is reported in Poem IX of the Gormlaith collection, especially stanzas six and ten:

> Gé do-c[h]uadar sin uile
> don bhioth bhuadhach bharrbhuidhe,
> is doilghe leam Domhnall dil
> do bheith aghaidh fo thalmhuin.
>
> Maircc do léicc a n-Ibh Fiachrach
> an mac builidh bínnbhriathrach,
> i ttír go n-iomad n-uiscce,
> in go ndaóinibh nair choisge.

["Though all these have gone from the glorious yellow-topped earth, sorer to me is it that dear Domhnall should be one night under the earth. Woe to her who allowed the gentle sweet-voiced lad to go into Uí Fiachrach, a land where water is plentiful and men are unruly."]

Drowning is not specifically mentioned but the reference to water in §10 is perhaps a hint which an earlier audience would have understood. Conell Mageoghagan seems to have made such an interpretation although there may have been other poems where the manner of Domnall's death was explicitly stated. Domnall is not recorded in the annals; as he evidently died in fosterage he may have been quite young.

The question of Gormlaith's poverty, expressed by Mageoghagan in terms which recall Henryson's description of Cresseid,[15] can be seen in several of the poems:

V, §7   Minic me a láim acc dreasaibh,
        as íad ag casadh fam cheartaigh,
        ni cara damh na droidhne,
        'sas biobhbha damh an drisóg.

["Often the brambles take hold of me, twisting about my rags; the thorn is no friend to me, and the briar is a foe."]

IX, §2   Tierce sa cách mo charuid,
        o nach bhfaicim ar Néll radhairc:
        ni cluin mo chlúas glan gle
        én ní fá ndénaim gaire.

["My friends grow fewer and fewer, since I no more have sight of Niall: my fair bright ear hears nothing at which I laugh."]

X, §5   Gan agam o nimh go lár
        acht léine bhán is brat cíar;
        a cCennanndas na cced ríogh
        bec an bhrigh mo bheith gan bhíadh.

["I have nothing between heaven and earth but a white smock and a dark cloak; in Kells of the hundred kings it matters little that I am without food."]

X, §11   Tug sisi damhsa anocht—
        nocha maith cumann nach ceart—
        dá deachmhadh do chóirce chrúaidh,
        da uigh chirce are mbúain da beart!

["She [Mór, the "wife of the abbot," who is addressed as a person, but Kells was known as Cennannus Mór and perhaps this is anthropomorphism] gave me tonight—an unfitting kindness is not good—two tenths of hard oats, two hen eggs taken from her clutch!"]

X, §14   Maircc do-ní díomas as ór,
        maircc, a Mhór, bhíos go neóid;
        da bhadhas acc díol na cclíar,
        noco rucc an Tríat[h] mo sheaód.

["Woe to anyone who is proud of gold, woe to anyone who is niggardly, O Mór. I had the poets in my pay until the Lord took my wealth."]

Finally, Mageoghagan's version of the death of Gormlaith is a paraphrase and abbreviation of the one in poem XI. His account is less clear and less dramatic than the poem's, because he omitted a few details, such as the reason for Niall's anger, but it is substantially the same. Like Mageoghagan, I shall paraphrase:

For 31 years since Niall died, I have wept seven hundred tears every night. Last night Niall said to me: "Stop your lamenting; the King of angels is displeased." I replied more angrily than ever before: "Why should the anger of the King of Heaven be against me while I am penitent?" "He created heaven and men and He does not desire their weeping." Niall turned away from me; I shrieked and threw myself after him. A yew bed post impaled me so that my heart split in the middle. God grant me death; wherever Niall is, may he and I be on one path.

Allowing for natural difficulties in comparing a prose paraphrase in English with verse quatrains in Irish, there seems to be a common literary tradition present in Mageoghagan's two expansions and in the poems of the Gormlaith cycle. Gormlaith is portrayed as a once-proud Queen of Ireland, reduced to poverty—friendless and living off the alms of Kells (a Leinster monastery) or of Cerball mac Muirecán's family. In AClon, however, we are also told of another of Gormlaith's adventures.

The story concerns a joke played on Gormlaith by her husband, Cerball. This Gormlaith, though, is not helpless or friendless: Cerball is made to pay for his little joke in a fitting manner. The story was censored in Murphy's edition. When the full account is read, the extent of Gormlaith's insult, the nature of Muirchertach's revenge, and the reason why Niall had to die before Cerball are all explained.

[936] Gormphley (of whom mention is made before) Queene of Ireland, and wife to Neale Glunduffe after that kinge Neale was slaine in the battle of Dublin by danes [Vikings] and Leinstermen, the kinge of Leinster caused privily kinge Neales stones irreverently to bee cutt off, and their cover to bee fleyed and conveyghed to his house of Naase, there to bee kept as a monument to keepe tablemen in. After the death of kinge Neale, Queene Gormphley married the k. of Leinster, whose name was Kearvall mc Moreagan, and vpon a time as the kinge of Leinster and Queene Gormphley were playeinge of tables in Naase aforesaid with condition yt whosoever would loose the game should beare this bagge of tablemen in his mouth vntill hee had wonne one game, which fell that Queene Gormphley lost the game; wherevpon shee was driven to putt the bagge to her mouth, little knowing what itt was or meant, save onely that it was a bagge. The k. seeing her in hand with the bagg, said bawdyly, that now shee carried in her mouth, that that shee received below diverse times before, and revealed vnto her how this bagg was k. Neales cover of his stones that hee kept as a monument in despight of all Vlstermen.

Wherevpon shee beganne somewhat inwardly grieved, concealed her grief for a time and sent privilye to Mortaugh mc Neale, who came with a company of Lusty and choise Vlstermen, cladd themselves with cowhides, and lay in the kinge of Leinsters parke att Naase, neere his pallace in their hides like cowes, to the end that the kinge vpon sight of them would take them for cowes. The k. after that hee had gotten out of his bedd, looked out att the window of his pallace, and seeinge soe many cowes lye couchant in his parke as Mortaugh brought men out of Vlster or the North to bee revenged, and thinkeing they had layen there all night, hee fell in a rage, and went himselfe amongst the cowes and was miserablie killed.

Mortaugh and his Vlstermen brought his bones with them to the North, and there artificially caused to bee made a payer of tables of the said kinges bones, which for a very long time after was kept as a Monument in the kinge of Vlsters house, and of these Cowhides, Mortaugh was ever after dureinge his Life named Mortaugh of ye Leather Coates. (Arm. MS, fol. 44ʳ)

A pair of tables refers to a backgammon board so I assume that Mageoghagan took that game to be a near equivalent of whatever word his source used. "Tables" and "playing of tables" also mean backgammon (the two halves of the board are termed "tables") and "tablemen" are obviously the very small pieces used in the game.

We had occasion above to note that Mageoghagan did not bother to reconcile the narratives' order of kings with that in the annals proper. It may be that a marginal note is an attempt at reconciliation. The marginalia in AClon are usually common to all the manuscripts and many are likely to have been in the lost original. A lengthy note beside the Gormlaith backgammon story is in both groups of manuscripts and deserves repeating here:

This tale cannott be true, for Gormphley was sooner maried to Cearvall then to king Neale, and that Cearvall was killed before she was married to k. Neale: butt the tale should be applied rather to some successor of Cearualls, who played with Queene Gormphly and was vsed by her means as here is sett forth. (Arm. MS fol. 44ʳ; BL MS, fol. 80ʳ⁻ᵛ; TCD MS, p. 97; NLI 767, p. 227, omits last clause after colon.)

There is, of course, no indication of the author. All that can be safely observed about this note is that it is in the text hand of all the manuscripts where it occurs. It could have been written any time between 1627 and 1660, and Mageoghagan (or possibly Terence Coghlan) is the most probable author of it.

The story cannot, contrary to the optimism of the marginal note, be placed in a historical context but it does have a literary context. In the Book of Leinster (pp. 257–59) there is a story in which Cerball insults Gormlaith by cutting off Cormac mac Cuilennáin's *head* after the Battle of Belach Mugna. Gormlaith's response this time was to flee to her father, Flann mac Maílsechlainn, and her avenger was Niall Glúndub. It is difficult to see how this alternate account of insult and revenge could have been confused with the first although there may well have been some influence between them.

In the list of stories which the professional poet was expected to know (Book of Leinster, p. 837) we find the title "Serc Gormlaithe do Niall" ("The Love of Gormlaith for Niall"). All three of Mageoghagan's additions to AClon would fit such a title, as would the Book of Leinster story and the poems published by Bergin. It is evident that Mageoghagan knew of a fuller legend than has survived. Although Bergin resisted the temptation "to regard the whole collection [of poems] as belonging to or founded on the lost historical romance called *Serc Gormlaithe do*

Niall," we can at least allow the possibility that the three AClon stories are based on it.

Conell Mageoghagan, then, combined legend and history in his discussion of Gormlaith, giving equal value to both. He and his reader must have seen the discrepancies. Why did he interrupt the annals to insert these extras? Why does he seem to have made no attempt to reconcile the different versions? Why did he *not* include other legends, such as those which surround the Rape of Dervorgilla in the twelfth century (which led to the invasion of Henry II)? A simple answer to the first question is that hardly anyone would sit down to read a set of annals for pleasure, and it was pleasure that was Mageoghagan's first goal: ". . . and if this my simple Labour shall in any way pleasure you, I shall hold myselfe thoroughly recompenced and my paines well employed . . ." (Arm. fol. [ii ᵛ]). Why, then, did he cast the greater part of his work in the form of annals? I doubt that we can ever do more than guess at the answers. The modern historian, in particular, is left in a quandary. So fashionable is it now to treat one's subject with deadly seriousness (for fear one will not otherwise be considered a serious historian) that the reader is virtually forgotten. Mageoghagan, then, poses a dilemma—and, in his indiscriminate love for his subject, perhaps sets an example as well.

Notes

1. Denis Murphy, ed., *The Annals of Clonmacnoise, Translated into English by Conell Mageoghagan* (Dublin: Royal Society of Antiquaries of Ireland, 1896). For a number of reasons this edition is inadequate for our purposes; all citations will therefore be taken from my forthcoming edition using all the manuscripts. Some silent capitalization and paragraphing are the only changes from the text. References are to the manuscript in the Public Library in Armagh (Arm.) supplemented from British Library Additional Manuscript 4817 (BL), Trinity College, Dublin, 673 (formerly F.3.19) (TCD), and National Library of Ireland Manuscript 767 (N7). For the relationships of these manuscripts see my "Manuscripts of the Annals of Clonmacnois," *Proceedings of the Royal Irish Academy* LXXXII, sect. C (1981), pp. 111–23. The title of the Annals of Clonmacnois can be traced to 1648.

2. J. H. Todd, ed. and trans., *Cogadh Gaedhel re Gallaibh, the War of the Gael with the Gall* (London: Rolls Series, 1867).

3. Whitley Stokes, ed. and trans., *Lives of the Saints from the Book of Lismore* (Oxford, 1890), pp. 24ff., 171ff. The manuscript, of course, has little to do with Lismore.

4. W. M. Hennessy, ed. and trans., *The Annals of Ulster* I (Dublin, 1887). The edition is not particularly accurate and I have frequently had recourse to the older and better of its manuscripts, Trinity College, Dublin, 1282 (H.1.8), to verify readings. A new edition and translation are forthcoming. The dates given by Hennessy after 488 are one year behind the true date, so AU's 912=913 A.D.

5. Marcellinus Comes, *Chronicon ad a. DXVIII continuatum ad a. DXXXIV. Additamentum ad a. DXLIII*, in Theodore Mommsen, ed., *Chronica minora saec. IV, V, VI, VII*, vol. II: *Monumenta Germaniae Historica*, auctorum antiquissimorum, tom. XI (Berolini, 1894), pp. 37–108.

6. Lil nic Dhonnchadha, ed., *Aided Muirchertaig meic Earca* (Dublin, 1964); Whitley Stokes, ed. and trans., "Aided Muirchertaig meic Erca," *Revue celtique* XXIII (1902), pp. 395–437.

7. Seán Mac Airt, ed. and trans., *The Annals of Inisfallen* (Dublin, 1951).

8. Whitley Stokes, ed. and trans., "The Annals of 'Tigernach'," *Revue celtique* XVI (1895), pp. 374–419; XVII (1896), pp. 6–33, 116–263, 337–420; XVIII (1897), pp. 9–59, 150–303, 374–91.

9. W. M. Hennessy, ed. and trans., *Chronicum Scotorum* (London: Rolls Series, 1866). The edition is not entirely accurate and I also used Trinity College, Dublin, 1292 (H.1.19).

10. John O'Donovan, ed. and trans., *Annála Ríoghachta Éireann. Annals of the Kingdom of Ireland compiled by the Four Masters*, 7 vols. (Dublin, 1851). Cp. Royal Irish Academy Stowe Manuscript C.iii.3.

11. Joan Radner, ed. and trans., *Fragmentary Annals of Ireland* (Dublin, 1978); John O'Donovan, ed. and trans., *Three Fragments of Annals of Ireland* (Dublin: Irish Archaeological and Celtic Society, 1860).

12. See F. J. Byrne, *Irish Kings and High-Kings* (London, 1973), pp. 213–14.

13. R. I. Best, Osborn Bergin, and M. A. O'Brien, eds.,*The Book of Leinster*, 5 vols. (Dublin, 1954–67), p. 182. The pages and lines are numbered consecutively through the five volumes. The edition is incomplete and untranslated. Further references will be noted in the text.

14. Osborn Bergin, ed. and trans., "Poems Attributed to Gormlaith" in Osborn Bergin and Carl Marstrander, eds., *Miscellany Presented to Kuno Meyer* (Halle a. S., 1912), pp. 343–68; reprinted in Osborn Bergin, *Irish Bardic Poetry*, comp. and ed. David Greene and Fergus Kelly (Dublin, 1970), pp. 202–15, 308–15. I refer to the poems by their numbers, which remain the same. See also Brian O Cuiv, ed. and trans., "Three Middle-Irish Poems," *Eigse* XVI (1975–76), pp. 9–12; and J. V. Kelleher, "On a Poem about Gormfhlaith," *ibid.*, pp. 251–54.

15. Henryson, a late fifteenth-century Scottish poet, in *The Testament of Cresseid*, wrote a "conclusion" for Chaucer's *Troilus and Criseyde* in which Cressid, spurned by Diomedes, curses Venus and for this blasphemy is struck down with leprosy. She ends her life in a leper colony (with her inferiors) accepting alms from Troilus, who does not recognize her. This version is quite different from Shakespeare's play, which is closer in its characterization to Chaucer.

A Question of Feminine Identity / *Paul Smith*

In the current and urgent effort to formulate a radical critique of cultural institutions, two areas of entrenched patriarchal influence have come under close scrutiny by feminist commentators—psychoanalysis and literary studies. Appropriately enough, it is the question of feminine identity that continually poses itself in both fields, as literature and psychoanalysis are regarded as potentially privileged modes of expressing or forging identity. For feminism, as it tries to take stock of both these phallocratic institutions, the question has become: what identities are allowed to women and what identities should women now claim?[1]

For many feminists it is simply a problem of ending the exploitation, objectification, and oppression of women in these institutions by bringing to women a more thorough consciousness of their worth. This has given life to a twofold enterprise, seen most clearly in America: first, filling in the gaps of a patriarchal tradition and history by inserting women's presences as a counter tradition; secondly, encouraging women's active use of present structures to ensure that the newly discovered women's tradition thrives and that it continues to have a corrective effect on patriarchal institutions. Thus, at the beginning of the current wave of feminist work in literary studies, Elaine Showalter encouraged these tactics to rectify the previously deficient relation of women to the dominant modes of literary studies and textual production, on the grounds that

> few women can sustain the sense of a positive feminine identity in the face of [male domination of curricula]. Women are estranged from their own experience and unable to perceive its shape and authenticity, in part because they do not see it mirrored and given resonance in literature.[2]

Unfortunately the crudity of the philosophy of literature embedded in founding statements of feminist criticism like Showalter's has not been everywhere improved upon. Nor, often, has it been even examined by feminist literary critics and teachers. The crucial emphasis for many feminists has become the achievement of a new and fairer equilibrium in literary curricula based on the recognition of women's *experience*, so that "woman" will see herself mirrored there in literary images. This desire can lead to, or arise from, traditional views of literary production where a text is assumed to be "imitating nature by revealing its essence in imaginative language." Such a fundamentally Aristotelian view of art carries with it ideas about "the awesome beauty of literature" and the "nobility of all human beings," and for feminist critics the merging of the two will be effected by the inclusion of women's writing in syllabi.[3] This constitutes a reformist program which partakes fully of the traditional literary ideology of "truth" and "communication." Thus, as Judith Kegan Gardiner puts it,

> Women writers *express* the experience of their own *identity* . . . often with a
> sense of urgency and excitement in the *communication* of *truths* just under-
> stood. . . . they communicate a consciousness of their identity.[4]

This ideology of the communication of truth, coming to consciousness, the expression of self and so on, is summed up by the latter writer as the need of women's
writing and criticism to ensure that "female experience is transformed into female
consciousness." The roots of such an ideology are apparent. The whole project has
received its imprimatur in the name "gynocritique"—with the assumption, one
presumes, of countering an "androcritique."[5]

The project is, of course, important on one level: the recognition given woman
against man is as attractive as it is necessary in the passes of a feminist strategy.
That is to say, so long as it is seen as a tactic with specific limits, such a project can
be (and has been) of use. However, when it is seen as an end in itself, as the
sufficient goal of feminist production, its ideology needs to be examined more
carefully. That ideology seems to me dangerous, caught up as it is in the assumptions that there *is* a coherent identity to express, that there *are* truths to communicate, and that there *is* a consciousness to be raised. Furthermore, if such assumptions
are thought of as phallocratic and phallocentric, then this form of a feminist project
becomes inevitably compromised.

The dominance of the patriarchal system is exerted in and through signifying
practices, by the cultural production of meaning: thus any "female self-consciousness turning in upon itself attempting to grasp the deepest conditions of its own
unique and multiplicitous realities"[6] eventually must, as Virginia Woolf says, "dash
itself against something hard."[7] Something hard: the question of women's relation
to the phallus in its role as the organizing metaphor in patriarchal life. Women's
experience can only be experience as forged by and in patriarchy; women's truths
and identities are currently representable only in a symbolic field that is organized
on a principle of difference which works to exclude women and defend itself
against them.

The problem that continually arises in and confronts feminist writing and criticism is that the unique identities and multiplicitous realities being claimed ultimately devolve upon some faith in an essential female character or identity that
has been oppressed or suppressed by male domination. Such an identity is often
assumed to be the product of an archaic essence or specificity in the category
"woman," or is always already assumed by the practices which are supposed in fact
to produce it. In the latter case, there is the affirmation that a certain conceptualization of woman can be realized; that affirmation persuades the affirmer that the
realization has already occurred. In the former case, real, authentic "woman" has
apparently been put down in patriarchy so that (really, authentically) the problem
is nothing but one of women's false consciousness in a male world. Here a kind of
authentic being is assumed, resembling a chrysalis, one that will break into its true
form when its being and its consciousness happily coincide. Such an ideology might
turn out to be debilitating for feminism, just as it has been for the vulgar Marxism
with which some feminism shares such thoughts.

In short the goal of much feminist writing on literature seems often to be the discovery for 'woman' of some sort of "changeless essence [shining] through all the erasures of external change," as Susan Friedman's recent study of the poet H.D.'s writing would have it.[8] Much of this kind of work has been undertaken under the aegis—explicitly or not—of those forms of American psychology having as their general goal the adjustment of a coherent, whole, and self-valuing ego to a society which is seen to be structurally inimical to that ego. This appeal to the idealist notion of a coherent self has also been harnessed to a political strategy which sees the raising of consciousness, or the dispulsion of false consciousness, as the path to substantive change. Although this is a crude generalization of the history of American feminism in the sixties and seventies, it might nonetheless be an adequate description of its sources and of many of its modes of practice today.

The paths that feminists in France (and to some extent in Britain) have taken are quite opposed to those taken—until very recently and in certain contexts—by those in America. French feminism has bypassed, in blissful ignorance, the notions of genuine identity that have been so much promoted here. With guidance from radical political thinking, especially that of Althusser, they have done away with the whole problematic of false consciousness—itself an illusion, they would say. The French way of life has not enshrined the psychologistic notion of primary or core identity from which all experience would arise and to which it would refer back: the French have been able to do without that particular revisionist version of Freud's metapsychological theories. Instead, they have had to deal with a different body of Freudian revisionism—the work of Lacan and his much vaunted return to the word of Freud. Indeed, it might be said that the most fundamental difference between European and American feminisms has been in the stances adopted toward psychoanalysis.

It has not, of course, gone unnoticed by either French or American feminists that psychoanalysis' definition of the female subject can be read as being predicated upon the irremovable fixity of the phallus; that women are situated in psychoanalytic theory, as elsewhere, in the position of other in relation to a normative male self. The argument most often used by feminists against psychoanalysis in general, and Freud in particular, is the apparent reliance upon a theory of gender differentiation which would establish the male as plenitude and the female as deficiency. Psychoanalysis is understood to posit an intrinsic, somatic, and therefore psychical inferiority in women. Throughout the sixties—and to some extent in the seventies and eighties—that view of Freud's theories of sexuality seemed sufficient to feminist thinking and so psychoanalysis was often dismissed, as in Kate Millett's *Sexual Politics*, for its supposed desire to consolidate male oppression of woman as other.

The origin of this view of psychoanalysis is not difficult to discern. Freud's texts often flirt with exactly that normative phallocentrism they are so often accused of. On occasion, this phallocentric comportment is clearly the product of Freud's having to speak from within a social context that itself dictates the form of theoretical address. Even in the 1932 *New Introductory Lectures on Psychoanalysis* this is the case: there Freud remarks that "throughout history people have knocked their heads against the riddle of the nature of femininity" and that "to those of you who are women this will not apply—you are yourselves the problem." The historical tradition itself privileges the male as investigator of the feminine. It is also generally true that Freud chose to align himself with that tradition, electing in most cases to treat of male sexuality before going on to comment upon (and very often express his relative ignorance of) female sexuality. In one crucial text he unequivocally refers to "the fact of [women] being castrated"[9] and in another to their obligation to "react to the fact of not having received [a penis],"[10] seeming to establish a view of the genesis of subjectivity in both sexes as a function of the evidential presence or absence of a penis.

There is, however, room for at least a rereading of Freud, if not a defense. Part of that rereading or resituating was initially undertaken by Juliet Mitchell from a feminist perspective and by Jacques Lacan. Mitchell's principal argument is that, rather than prescribing a phallocentric order detrimental to women, Freud's work emerges from and more exactly describes such an order. The crucial epistemological function of her argument is that, in attacking Freud's supposed prescriptions, feminists are led to what she sees as the politically damaging gesture of foreclosing on the concept of the unconscious and so encouraging biologistic or psychologistic renditions of feminine identity. Her principal aim is to preserve the radical epistemological yield of Freud's work against the long line of Freud's followers (like Melanie Klein, for example) who, in order to overcome the difficulties of Freud's treatment of femininity, presuppose a natural or biological sexual division that takes precedence and preeminence over any unconscious processes of subjective construction. The fault that Mitchell finds with such theories is that, although they are often proposed as if on behalf of femininity, countering Freud's formulations of a deficiency in the female subject, they paradoxically return to a notion of a given sexuality which in no way helps explain women's oppression—much less offers practical political ways of ending it. Indeed, it might be said that such theories of the feminine stand unwittingly close to Freud's infamous statement—often quoted to his disadvantage—that "Anatomy is Destiny." Mitchell's point is that in the debate with Freud over the derogatory implications of his theories of penis-envy and the castration complex, analysts such as Klein, Ernest Jones, and Karen Horney have run the risk of distorting psychoanalysis' theoretical project and changing it into a tendentious one: "The issue subtly shifts from what distinguishes the sexes to what has each sex got of value that belongs to it alone."[11]

That subtle shift is what lies beneath the claims of Freud's commentators that sexual identity is not purely a product of the subject's passage through the Oedipal stage but takes shape before it. By positing pre-Oedipal specificity for the female subject and by claiming that in psychoanalysis' phallocentrism "the importance of the female organs [are] correspondingly underestimated,"[12] the early opponents of Freud's views began to construct an ethical path that many analysts have unhesitatingly followed, notably in the parade of American ego psychology. Ernest Jones' desire to have psychoanalysis establish a "sense of proportion" or fairness in dealing with female sexuality is emblematic of the liberal post-Freudian approach to the concepts of penis-envy, the castration complex, and the Oedipus. The ethical spirit that pervades the desire to demote the phallus from the privileged and dominant position it holds in Freud's work is the immediate source of the feminist rejection of Freud in the sixties—and it exhibits the same moral outrage. Freud's own contention, however, is that the work of psychoanalysis becomes distorted in such propositions. He maintains that Jones' work fails to "distinguish more clearly and cleanly between what is psychic and what is biological, [and tries] to establish a neat parallelism between the two." [13] The result of such a parallelism would be the explanation of sexual division on biological grounds and a reclaiming of parity between male and female bodies. The crucial psychical consequences of the imposition on the human subject of the paternal law would then be disregarded on behalf of a liberalist claim—an ethical claim—for a kind of somatic sexual equality.

Freud claims that "here the feminist demand for equal rights for the sexes does not take us very far." [14] The mere reversal or rebalancing of the phallocentric economy on the grounds of equality ignores the way in which both male and female subjects are constructed within that order. This sort of feminist demand concentrates more on the conception of a static nature of subjectivity than on attempting to understand its social construction. Freud points out that psychoanalysis properly "does not try to describe what a woman is—that would be a task it could scarcely perform—but sets about enquiring how she came into being." [15] His emphasis there on the construction of femininity—indeed, of all sexed subjectivity—allows a glimpse of the most productive implications of his thought. The genesis of subjectivity is the object of psychoanalytical investigation and Freud is clear that this does not allow given and biological factors to be decisive. Any view suggesting otherwise will have as its necessary corollary a righteous moralism —such as that of Jones—which ultimately finds its roots and guarantees in traditional notions about the species, where cultural exigencies are seen as mere impositions upon the natural character of the human. Against such a traditional paradigm of truth and falsity, Freud inaugurates an investigation of the dynamic construction of the fictional and a dismantling of the static economy of the natural. [16]

It would nonetheless be fair to say that whatever moralistic and normative characteristics there are in Freud's thinking represent (or are the symptom of) his own unconscious difficulties with female subjectivity. [17] Luce Irigaray, in an extended critique of Freud's lecture entitled "Femininity," points out several times that Freud's logic goes astray when he talks of women: "Il aura . . . surtout quand il y sera question de la femme, subrepticement interrompu le fil de son raisonnement, de sa logique." [18] He tends, for example, to talk of the mystery of woman's sexuality as if male sexuality were perfectly clarified, and at the same time describes feminine sexuality in the pre-phallic phases as if it were the same as the masculine. In other words, the primary bisexuality that he insists on for both genders is fundamentally masculine—there is one libido and it is masculine in character. Irigaray is probably right in suggesting that Freud's androcentric bias is more apparent here than in his dealings with the Oedipus complex, castration anxiety, and penis-envy. But she objects to the total picture of feminine development which she reads in Freud: a pre-Oedipal sexuality that is essentially masculine and a post-Oedipal sexuality that is castrated masculinity—"phallisme valeureux, et phallisme chatré . . . désir 'viril' pour la mère, et 'envie' du pénis du père." [19]

Irigaray's early critique of Freud—in fact her doctoral thesis—often tends toward the compensatory moralism apparent in Jones and the American feminists. Her question for Freud's text is finally the same as theirs: What do women have of value that is specific to them and why did Freud neglect it? When she asks rhetorically why Freud did not consider womb-envy or breast-envy, she operates with the same reversal in mind as that which prompts Jones' desire for "fairness" and his introduction of the notion of a specifically feminine libido in the debate with Freud. The term *concentric*, coined by Bela Grunberger, marks such a trend, opposed to the phallocentric in a simple reversal. The concentric is that which is regarded as specifically feminine in the unconscious and is used in reference to the female's pre-Oedipal sexual organization. Ultimately in Jones and in Irigaray's *Speculum*, that specificity is founded on somatic detail: there is a biological determination of sexuality through the sexed organs. (It may be objected that Jones and Irigaray differ in that the former will stress the primary genital organs whereas Irigaray talks of the whole female body in its specificity. Nonetheless a biological or a somatic specificity is posited, and if there is a difference in the foundations of each conception, it is not one that Irigaray makes apparent in her early work.)

Beyond this return to the specifically feminine organization of the pre-Oedipal, or to the woman's privileged relation to pre-Oedipal sexuality before the imposition of the symbolic, there is another problem raised by Irigaray's formulations—the problem of the passage between the two terms she is trying to marshall, *phallisme valeureux* and *phallisme chatré*. If woman's relation to the pre-Oedipal imaginary, her relation to the maternal body, is to be revised in its terms (from *phallisme valeureux* to *conisme valeureux*, perhaps), is this not merely an attempt to define woman as outside the symbolic realm, outside the imposition of culture on the subject? Does it not reassert the old moral repartition not only of nature and culture, but of man and woman? Would not a *conisme valeureux* foreclose woman's entry into the symbolic and maintain her in a state of primary narcissism, structured in an imaginary unity with the maternal body? I will return to Irigaray's later attempts to deal with such questions; for the moment it should be clear that what is involved here is the whole question of woman's subjectivity in or to signifying practices, in or to language. Irigaray's *Speculum*, recommending the investigation of what she calls *une scénographie somatique* of femininity, has much in common with the work of post-Freudian commentators both in its insistence on some form of pre-symbolic (or extra-symbolic) subjectivity for women and in that it makes recommendations for a specifically feminine place in the unconscious, relying on a notion of women's unique access to language and the body.[20]

The desire to posit a sexual identity for women which is not constituted in relation to the phallus but which exists in or as a result of the pre-Oedipal, although a strategical part of the effort to specify the feminine, almost invariably carries a suggestion of innate human characteristics that act as the locus of values in arguments like Jones'. These characteristics or qualities are presumed to be submitted to, or distorted by, the subject's passage into the cultural world. When Irigaray claims in her early work that "la femme renonce à son insu à la spécificité de son rapport à l'imaginaire" in order to be able to speak at all, she reifies some kind of pre-symbolic being in much the same way as do feminists whose arguments are very different.[21] Nancy Chodorow, for example, reifies and *evaluates* the subject's capacities (such as capacities for "relatedness" and "intimacy" or generally for a "sense of connectedness" in the pre-Oedipal stage.[22] Dorothy Dinnerstein bemoans the "tendency to renounce the sensuous-emotional world of our early childhood."[23] In feminist accounts of this variety, because of woman's special and incompletely repressed relation to the maternal body, female subjectivity comes to be seen as "not so independent of its emotional origins" as its male counterpart.[24] Even though Chodorow, for example, wants to claim that her work is devoted to stressing the historical and social dimensions of subjectivity's construction, she ahistorically and asocially emphasizes this pre-Oedipal stage in such a way that it becomes an absolute and invariable determinant and is linked directly to bodily specificity. Chodorow makes statements of the following sort:

> We can conclude that the establishment of an unambiguous and unquestioned gender identity and realistically sexed body-ego is a pre-Oedipal phenomenon.

> The basic feminine sense of self is connected to the world, the basic masculine self is separate.[25]

Such claims find an echo in work done by clinical psychologists like Carol Gilligan whose claim that men relate antagonistically and women with caring relies upon some notion of male and female identity as constant and ineluctable entities that the social merely reflects and reinforces.[26] There the entry into the social, symbolic realm is not anything more than the affirmation and confirmation of already existing "core identities" in men and women. Gilligan in effect offers the empirical justification for a tendency that is found also within psychoanalysis itself, the tendency to ignore the functional—indeed, junctional—intervention of language in the construction of sexed subjects. The orthodox psychoanalytic counterpart to her claims is illustrated by a recent college textbook's claim that "Freud believed that children are first able to differentiate the sexes [at the phallic phase], an ability that we now know exists much earlier."[27]

Freud, of course, is insistent that gender identity cannot be established before the passage through the Oedipus complex and his thinking is echoed in Lacan's affirmations that nothing in the unconscious accords with the body and that nothing like the ego pre-exists the symbolic. The upshot of this emphasis is that the phallus and its signification are crucial to the development of gendered identity. This is the avenue that Lacan followed to arrive at an account of subjectivity fundamentally hostile to any suggestions of innate human characteristics, one which throws the whole responsibility for the division of the sexes onto language and the subject's unconscious representations.

Freud had always suggested that such questions were the way through which any proper conception of the unconscious should pass. Indeed, one of psychoanalysis' crucial discoveries remains that the unstable representations constituting the unconscious are always a threat to stable identity. As Lacan states:

> It is a question of recovering, from the laws governing that other scene which Freud designated . . . as that of the unconscious, the [representational] effects that are discovered at the level of the chain of materially unstable elements that language consists in.[28]

These effects of representation are never deducible as corresponding to any prelinguistic identity or coherence in the subject, but are organized only according to the logic of the signifier which is actually what constitutes the subject. Within that logic the phallus holds sway, acting metaphorically as the guarantor of fixed meaning and thus of identity. It is in relation to the organizing function of the phallus as signifier that the subject takes its constitution.

The provocation and upshot of Lacan's conception of the subject are obvious. The subject is no longer conceived of as a given entity, sexed or not, embodying some authenticity upon which the social merely inscribes itself. Immediately, Lacan's notions challenge not only all claims for truth and authenticity as the subject's ground, but also the notion of false consciousness. Durable propositions concerning the originary, imaginary identity of the subject cannot be deduced from Lacan's theories in which the fictional nature of all claims to stable and unified identity is underscored. Insofar as it is the phallus that initiates and guarantees all such claims to identity, then the fictional nature of that authority (paternal authority) can also be stressed. The privilege that the phallus holds in defining sexual identity is automatically put into question at the same moment as its privilege in instituting fixed meaning.[29]

What Lacan does stress, however, is the overriding and fraudulent dominance of the phallus. In this, his conception of the subject is pessimistic and somewhat fixed. Since the subject is posited as receiving the authority of the phallus through language and the unconscious organization of the Name-of-the-Father, it appears to have no way of altering an inevitable history. This tends to encourage a conception of the authority of discursive structures that is ultimate: the phallic nature of cultural and linguistic organization is taken as decisive and static, having no alternative and no explicable history. If the problem with feminist objections to psychoanalysis is that they have tended to posit a pre-symbolic reality which might be characterized as a sort of undifferentiation and solipsism, incapable of accounting for desire or of offering anything more than a transcendentalist politics, then psychoanalysis' problem has been its submission to the necessity of the law of the father. In other words, psychoanalysis is caught in its inability to conceptualize difference except as a polarization defined, established, and presided over by phallic law.

So it may be said that feminist objections to psychoanalysis and its view of femininity, attempting merely to counter what it sees as a consolidation of phallocratic privilege by proposing a kind of equal and opposite specificity and privilege for femininity, often fail to take seriously into account the force and intricacy of the unconscious construction of gendered subjectivity and its representations. The theoretical equalization of privilege is effected by resort to often mystical, usually naturalistic descriptions of femininity which cannot but elide the problem of the imposition of the symbolic realm.

Psychoanalysis, on the other hand, is always susceptible to another form of feminist argument which would berate it for its inability to offer an explanation of gendered subjectivity without recourse to the phallic paradigm where the symbolic is merely the symptom of a social order that is always already phallic. Even if Lacanian psychoanalysis has made possible a move away from a strictly Freudian insistence on the 'fact' of castration for women, its subsequent (nay, consequent) submission to the concept of symbolic castration, said to underlie all subjectivity, tends toward the pessimistic and proffers nothing so much as a monolithic and overriding symbolic order which is rigidly phallocratic. While Lacan's difficulties with his own phallic authority as male and teacher might constitute for him the limits of any possible masculine exploration of phallic privilege, the fact that he is always unable to effect a depriviliging and must always finally attest to the impossibility of doing anything but accepting the strictures of the phallocentric order has not always pleased his feminist colleagues.

The central moment in the construction of gendered sexuality in Lacan's theories is still the Oedipal moment. The recognition of the mother's lack of a penis initiates the conception of difference, a sexual division which has signification:

> The ways of what one must do as a man or as woman are entirely abandoned to the drama, to the scenario, which is placed in the field of the Other— which, strictly speaking, is the Oedipus complex.[30]

The Oedipal moment is the moment of entry into the symbolic order where the subject is reduced to the function of a signifier "in the field of the Other." In other words, the recognition of sexual difference is mapped onto a system of signification, language itself—which analogously operates by the structuring of differences. Just as language produces meaning only through the difference between signifiers, so gendered subjectivity is attained by a similar recognition of difference. Lacan is always at pains to make clear that the two processes inform each other so thoroughly that there can be no such thing as a sexed being before the subject's entry into the system of difference that is language. In Lacan's thinking, then, the Oedipus complex imposes the structural organization of sexuality upon the subject with the structural necessity of speech. This dual imposition that comes with the subject's entry into the symbolic realm is a submission to the Law-of-the-Father instituting separation both from the mother and from the realm of the imaginary symbiosis of self and other.

Lacan accepts and extends Freud's view of the differing male and female passages through the Oedipus and thereby posits differing relations for males and females to the symbolic realm. His important and provocative offering lies in his linking the

Oedipus complex with the structural demands of language. While it seems to be the case that an actual, empirically evident recognition of sexual difference—a sighting of the "fact" of castration—is crucial to Lacan's theories, the link with the entry into language allows him to stress the fictional or metaphorical nature of sexual division and of all the social privileging that is founded upon sexual distinction. It is this symbolic dimension of the Oedipal imposition that is all-important in Lacan's work, and its force needs to be kept alive in any reading of Lacan.

One of the most important and fundamental of Lacan's metaphorical explanations of the genesis of subjectivity is "the mirror stage," when the infant first sees itself reflected in a mirror and begins to construct a plenary image of itself. At the same time, it inaugurates a basic split in identity, since the image and the body are not the same entity, even if they look alike. Lacan's notion of the mirror stage is strangely preempted by Virginia Woolf's assigning what she calls "a looking-glass vision" to men in *A Room of One's Own*. For Lacan, as apparently for Woolf, the identification the subject makes in the mirror with its own image is a founding and supporting moment in the construction of the ego. The subject sees itself in the mirror as both self and other—self, insofar as it can say, "this is me"; other, in that it has to say, "that's me there, not actually my body." The mirror stage constructs what Lacan, after Freud, calls the I-ideal, the component of the ego that, while evidently constructed as an imaginary coherence for the subject, also relentlessly and consistently opens up a gap between self and other—the gap upon which all representation must build itself. The mirror phase actually institutes the subject's entry into language, the field of the other. "Take that 'looking-glass vision' away," says Woolf, "and man may die like the drug fiend deprived of his cocaine."

But the presence, the self-ness of that image is nothing more than a comforting representation of the self as a unity, a whole. It authorizes and supports, in Woolf's words, that "self-confidence, that self-assurance that have such profound consequences in public life and lead to such curious notes in the margin of the private mind." Those curious notes: the inscription of the unconscious at the founding moment of the ego; the process of repression that is the very price paid for identity or for the illusion of a coherent self. Woolf's general points are much the same as Lacan's: that the sufficiency of the mirror image is based on a misrecognition—Lacan's *méconnaissance*—which inaugurates the process of the subject's being brought into place ("interpolated," in Althusser's word) in the symbolic. Both Woolf and Lacan underline the fictional nature of this ego and claim that it is simply that which is demanded by "public life" or the symbolic realm.

The difference between the two is that Woolf specifically ascribes this delusory figure to the male of the species, whereas for Lacan it becomes the fundamental fiction for subjects of both sexes. Woolf seems to assume that for women there is some identity that is not part of, that lies outside, the "looking-glass vision." Lacan on the other hand is adamant that nothing like a sexed ego preexists the symbolic and in this he follows Freud who says that masculinity and femininity are but conventional assignations.

Woolf's view of the matter is implicit in the following phrases: "So I reflected . . . looking at the people in the street. The looking-glass vision is of supreme importance." The people in the street are explicitly men, going about their *business* in the male world. The looking-glass vision is their enabling fiction, the mechanism that allows them to regard themselves as sufficient. But instead of finding a similar reassurance by looking into the mirror, women, according to Woolf, undertake their own reflections from a place that is different from man's fictitious space. That place is surely Woolf's "room of one's own," a spot somewhere outside of the phallocratic world. From there, however, Woolf imagines that woman can *buy into* that masculine economy with something like "five hundred pounds a year."

What I think Woolf promotes here is an implicit vision of woman's own space as one apart from the symbolic realm, a space which Lacan dubs the "imaginary" —a realm theoretically free of the phallus' imposition and thus free of the specular construction of the subject at the mirror stage. If, then, for Lacan, there is no sexed being before the Oedipus complex and nothing like a unified ego before the mirror stage, for Woolf there is "woman" before both. Women are thus liberated to reclaim access to the room of the imaginary—needing only the means to buy into the symbolic of which they are not "really" a part.

It is exactly this tension between the imaginary and the symbolic (crucial to Lacanian theory) and the question of woman's relation to both that has interested French feminists. How are the imaginary and the symbolic constructed differently for women, in women? And so the question, not of *what* identity can be claimed for women but the question of how any identity, any sense of self-as-woman, might operate. For these feminists Lacan's work has been advantageous in its mapping out of the phallocentric order of the symbolic in a way which will allow discussion of the history of the individual subject, the story of its construction in the world of language and culture. In other words, Lacan's work allows discussion of the tyranny of the ideology of the symbolic realm—ideology conceived of here as in Althusser, not as a collection of ideas that circulates, but as a material practice in, on, and for the subject who is interpolated into his or her proper place. For Lacan's feminist followers ideology is to be seen as putting into practice a general social process or law, residing in language. Thus the production of the subject is primarily a matter of positionality in language.

This opening of the field does not, however, allow Lacan to take any openly avowed position of privilege in the discourse of these feminists. Writers such as Hélène Cixous and Luce Irigaray claim that Lacan's work still clings to a phallocentric, anti-woman model. Even if it has allowed a clearer understanding of the subject's actual construction, its gesture of returning to Freud necessarily includes a heavily deterministic and pessimistic element—the acceptance of the predetermined power of the logos and the relative stability of phallocentric rule. Thus we find in Cixous, Irigaray, and others, direct and indirect attacks on Lacan for persistently defining woman in relation to the phallus. This seems to preclude their accepting entirely Lacan's claim that the subject's identity is only a construction passed through the symbolic (never a given entity or a primary or core identity).

Cixous' best-known text is "The Laugh of the Medusa." There she appears at first to take it for granted (with Lacan) that the symbolic world is a phallocentric organization constructed in the tight knot of "a libidinal and cultural—hence political and typically masculine—economy."[31] Her argument with Lacan, however, is over the question of woman's relation to language. Cixous rejects the Freudian and Lacanian proposition that woman is necessarily in negative relation to the cultural world. She wants that male economy to be, as she puts it, *dépensé*: dépensé as in un-thought, de-thought; and *dépensé* in the sense of spent, spent by the production of a feminine discourse which would act as the "precursory movement of transformation in social and cultural structures."[32] This desire to destructure the male economy is clearly more radical than Woolf's gilt/guilty relation to it; it is not a question of Woolf's thrifty ten shilling notes, but more an exhaustive spending, one without reserve. The spending here refers also to the orgasmic energy of women's bodies—spending without end, orgasm without end—so that the libidinal as well as the economic structures are to be undone at one fell swoop by the female body.

Instead of buying a stall in the male economic show, Cixous wants to expose the male economy to a run, an uncontrollable effusion that will cause the collapse of all the stocks, the devaluation of the phallic stakes, and the structuring of a new economy. As Jane Gallop says: "For Cixous, the heroine is she who breaks something . . . compromise attaches to the one who is shut up."[33] In other words, the woman shut in her room or the woman enclosed and silenced in a putative identity who thriftily buys into the male economy is accepting it, compromising herself with its stakes. For Cixous, if the subject is formed in language and yet is never definitively fixed, then a destructuring of the language will forge new subjects. Woman has the potential of continually opening up the symbolic, not expressing herself from the base of an identity, but positing herself as a continually changeable relation to the symbolic.

It is perhaps not very surprising that Cixous' text, when reprinted in a recent *New French Feminisms* anthology, was placed under the rubric "Utopias." Probably that assignation was meant to refer to Cixous' willingness not to take a fixed position or express a final configuration of "woman." Less kindly, it might refer to the affirmative and hopeful nature of Cixous' project which has been described by Elaine Showalter as "a significant theoretical formulation" of the question of woman's relation to language, but one which is "a Utopian possibility rather than an actual literary practice."[34] As a strategic or tactical necessity, of course, Cixous' writing works: it predicates future possibilities on the disruption of all notions of psychic identity and, insofar as it refuses to fall back on the idea of a primary bank of subjectivity, it constitutes a necessary objection to simplistic feminist notions of identity. Cixous' claim is that there is no firm and capacitating self for us to express, but only relations to an overbearing symbolic world, relations to a language that needs to be explored and broken, destructured and exhausted.

The utopian project is always fraught with theoretical problems. With Cixous, perhaps the most glaring of these is that in her tactical urgency and through the undoubted necessity of establishing real women's access to cultural modes, she is led to presuppose a category "woman." Not only is the teleological impulse somewhat idealist here, but Cixous might also be said to fall into the trap of another kind of fixed identity. Although she does not rely upon a notion of a fixed female psychical identity, she fixes woman as a function of the female body. She almost mystically conceives of woman's body as infinitely capable of pleasure, "a thousand and one thresholds of ardor." And with this body there comes a privileged relation to language: "More body, hence more writing." [35] She would unproblematically attach woman's body to what Lacan says corresponds to desire itself—the metonymic axis of language, the free flow of signifiers in an endless run, unimpeded by the imposition of the signified.

When Lacan establishes the assignation of the two Jakobsonian poles of language—metonymy and metaphor—to, crudely speaking, "Desire" and the "Law" respectively, his claim is that no meaning can exist for the subject outside of the imposition of the metaphoric axis upon the metonymic. Desire in language can never be totally uninhibited: the signifier must always be halted and anchored, arbitrarily and temporarily. Language's functioning between the metonymic and metaphoric axes means that neither the male nor the female subject is free of language's laws in the production of meaning. Furthermore, there are few indications in the structured functioning of utterance for either sex which indicate that this utterance has to have been produced by a woman or by a man. Our positions as men and women are not more than superficially marked and can be differentiated only at the level of the unconscious where we are interpolated as sexed subjects. In other words, it is in submitting to the dominance of the symbolic that we produce meaning and are ourselves produced as subjects.

Cixous never attempts to account for the fact that any utterance, whether produced by a male subject or female subject, is located in the symbolic as a function of language itself. In presupposing the category "woman," Cixous calls into existence a new entity whose specification is also the affirmation of a set of unactualized practices in language. Here the statement "more body, hence more writing" must be taken as an imposition of will, one also reflected in the multiple uses of the future and conditional tenses in Cixous' work. The anticipatory urgency of Cixous' work should, I think, be critically viewed in the context of the political options that it forecloses, just as it must be recognized as a valuable strategical and rhetorical enterprise.

Not only does Cixous' affirmation tend to idealize language—simultaneously seeing it as something it is not and as the locus par excellence for social change—but it feigns to ignore the historical fact that it is precisely women's bodies that have been the object of patriarchy's most deep-seated fears and oppressive processes. It is woman's body that is repressed by men in their own unconscious. Cixous offers no substantial reason and no practical demonstration for how and why it is that she can claim for women an especially privileged relation to the body and to desire in language. Furthermore, any epistemology founded upon the notion of the body and attempting to foreclose the radical mediations of the social and the symbolic, can end up positing the most totalitarian form of politics. An example of this might be the poet Ezra Pound in whose work the coherence and self-sufficiency of the body acts as a guarantee for the efficient transmission of truth from one person to another, ignoring the problems of a symbolic order. Language becomes the totally transparent vehicle for the expression of, in Pound's case, a special historical truth.[36] In Cixous' case the truth transmitted is that of woman's identification with her anatomy. We are returned, strangely enough, to one of Freud's most controversial statements, "Anatomy is Destiny."

If Cixous' work is surrounded by a certain aura of celebration—even of mystical ritual—it has the virtue of necessity: the pure rhetoric of a proposal of the feminine is a discursive ally in any attempt to oppose dominant structures. But the pitfalls of such rhetoric are obvious and legion, familiar to any liberationary project. The inversion, however principled, of a given system or economy rests inside that same economy and can, by dint of that fact, be reappropriated and recuperated by the existing structures. In Cixous' case even a certain enthusiasm for deconstruction, and her desire to get beyond modes of thought subjected "to a two-term system, related to 'the' couple man/woman," have not allowed her to entirely refuse those modes.[37] It is this danger I try to point out in her work, hoping that alongside such risky operations there will exist work which will more self-consciously resist being pulled back into, and more thoroughly invalidate, the system of masculine oppression.

The work of Luce Irigaray is in some sense more thorough than that of Cixous, even though it ostensibly appears to operate in the same area. Irigaray extends Cixous' notions of the body in order to radicalize them. After her thorough critique of Freud in *Speculum*, her writing takes up the task of reconceptualizing difference outside the metaphor of the phallus. She proposes that "woman"—the category again—exists in some irreducible manner that has not yet been permitted to conceptualize itself in patriarchal, logocentric thought; that this irreducible form should be able to act as the means by which women enunciate themselves as the *subjects* of the quest for femininity, without the encumbrance of the masculine typologies which inevitably establish woman as the object of inquiry into femininity; and that this feminine essence will be found by reconceptualizing the female body in such a way that the reductive force of the phallic metaphor will be countered.[38]

Although there is some similarity between Cixous' celebrated characterization of the female body as "a thousand and one thresholds of ardor" and Irigaray's equally well-known description of female sexuality as "two lips kissing," there is perhaps a difference.[39] Cixous' phrase is an ethically and morally charged description which posits a pluralistic vision against the oppositional bases of logocentric thought and the unicity to which the phallic metaphor reduces all life. In that sense Cixous' strategy is yet another oppositional one. Irigaray's, on the other hand, is a philosophical attempt to think of woman's body beyond the terms of same and other. Irigaray sees the necessity not just of reinserting the female body into the male economy as a kind of provocative rhetoric, but also of envisaging it in a way by which it will not be reduced or appropriated by the phallicized system of language in which it is traditionally caught. She is, quite simply, attempting to conceptualize difference outside of the relation to the phallus. Irigaray has worked on the deconstructive lesson that Cixous has avoided in her desire to see written language as a privileged synecdoche for all forms of signifying practice, merely countering its logocentric manners.[40] Irigaray's "two lips kissing" is, as Jane Gallop has argued, not even a description of the female body in male, "phallological" terms:

> In phallo-logic the female genital is either a clitoris, phallic-same, or a vagina, phallic-opposite. . . . This either-or, same or opposite, always seen according to phallic parameters, has constituted the alternatives for the representation of female genital anatomy. . . . Irigaray seems to be advocating a female sexuality that replaces the anxious either-or . . . ultimately choosing *not both but neither.*[41]

If it is the symbolic trap which persuades us that we can see coherence only in the phallus—with pluralism, random or organized, as its economic bedmate—we might be able to alter the dictates of the symbolic by refusing to be reduced by our bodies, male or female, to the descriptions they offer. The aim is not to claim a privileged essence for women's "two lips" but to propose a different construct: neither dualism nor reference to a knowable body, but a disavowal of the terms of phallological discourse altogether.

The fact that Irigaray's attempts to change the logic of phallic culture take as a base the female sexuality that has been prohibited because of its irreducibility—"Son sexe est fait de deux lèvres. . . . elle est déjà deux—mais non divisible en un(e)s"—does not mean that she is engaged in the same operations as Cixous.[42] However, the reference to female sexuality is made, like that of Cixous, in the context of an ethical objection to the male body and in the spirit of political utopianism: female sexuality is mystically celebrated, its radical multiplicity having a disruptive potential far in excess of even the most careful political efforts.[43] The terms of Irigaray's attempts to dismantle phallocratic modes of thought run the risk of promoting a politics where "woman" is disruptive because she is in excess of the modes of male culture, and where that excess is tied to a physical referent.

Ironically there is a point at which Cixous and Irigaray—even if it is inaccurate to say that they accept the Freudian notion of anatomical destiny—can be seen to agree with the work of Lacan, despite their continual anti-Lacanian insistence. Their interpretation of the notion of feminine *jouissance* is akin to what Lacan expresses when he states that "I believe in the *jouissance* of women in so far as it is *en plus*," something more, something excessive and beyond the legislation of patriarchy.[44] This function as something *en plus* is redolent of nothing so much as the function of the id in Lacan's work. Indeed, Lacanian psychoanalysis can be seen as the positing of an unstable opposition between ego and id in such a way that the (male) ego can control the id by loving it, by calling it woman, or by calling woman it (id, Lacan's *ça*).

For Lacan, woman is *id*-entified, made into that other excessive function within the patriarchal order: the unconscious processes themselves. Woman *is*, then, that which is repressed because she is ineluctably associated with her body's sexual potential, an *en plus* beyond phallic law. Lacan importantly announces that "the id (*ça*) is elaborated in the female manner" and stipulates a category "woman" not unlike Cixous' and Irigaray's when he assigns a "supplementary *jouissance*" to women, linking it with the elaboration of the id.[45] Lacan's most radical and provocative statements about the precise nature of woman align her with a naturally unknowable essence that belongs to the order of the truth:

> I just don't know how to conduct myself with truth, any more that I do with women. They're both the same thing . . . and I've got a taste for them both.[46]

Lacan, revealing his heterosexuality, exhibits his taste for women by actually devouring them, assigning them a place outside of what is knowable, outside the productions of the symbolic. In *Encore*, which contains his most thorough meditation on female sexuality, Lacan reduces woman to a kind of natural resource to be identified with her sexuality, identified with her tasty body that can be mined to the satisfaction of the male economy. Cixous and Irigaray run the risk of falling into that open-cast mine if they agree to define "woman" as a somatic function and thus become part of the material used by the male economy for its stocks and shares: any merely affirmative action in their writing would be recuperable by the male economy. Irigaray's insistence on an almost exclusive, separatist feminism, what she calls *l'entre-femmes*, could consolidate a convenient definition of woman as essence, as bodily specificity constituted as a group—all the women herded together where they can be seen plotting to become what they are already seen by patriarchy to be (disruptive, garrulous, irrational, sexually uncontrollable, unknowable to man). The male economy has never needed to *buy* that: it simply and always appropriates it.

It seems to me important that, as the valorization of the feminine is undertaken and taken seriously, feminist theory should be increasingly aware of the difficulties of purely inversionary tactics. At very least those tactics should proffer themselves as provisional and not as the reification of the as yet unrealized category of a "woman." Most of all, the trap of proposing a femininity outside of the symbolic world might be carefully scrutinized so that women embracing it are not left alienated from any potential and practicable attempts to change that symbolic realm: to be left outside of it does nothing to ease the very real oppression of very real women in all parts of the world.

It would perhaps be most useful to propose a kind of feminism that will operate against patriarchal institutions, culture, and logic with a twofold strategy. This would involve not only valorizing woman—and avoiding or being very circumspect about the way in which such valorization can be recuperated—but also working on an analysis and a consequent politics for feminism in such a way as to recognize and exploit the contradictions inherent in dominant practices. The second path involves, of course, recognizing the implication of women and men within a symbolic order which oppresses both.

Such a strategy has been proposed by Gayatri Spivak under the rubric of a practice that will be against sexism and for feminism:

against sexism, where women unite as a biologically oppressed caste; and *for* feminism, where human beings train to prepare for a transformation of consciousness.[47]

Spivak's program is an important one, but its terms need to be examined. If the slogan against sexism urges the necessity of seeing women unite as a biological caste, it also carries the possibility of itself becoming a sexism, privileging one biological group, one sex over another. As the editorial group of the journal *Questions Féministes* points out, it remains true that although

> it is worthwhile to expose the oppression, the mutilation, the functionaliza-
> tion, and the objectification of women's bodies . . . it is also dangerous to put
> the body at the center of a search for female identity. Furthermore, the notions
> of Body and Otherness merge easily since the most evident difference between
> men and women . . . is indeed the difference in bodies. That difference has
> been used to justify total domination of one sex over the other.[48]

And that difference could be used, of course, all over again.

It should be said Spivak's proposals are made in order to suggest a view of women's oppression in terms of "symbolic clitoridectomy" and can be seen as an attempt to recast conceptualizations of difference through the phallus. Yet they return to a call for women to unite on a biological front and, in a familiar way, propose women's bodies as the ciphers of a natural excess. Spivak's program very easily becomes, if not intentionally, a plea for women's bodies because of their fundamental and even essential asymmetry. The locus of the argument can perhaps be seen in Spivak's reference to the work of the feminist socio-biologist, Evelyne Sullerot, who states that a feminist interpretive system must be built from "observations based on reality" and that "one is indeed born a woman."[49]

The aim of a feminism that would be "against sexism and for feminism" is perhaps, then, bound to flirt with a certain notion of biological specificity. Spivak herself has been heard to propose that women "take the risk of essence" in order to effect substantive efficacy in feminist practice.[50] However, the work of the feminist psychoanalyst Michèle Montrelay seems to me to offer ways of not having to take that risk. Montrelay's work is not widely read in the United States. No part of her book, *L'Ombre et le nom*, has appeared in a North American translation, though Jane Gallop has paid some close attention to it in her work. One part of it, a section called "Inquiry into Femininity," has appeared in translation in Britain, but only with a critique of its positions by the British feminist, Parveen Adams. Stephen Heath's article "Difference," almost a classic text for feminist theory, is also critical of Montrelay's thesis. I want here to disagree with the British feminist reading of Montrelay on the grounds that it ignores some of the tensions in her work and forecloses on the possibility of establishing the twofold strategy I have mentioned.

Heath closely relates Montrelay's work to that of Cixous and Irigaray. He assumes, for example, that when Montrelay asks "is not the 'adult' woman one who reconstructs her sexuality in a field which goes beyond sex?" she is aligning herself with statements such as Irigaray's "woman has sexes everywhere." Similarly, her statement that "woman's sexuality is capable of remaining apart from all repression" is related to Lacan's id-entification of woman. The core of her book, the proposal that "femininity is the downfall of interpretation" and "the ruin of representation," is seen as another risky expression intended to valorize "woman" through the qualities of excess and disorder that patriarchy easily recuperates or oppresses.[51]

Heath reads Montrelay as if he were confronted by another version of the feminine essence that he sees proposed in Lacan, Cixous, and Irigaray. But in fact the argument of Montrelay's book is more complicated than Heath's reading. It is true that she sees femininity and women's identity as being involved with a specific mode of sexuality, one constructed as radically other to the phallocentric order. But she never claims that women can do away with the symbolic order by simply flooding it, or by reversing it, or by holding back from it. Rather, she seems firmly aware of the production of women's sexuality and language within the constraints of the symbolic.

For Montrelay difference in male and female subjectivity is to be explained through the unconscious processes as they form and inform the subject's access to language and to the cultural world. She continually stresses that for men the price of the symbolic, the price of representation, is the repression of castration anxiety. This includes both a mourning for the sacrifice made to the Law-of-the-Father and a disavowal of the loss. She claims that conventional sexual difference resides in the fact that a woman, having lost only that which she never had in the passes of the Oedipus, does not undergo the same repetition of repression as is a man's lot. Rather, her access to the symbolic is gained with the mere price of a sublimation— a sublimation of the reality of her body. Because of men's relation to the phallus, one of homomorphism, the symbolic demands of them the repression of the Oedipal conflict and of separation from the mother. Montrelay claims that grand-scale repression is not required of women since their relation to the phallus is heteromorphic.

Some of the many consequences of Montrelay's arguments can be drawn from the recognition that patriarchy is erected and upheld by the price of men's repression. The difference between repression and sublimation—the latter always more easily undone—allows women less constrained access to their own bodies. The specificity of those bodies is immaterial in the sense that Montrelay does not allow her explanation of sexual difference to come down to a difference of bodies. Even more than Lacan, who allows for continual vacillation between the notion of the phallus as symbolic and the existence of the real penis, Montrelay affirms the absolutely symbolic or metaphoric function of the phallus. The phallus is only that which organizes social life—it cannot be collapsed into the specifications of male bodies. Both women and men are subject to the rule of the phallus, but at different psychical cost. Women's advantage is their ability, by virtue of being more capable of reaching the reality of their bodies than are men, to short-circuit the economy of the masculine world. Thus Montrelay's feminism maintains the valorizing impulse that is tactically and philosophically necessary for feminist theory but does it without recourse to specific physical difference: what is at stake is women's access to their bodies and not the specificity of those bodies themselves. The argument is one against sexism, against the reduction of sexuality to the one or the other; against too, the societal privileging of masculine sexual control which comes to be seen as a frightened and anxious repression of bisexuality.

Montrelay's proposals, based firmly in Lacanian analysis, but which neither mystify (or re-mystify) femininity nor allegorize it in the manner of Derrida or Cixous, seem to me to be capable of producing the utmost confidence and optimism against sexism and for feminism. Montrelay implies that women are not simply the other for men, but have access to a specific mobility—a mobility which is the "ruin of representation," the possibility of transgressing and breaking down the symbolic structures under which we all live.

L'Ombre et le nom, the shadow and the name: the imbrication of the two establishes a specifically feminine process of identity, an identity that is only imperfectly legislated in a patriarchy whose fundamental effort is to put men in their place or to fix them in a coherent identity. Montrelay's notion of feminine identity is one of vacillation, unfixity. In some senses it is a notion very close to Julia Kristeva's descriptions of those semiotic practices that cut across and transgress the fixity of the symbolic—a kind of metonymic route left negligently open by the symbolic realm and which constitutes a contradiction or a flaw in the weave of hegemonic structures. It also accords well with what Jane Gallop says about the relation of identity to feminism:

> Both psychoanalysis and feminism can be seen as efforts to call into question a rigid identity that cramps and binds. But both also tend to want to produce a "new identity," one that will now be adequate and authentic. I hold the Lacanian view that any identity will necessarily be alien and constraining. I do not believe in some "new identity" which would be adequate and authentic. But I do not seek some sort of liberation from identity. That would lead to another form of paralysis—the oceanic passivity of undifferentiation. Identity must be continually assumed and immediately called into question.[52]

What further strikes me as important in Montrelay's work is that her reading of psychoanalytic theory leads her to suggest that the opposition between repressed men and sublimated women is not a fixed opposition. Believing firmly in the Freudian thesis of bisexuality, she theorizes that as women undo the sublimation they have been led into, men should undo the repression that is their lot in patriarchy. In other words, a metonymic passage between identities is available to both men and women. Both the imaginary and the symbolic can be rewritten since neither is coherent or finally constitutive—there is never one without the other for either men or women.

Montrelay sees some of the writing by men like Bataille, Klossowski, or Jabès as crucial acts of murder against the fixity of the symbolic realm, attempts to undo male repression, recognizing what she calls the *odor di femina* that remains with each of us. *Odor di femina*: the smell of woman, Montrelay's own trail perhaps, traditionally causing only anxiety, abhorrence, and repression in men. I suppose that I want to say that this odor is everywhere, at the thresholds of my own repressive mechanisms and constructions, and it is a scent that needs to be followed. Not to liberate or valorize the id, not to find the woman inside men, but merely to recognize that what has been oppressed and repressed is everywhere. When Lacan says that woman is *pas-toute* in relation to the phallic economy—not everything, not all, not whole—I want to read a pun there: *pas-tout* becoming *partout*, everywhere. Recognizing the scent of it then becomes man's job as much as woman's.[53]

Men, it's true, still have everything to say about their own sexuality, their own unconscious, their own supposed identities, since the funding repression in phallocentric economy is ours and ours alone. For me, then, the project becomes a task—that of recognizing the tyranny of the symbolic world, but noticing for women and for men that the phallocentric order is itself riddled with contradictions, with the traces of imperfect repression; it is an order that is always on the defensive and covers up its repressive deficiencies with an art that comes from centuries of use. But we can attack its defenses: not by forging a grammatically symmetrical identity for women, but more exactly by exposing, exploiting, and exacerbating the signs of weakness in the defenses, dismantling phallocracy brick by brick, person by person.

Notes

1. A version of this paper was presented as a talk at Wesleyan University's Center for the Humanities in October 1982. I want to thank the audience there for its responses, which have helped me revise the paper—I think for the better. I have special reason to thank Christina Crosby for her direct and indirect participation in the revisions, my students in a class on feminist theory and practice in the arts who both provoked and stimulated me for a semester, and Jane Gallop, whose work has been crucial to my own.

2. Elaine Showalter, "Woman and the Literary Curriculum," address to the MLA Commission on the Status of Women (1969).

3. C. R. Swift, "Once More Unto the Breach of Western Literature Courses," *Women's Studies Quarterly* 9/4 (1981).

4. Judith Kegan Gardiner, "On Female Identity and Writing by Women," *Critical Inquiry* 8/2 (1981). My emphases.

5. Elaine Showalter, "Feminist Criticism in the Wilderness," *Critical Inquiry* 8/2 (1981).

6. Annette Kolodny, "Dancing Through the Minefield," *Feminist Studies* 6/1 (1980).

7. Virginia Woolf, *A Room of One's Own* (New York: Harcourt Brace Jovanovich, 1977).

8. Susan Friedman, *Psyche Reborn* (Bloomington: Indiana University Press, 1981), p. 109. For a more detailed critique of the assumptions and practices of feminist critics such as Friedman, see my article, "H.D.'s Identity," forthcoming in *Women's Studies*.

9. Sigmund Freud, "Feminine Sexuality," in *The Standard Edition of the Complete Psychological Works of Sigmund Freud*, trans. and ed. James Strachey, vol. XXI (London: Hogarth Press, 1961).

10. Sigmund Freud, "An Outline of Psychoanalysis," in *The Standard Edition*, vol. XXIII (London: Hogarth Press, 1964).

11. Juliet Mitchell and Jacqueline Rose, eds., *Feminine Sexuality: Jacques Lacan and the Ecole Freudienne* (New York: Norton, 1982), p. 20.

12. Ernest Jones, "The Early Development of Female Sexuality," *International Journal of Psychoanalysis* 8 (1927), p. 438.

13. Sigmund Freud, uncollected letter printed in *Psychiatry* (1971) and entitled "Freud and Female Sexuality: A Previously Unpublished Letter."

14. Freud, "Feminine Sexuality."

15. Sigmund Freud, "New Introductory Lectures on Psychoanalysis," in *The Standard Edition*, vol. XXII (London: Hogarth Press, 1964).

16. Freud's thought is not, of course, untroubled by contradictions in this respect: the natural is frequently reified in his writings in the shape of the inherited unconscious component of the id and the normative demands of the cultural often act as the compelling force behind Freud's recommendations for actual analytic practice. And yet when Freud gives way in the face of one of his most long-standing theoretical difficulties (namely, the question of phylogenetic traces in the psyche) by seeing himself "obliged to regard such traces as part of the *archaic heritage* which a child brings with him into the world" (see "An Outline of Psychoanalysis"), it should be remembered that it is nonetheless Freud himself who consistently protested against the biologic tendencies of psychoanalytic theory. Even if Freud speaks of the "sick ego" that needs to be returned to its "normal functions," he is also at pains to make clear that cures cannot be affected if the analyst is "tempted to become a teacher, model and ideal"; such moralistic undertakings are not, according to Freud, "the analyst's task in the analytic relationship." Through a reading of Freud's dealings with the question of homosexuality, an especially good case can be made for his refusal to submit to biologism. Such a reading has been made—with particular reference to Freud's letters to Putnam—by Henry Abelove. I am grateful to have had the chance to read Abelove's unpublished article, "Freud and Homosexuality."

17. Especially interesting on Freud's problems of this sort is Sarah Kofman's *L'Enigme de la femme* (Paris, 1980) which—although it is somewhat obvious and jaded in its analyses—will probably remain a standard critique of Freud's dealings with his own unconscious.

18. Luce Irigaray, *Speculum de l'autre femme* (Paris: Editions de Minuit), p. 17. "Especially when woman is in question, Freud's reasoning, his logic, becomes suddenly interrupted."

19. *Ibid.* "Validated phallicism and castrated phallicism . . . 'virile' desire for the mother and 'envy' of the father's penis."

20. *Ibid.*, pp. 155–56. "A somatic scenography." It is ironic that Lacan's Ecole Freudienne ejected Irigaray for exactly the reasons that caused Freud's disagreement with Jones and others more than fifty years before—a dispute over the question of a specifically feminine unconscious or unconscious component.

21. *Ibid.*, p. 165. "Woman unwittingly renounces the specificity of her relation to the imaginary."

22. Nancy Chodorow, *The Reproduction of Mothering* (Berkeley: University of California Press, 1978), p. 169.

23. Dorothy Dinnerstein, *The Mermaid and the Minotaur* (New York: Harper and Row, 1976), p. 32.

24. Chodorow, *The Reproduction of Mothering*, p. 169.

25. *Ibid.*, pp. 158, 169.

26. See C. Gilligan, *In A Different Voice* (Cambridge, Mass: Harvard University Press, 1982).

27. J. A. Talbott, "Development," in *Introducing Psychoanalytic Theory*, ed. S. L. Gilman (New York: 1982), p. 27.

28. Jacques Lacan, *Ecrits: A Selection* (New York: Norton, 1977), p. 285.

29. See Jane Gallop, *The Daughter's Seduction* (Ithaca: Cornell University Press, 1982), especially "Of Phallic Proportions: Lacanian Deceit."

30. Jacques Lacan, *The Four Fundamental Concepts of Psychoanalysis* (New York: Norton, 1977), p. 204.

31. Hélène Cixous, "The Laugh of the Medusa," in *New French Feminisms*, ed. Elaine Marks and Isabelle de Courtivron (New York: Schocken, 1981), p. 249.

32. Hélène Cixous, "Castration or Decapitation," *Signs* 7/1 (1981).

33. Gallop, *The Daughter's Seduction*, p. 136.

34. Showalter, "Feminist Criticism in the Wilderness," p. 185.

35. Cixous, "The Laugh of the Medusa," pp. 256–57.

36. See for further elaboration my *Pound Revised* (London, 1983).

37. Cixous, "Sorties," in *New French Feminisms*, p. 91 and note.

38. Luce Irigaray, *Ce sexe qui n'en est pas un* (Paris: Editions de Minuit, 1977) and *Et l'une ne bouge pas sans l'autre* (Paris, 1979).

39. Irigaray, "This Sex Which Is Not One," and "When the Goods Get Together," in *New French Feminisms*.

40. The recent and somewhat problematic confluence of Derrida, deconstruction, and feminism is discussed at length by Gayatri Spivak in "Displacement and the Discourse of Woman," in *Displacement: Derrida and After*, ed. Mark Krupnick (Bloomington: Indiana University Press, 1983). Spivak's critique of Derrida's use of woman as the figure of displacement par excellence quite correctly criticizes the fact that the material of specificity of women's bodies is denied them by Derrida's figurations. Equally important in this connection, I think, is that Derrida tends to allegorize "woman" in a way that is entirely in keeping with his anti-social textual strategies. To the extent that Derrida's critique of the will to power in any discursive practice itself becomes a mastering discourse such an allegorizing becomes an inevitable—perhaps covertly desired—symptom of masculine, controlling tendencies.

41. Jane Gallop, "Quand nos lèvres s'écrivent: Irigaray's Body Politic," *Romanic Review*, 74/1 (1983); Gallop's italics.

42. Irigaray, *Ce sexe qui n'en est pas un*, p. 25. "Her sex is constituted of two lips . . . she is already two—but not divisible into one(s)."

43. In her two texts in *New French Feminisms*, Irigaray reduces the male body to the function of a "violating penis" which finds the vagina as nothing more than a "substitute for the little boy's hand" (p. 100); she also insists on the rigid separation of existing political and social oppositional groups from her proposed politics of the female body (p. 105).

44. Jacques Lacan, *Le Séminaire XX: Encore* (Paris: Seuil, 1975), p. 71.

45. *Ibid.*, pp. 68–69.

46. *Ibid.*, p. 108.

47. Gayatri Spivak, "French Feminism in an International Frame," *Yale French Studies* 62 (1981), p. 170.

48. Editorial collective, "Variations sur des thèmes communs," *Questions Feministes* 1.

49. Evelyne Sullerot, in *New French Feminisms*, pp. 157–58.

50. I quote this from several of Spivak's many interventions in sessions of the 1982 MLA conference in Los Angeles.

51. Steven Heath, "Difference," *Screen* 19/4 (1978/79), p. 72. Montrelay's "Inquiry into Femininity," from *L'ombre et le nom* (Paris, 1978), appeared with Adam's "Representation and Sexuality," in *m/f*, 1.

52. Gallop, *The Daughter's Seduction*, p. xii.

53. Lacan, *Encore*, p. 13.

Hawthorne's Letter / *John Dolis*

When Hawthorne discovers the Letter in the attic of the Custom-House, he does precisely what the technological attitude demands. He seeks to understand the object by means of analysis: "This rag of scarlet cloth . . . on careful examination, assumed the shape of a letter. It was the capital letter A. By an accurate measurement, each limb proved to be precisely three inches and a quarter in length."[1] Yet this solitary mark, discovered in the attic, refuses to assign itself to rational design: "Certainly, there was some deep meaning in it, most worthy of interpretation . . . but evading the analysis of my mind" (I: 31). For its significance Hawthorne must go from the "attic," or head, to what technology would deem the "cellar," the heart: "While thus perplexed,—and *cogitating*, among other hypotheses . . . *I happened to place it on my breast*. It seemed to me,—*the reader* may smile, but *must not doubt my word*,—it seemed to me, then, that *I experienced a sensation not altogether physical*, yet almost so, as of burning heat" (I: 31–32, italics mine). Here Hawthorne clearly opposes the authority of the *logos* to the traditional logic of the head. It is understood—and not to be doubted—from the outset, that the meaning of the sign is excavated from the logic of the heart: the correspondence between subject and object is primordially grounded in expression. Moreover in its initial design, the Letter falls away from its original place, from its location as circumscribed by Surveyor Pue's manuscript: "In the absorbing contemplation of the scarlet letter, I had hitherto neglected to examine a small roll of dingy paper, around which it had been twisted. This I now opened, and had the satisfaction to find, recorded by the old Surveyor's pen, a *reasonably* complete explanation of the whole affair" (I: 32, italics mine). We need not be reminded of the extent to which these "half a dozen sheets of foolscap" (I: 33) constitute the authority and domain of rationality in its entirety: so much for reason. This too accounts for the emphasis Hawthorne gives to the imaginary which allows the actual to be appropriated by the logic or affective significance of the heart. This is what happens with the Letter. Indeed one might say that in its very fall from the grace of this original manuscript, the Letter itself is inaugurated into si(g)n. In falling out of his-story (Surveyor Pue's), from the place in which its initial inscription is circumscribed, the Letter needs to be recovered in Hawthorne's own story. For in sliding off the page, the Letter itself does nothing less than fall into the white space of a new margin.[2]

We are recalled to Hester's own predicament beside the brook: "By this time Pearl had reached the *margin* of the brook, and stood on the farther side, gazing silently at Hester and the clergyman, who still sat together on the mossy tree-trunk, waiting to receive her" (I: 207–8, italics mine). When Hester hastens Pearl to retrieve the Letter, and is refused, she remarks to Dimmesdale:

"Was ever such a child! . . . O, I have much to tell thee about her. But, in very truth, she is right as regards this hateful token. I must bear its torture yet a little longer. . . ."

With these words, she advanced to the *margin* of the brook, took up the scarlet letter, and fastened it again into her bosom. Hopefully, but a moment ago, as Hester had spoken of drowning it in the deep sea, there was a sense of inevitable doom upon her, as she thus received back this deadly symbol from the hand of fate. She had flung it into infinite space!—she had drawn an hour's free breath!—and here again was the scarlet misery, glittering on the old spot. (I:211, italics mine)

Here we stand witness to the return of the repressed: the Letter comes back to Hester once again from out of the other, its original source of meaning. Here too issues the locus of what Lacan refers to as the "real"—that which always comes back to the same place and before which all symbolic discourse falters. Constantly held in abeyance, it is "another locality, another space, another scene": the encounter in as much as it is missed.[3] So with the forest scene in general: its significance resides in what is missing. In place of the Letter, Pearl but indicates its absence—as Hester observes: "Pearl misses something which she has always seen me wear" (I:210). Amid a circular round of pointing [Pearl to Hester: "Pearl stretched out her hand, with the small forefinger extended, and pointing evidently towards her mother's breast" (I:209); Hester to the Letter: "'Pearl,' she said, sadly, 'look down at thy feet! There!—before thee!—on the hither side of the brook!'" (I:210); and so in turn to Pearl: "She extended her hand to Pearl" (I:211)], amid this encapsulated round of substitution and displacement of the signifier, the margin of the stream again returns the Letter in its absence, reflecting only the margin of the Letter. "The child turned her eyes to the point indicated; and there lay the scarlet letter, so close upon the margin of the stream, that *the gold embroidery was reflected in it*" (I:210, italics mine). In this reflection the Letter itself is plainly absent. Only with Hester's Letter finally back in place does Pearl acknowledge her as mother: "Now thou art my mother indeed! And I am thy little Pearl" (I:211).

It is further to be remarked, amid this round of nomination in the very presence of Dimmesdale, that the name of the father is here occluded—and this despite the many lessons in catechism in response to which Pearl repeatedly demands her origins:

"Tell me, then, what thou art, and who sent thee hither?"

"Tell me, mother!" said the child, seriously, coming up to Hester, and pressing herself close to her knees. "Do thou tell me!"

"Thy Heavenly Father sent thee!" answered Hester Prynne.

But she said it with a hesitation that did not escape the acuteness of the child. Whether moved only by her ordinary freakishness, or because an evil spirit prompted her, she put up her small forefinger, and touched the scarlet letter.

"He did not send me!" cried she, positively. "I have no Heavenly Father!"

"Hush, Pearl, hush! Thou must not talk so!" answered the mother, suppressing a groan. "He sent us all into this world. He sent even me, thy mother. Then, much more, thee! Or, if not, thou strange and elfish child, whence didst thou come?"

"Tell me! Tell me!" repeated Pearl, no longer seriously, but laughing, and capering about the floor. "It is thou that must tell me." (I:98)

Without a history, Pearl lacks a story of her own. And yet it is logically appropriate that she should omit the name of the father, for it is she who—by upholding the (Puritan) law, demanding with her "singular air of authority" (I:209) that Hester return the Letter to its place—usurps the very place of law itself. In place of the father (the law), she presumes to fill the gap—and does so as an imposter, as but "the freedom of a broken law" (I:134). Indeed desire emerges in this very margin where demand becomes separated from need.[4]

For Hawthorne, also, who—on the margin of discourse, upon the threshold of the Custom-House—seeks to father the Letter as his own, there arises the question of authority. In respect to the Letter, which has fallen out of another manuscript, Hawthorne is acutely sensitive to the demands of authorship. When first he broaches this issue in conjunction with the meaning of historical authenticity, he disclaims responsibility for the story by assuming the posture of editor: "It should be borne carefully in mind, that the main facts of that story are authorized and authenticated by the document of Mr. Surveyor Pue" (I:132). The history of the Letter represents an interruption in Hawthorne's story. This false submission to the authorization of another occupies the very place in which we would expect to see the author's signature. But if he disowns the Letter, Hawthorne must disown *The Letter* as well: "The original papers, together with the scarlet letter itself,—a most curious relic, —*are still in my possession*, and shall be freely exhibited to whomsoever, *induced by the great interest of the narrative*, may desire a sight of them" (I:32–33, italics mine). Thus in the very next breath he disclaims his initial disclaimer so that he might reclaim the story as his own:

> I must not be understood as affirming, that, in the dressing up of the tale, and imagining the motives and modes of passion that influenced the characters who figure in it, I have invariably confined myself within the limits of the old Surveyor's half a dozen sheets of foolscap. On the contrary, I have allowed myself, as to such points, nearly or altogether as much license as if the facts had been entirely of my own invention. What I contend for is the authenticity of the outline. (I:33)

What then is the truth of history? As Lacan cautions, "Any statement of authority has no other guarantee than its very enunciation, and it is pointless for it to seek it in another signifier, which could not appear outside this locus in any way."[5] The authorial "I" occasioned by Surveyor Pue's history cannot accede to itself by being designated. It is, rather, the constant reminder of the (w)hole text

(*The Scarlet Letter*). Hawthorne's authority is nothing less than the white page which stands before him: it remains to be written. Here he will mark out his own paternity—the authority by which he will transcend laws external to himself, both Puritanical and political.

The entire Custom-House moves away from this oppressive impotence toward manhood. Heretofore, and indicative of his tenure as Custom-House official, Hawthorne's signature has never been his own, but rather the mark of Uncle Sam's seal. At the same time, he is everywhere circumscribed by a paternity of impotent old men: "I doubt greatly—or rather, I do not doubt at all—whether any public functionary of the United States, either in the civil or military line, has ever had such *a patriarchal body* of veterans under his orders as myself" (I:12, italics mine). In this debilitating context, Hawthorne would carve out or inscribe the text of himself:

> An effect—which I believe to be observable, more or less, in every individual who has occupied the position—is, that, while he leans on the mighty arm of the Republic, his own proper strength departs from him. He loses, in an extent proportioned to the weakness or force of his original nature, the capability of self-support. . . . Conscious of his own infirmity,—that his tempered steel and elasticity are lost,—he for ever afterward looks wistfully about him in quest of support external to himself. . . . Uncle Sam's gold . . . has, in this respect, a quality of enchantment like that of the Devil's wages. Whoever touches it should look well to himself, or he may find the bargain to go hard against him, involving, if not his soul, yet many of its better attributes; its sturdy force, its courage and constancy, its truth, its self-reliance, and all that gives the emphasis *to manly character*. (I:38–39, italics mine)

And though his own prognosis confirms that he has taken a turn for the worse, Hawthorne is nevertheless able to prescribe the cure: "I had ceased to be a writer of tolerably poor tales and essays, and had become a tolerably good Surveyor of the Customs. That was all. But, nevertheless, it is any thing but agreeable to be haunted by a suspicion that one's intellect is *dwindling away*" (I:38, italics mine). That is, as an official representative of conventional authority, Hawthorne's very own manhood is shrinking to aught: "I began to grow melancholy and restless; continually *prying into my mind*, to discover which of *its poor properties were gone*, and what degree of detriment had already accrued to the remainder. I endeavored to calculate how much longer I could stay in the Custom-House, and yet go forth *a man*" (I:39–40, italics mine). As things stand (or, in this case, fall), he is not even the remainder of himself.

Herein, too, we discern the very trace of the signifier as the desire of otherness: in this bind Hawthorne is divided against himself. On the one hand he would like to resign: "In view of my previous weariness of office, and vague thoughts of resignation, my fortune somewhat resembled that of a person who should entertain an idea of committing suicide" (I:42). On the other hand he feels compelled to assign himself as his own man, to inscribe his own signature, to rise from the political (mis)fortune of his dismissal from office—"*My own head* was the first that *fell*" (I:41, italics mine)—and therefore employs the Custom-House pre-text as the very ground from which he will figure forth as his own authority and deploy his own text. As a (w)hole, he offers his public this autobiographical sketch as the "POSTHUMOUS PAPERS OF A DECAPITATED SURVEYOR" (I:43), and this he undertakes with self-effacing mockery: "The moment when *a man's head drops off* is seldom or never, I am inclined to think, precisely the most agreeable of his life" (I:41, italics mine). Indeed the public voice of conventional authority would have it no other way: "Meanwhile, the press had taken up my affair, and kept me, for a week or two, careering through the public prints, in my decapitated state, like Irving's Headless Horseman; ghastly and grim, and longing to be buried, as a politically dead man ought" (I:42–43). Over and against the decapitation of his public person, however, Hawthorne would yet stand up. And toward its climax he therefore inserts his own private part: "The real human being, all this time, with *his head safely on his shoulders*, had *brought himself to the* comfortable *conclusion*, that every thing was for the best; *and, making an investment in* ink, paper, and *steel-pens*, had *opened his* long-disused *writing-desk, and was again a* literary *man*" (I:43, italics mine).[6]

Unlike the blissful couple of Edward and Ellen in *Fanshawe*, who, at the end of the romance and the beginning of Hawthorne's career, were content to leave "no name behind them" (III:460), Hawthorne is now committed to the opposite. It is the problem of nomination repeated in Dimmesdale's failure to admit his own paternity to Pearl. Although for Dimmesdale it is a matter of seven years, for Hawthorne it is simply a matter of several pages before he confesses to the lie of editorship and reveals the truth of authorship. Toward the conclusion of the Custom-House sketch Hawthorne is ready both to admit his indebtedness to the other (Surveyor Pue) and to declare the authority of his own name.

> As the public disapprobation would weigh very heavily on him, were he conscious of deserving it, the author begs leave to say, that he has carefully read over the introductory pages, with a purpose to alter or expunge whatever might be found amiss, and to make the best reparation in his power for the atrocities of which he has been adjudged guilty. But it appears to him, that the only remarkable features of the sketch are its frank and genuine good-humor, and the general accuracy with which he has conveyed his sincere impressions of the characters therein described. . . . *The sketch might*, perhaps, *have been wholly omitted, without loss to the public,* or detriment to the book; but, having undertaken to write it, he conceives that it could not have been done in a better or a kindlier spirit, nor, so far as his abilities availed, with a livelier effect of truth.
>
> *The author is constrained*, therefore, *to republish* his introductory sketch *without the change of a word.* (I:1–2, italics mine)

Need we add that this constraint is now of his own making, the progeny of his own authority? What might have been wholly omitted without loss to the public has been included at the public exclusion—and this for the sake of fathering the self.

We detect in this bind a structure not unlike that which Derrida calls "differance," and which Gayatri Spivak transcribes as "*pre*monition" and "*post*ponement."[7] If the sign can be said both to defer itself and differ from itself, the same can be said of the signifier named "Hawthorne." In the Custom-House sketch, he clearly seeks to understand the significance of his own existence, but he is divided in his dual role as editor and author. Similarly the ambivalent tone of "The Custom-House" discloses Hawthorne's ambiguous attitude toward his Puritan ancestry. He would simultaneously recognize and disown both story line and family line. Furthermore he repeatedly delays the fact that he must stand up to this story as his own, that he must at last sign his own name to it. He is, of course, aware from the outset that his story excludes a privileged authorial position, that its beginning, in fact, originates elsewhere and is ultimately inaccessible. "As regarded its origin, there were various explanations, all of which must necessarily have been conjectural" (I:258). We are repeatedly cautioned regarding this genealogy. If he is ever to come into his own, Hawthorne realizes that he must recognize his source of identity in the other. The source of his story is not his own doing; yet if one tries to follow it back to an absolutely certain origin, the trace of its historical inscription becomes irrevocably lost in pre-historical discourse—that is, in gossip, in what is passed down or passed along by word of mouth. Such is his original source of indebtedness: "The authority which we have chiefly followed—a manuscript of old date, drawn up from the verbal testimony of individuals, some of whom had known Hester Prynne, while others had heard the tale from contemporary witnesses" (I:259–60). And such is the testimony to which Hawthorne's signature at last bears witness: from the beginning, his story is inscribed within the other.

If Hawthorne's story immediately obtains from Surveyor Pue's history, history itself nevertheless appears all the more problematic when we recall its intimate resemblance to story. For while Hawthorne initially remarks its status as official, a closer examination reveals "more traces of Mr. Pue's mental part, and the internal operations of his head, than the fizzled wig had contained of the venerable skull itself. They were documents, in short, not official, but *of a private nature*, or, at least, *written* in his private capacity, and apparently *with his own hand*" (I:30, italics mine). Hawthorne undermines that easy epistemology which relegates knowledge to the simple accumulation of facts. In doing so, he also speaks against the authority of his Puritan ancestors whose judgment would condemn him to insignificance: "an idler like myself. . . . A writer of story-books" (I:10). Indeed, from the beginning, fact is put in doubt for when he measures the Letter (three inches and a quarter in length) it tells him nothing. While the proper measurement of a thing gives us its correct form, its meaning remains absent. The signifier considered in and of itself is nothing but the isolated subject taken by itself: the subject objectified. Thus would reason reduce meaning to the integer of self-identity. A fact is therefore meaningless precisely to the extent that it coincides with itself; identity does not give rise to meaning, but rather—like meaning itself—arises from discrepancy. Similarly the question of self-identity leads every character in *The Scarlet Letter* to another: Chillingworth returns to Dimmesdale (in whom he forecloses on himself); Pearl returns to Dimmesdale (in whom she finds herself); Hester returns to Dimmesdale (in whom she sustains herself); and Dimmesdale returns to each (for whom he names himself). It happens as no accident, moreover, that each and every one desires to know the name of the father, in whom there resides the locus of authority as the source of any and all identity. In this regard identity itself is always a fiction; a text whose context, whose very pre-text, needs to be delineated; a story whose knot might "induce the beholder to attempt unravelling it" (IV:306). History too reveals its origins in story, in fiction, in narration. As Arthur Danto observes: "To exist historically is to perceive the events one lives through as part of a story later to be told." [8] In *The Marble Faun* Hawthorne cautions his "Gentle Reader" about the fragile structure of his woven narrative, the tapestry of his story:

> If any brilliant or beautiful, or even tolerable, effect have been produced, this pattern of kindly Readers will accept it at its worth, without tearing the web apart, with the idle purpose of discovering how its threads have been knit together; for the sagacity, by which he is distinguished, will long ago have taught him that any narrative of human action and adventure — whether we call it history or romance — is certain to be a fragile handiwork, more easily rent than mended. The actual experience of even the most ordinary life is full of events that never explain themselves, either as regards their origin or their tendency. (IV:455)

In this way, too, Hawthorne's superficial observance of historical objectivity often merely constitutes an ironic posture. Like Goethe and Tieck, he delighted in destroying this objectivity at every opportunity. Indeed he frequently satirizes the past as a value in itself. Whereas, for example, only one glass of whiskey suffices to produce the rather doubtful "Edward Randolph's Portrait," the story of Lady Eleanor represents the product of three glasses of madeira.[9] Likewise the stamp of historical authority lies in the personal or private domain, though for its institutionalization (that is, in order to become a fact) it clearly requires the public consent. That Hawthorne appreciates this bind is all the more ironic insofar as he, like Surveyor Pue, has authorized official governmental transactions by means of a meaningless stamp, an imprimatur which bears his name — "imprinted . . . with a stencil and black paint" (I:27) — but not his signature. By an ironic *dédoublement* of perspective, he speculates that his fiction alone, and not his official public activities, may lead to the discovery and preservation of any meaningful identity — that his stories might become, in turn, "*materials of* local *history*" (I:28, italics mine).[10]

By the time that Hawthorne finally signs his name to the work, we are aware that his ironic signification already contains within it the possibility of meaning its opposite. Discourse, by nature, displaces the insignificant correctness of fact with the sign of fiction. Witness, for example, Hawthorne's "conclusion" regarding the further adventures of the Letter in the transformed shape of Pearl: "But, in no long time after the physician's death, the wearer of the scarlet letter disappeared, and Pearl along with her. For many years, though a *vague report* would now and then find its way across the sea, — like a shapeless piece of driftwood tost ashore, with the *initials of a name* upon it, —*yet no tidings* of them *unquestionably authentic were received*" (I:261, italics mine). Over and against these vague reports bearing but the initials of a name, Hawthorne's final signature commends us to the discursive fabric of all authority.[11]

Regarding its claim to authority the text refers us purely and simply to the domain of good faith and interpretation. So Hawthorne concludes with respect to Pearl's correspondence with Hester, letters that locate Pearl within another story, another context, yet one for which he implicitly claims authority as well: "In fine, the gossips of that day believed, — and Mr. Surveyor Pue, who made investigations a century later, believed, — and one of his recent successors in office, moreover, faithfully believes, — that Pearl was not only alive, but married, and happy, and mindful of her mother" (I:262). Authority therefore displaces the lineage of fatherhood with the discursive knot of textuality. Language constitutes the beginning of another enterprise, an intentional structure signifying a series of displacements: language replaces genesis with paragenesis, origins with beginnings, continuity (the line) with contiguity (the knot). Textuality transforms an original object whose significance is fixed into a beginning intention, whose significance is open and multiple.[12] The emerging intention to mean, when it is bequeathed to language, strays toward multiplicity, permitting the possible forms of discourse to merge one into the other.

Because meaning is grounded in intentionality, authority primordially refers us back to self-expression — the fictive or fabricated correspondence between subject/object, signifier/signified — always against a background of repression. As Freud observes of the *Hexateuch*, there is violence in texts:

> Almost everywhere noticeable gaps, disturbing repetitions and obvious contradictions have come about — indications which reveal things to us which it was not intended to communicate. In its implications the distortions of a text resemble a murder: the difficulty is not in perpetrating the deed, but in getting rid of its traces. We might well lend the word "Entstellung" [distortion] the double meaning to which it has a claim but of which today it makes no use. It should mean not only "to change the appearance of something" but also "to put something in another place, to displace." Accordingly, in many instances of textual distortion, we may nevertheless count upon finding what has been suppressed and disavowed hidden away somewhere else, though changed and torn from its context.[13]

This textual disruption is due to the discrepancies inherent in the sign itself. Pearl's nature, as the Letter in another form, articulates this broken law of signification: "It lacked reference and adaptation to the world into which she was born. The child could not be made amenable to rules. In giving her existence, a great law had been broken" (I:91). Meaning emerges from this violent gap in signification. A consciousness of the facts can therefore never account for the fact of consciousness: the self-reflexive subject reveals that its identity in no way coincides with itself, but rather is constituted by another in its origin. This otherness represents the boundary of the self as signifier of desire.

It is precisely the missing or absent beginning which presents the crisis of Pearl's identity: she would know the other by whom she has initially been authorized. Lacking this knowledge, she can nonetheless occasion the significance of the lives surrounding her by means of substitution. In respect to her parents, for example, Pearl knots the chain of signification, "herself a symbol, and the connecting link between those two" (I:154). She is the other whose substitution guarantees one's being, the bond of identity for both Hester and Arthur: "In her was visible the tie that united them. She had been offered to the world, these past seven years, as *the living hieroglyphic*, in which was revealed the secret they so darkly sought to hide, —*all written in this symbol*, —all plainly manifest, —had there been a prophet or magician skilled *to read* the character of flame! And Pearl has the oneness of their being" (I:206–7, italics mine). Significance here emerges from the insertion of one signifier in place of another. When Hester discards the Letter (Pearl) in the forest, this alters the relationship insofar as Dimmesdale takes its (her) place: "The stigma gone, Hester heaved a long, deep sigh. . . . O exquisite relief! She had not known the weight, until she felt the freedom" (I:202). Here Hester assumes the very freedom she had for so long postponed, "the freedom of a broken law" (I:134) which Pearl represents and yet dissembles in herself. Similarly Hester's self-expression occasions the premonition of Dimmesdale's self-repression. Thus, when Hester returns the Letter to its initial place, when Pearl once again occupies the place next to her mother, Dimmesdale is, in turn, recalled to the displacement of himself—the way in which the real, as Lacan defines it, always comes back to the same place:

> As the minister departed, in advance of Hester Prynne and little Pearl, he threw a backward glance; half expecting that he should discover only some faintly traced features or outline of the mother and the child, slowly fading into the twilight of the woods. So great a vicissitude in his life could not at once be received as real. . . . And there was Pearl, too, lightly dancing from the margin of the brook, —now that the intrusive third person was gone, —and taking her old place by her mother's side. So the minister had not fallen asleep, and dreamed. (I:214)

By the same token, that is, in the displacement of the Letter by Pearl, Dimmesdale feels "this indistinctness and *duplicity of impression*" (I:214, italics mine) within himself, though it has *yet to be expressed*:

> The *intervening space* of a single day *had operated on his consciousness* like the lapse of years. . . . Before Mr. Dimmesdale reached home, his inner man gave him other evidences of a revolution in the sphere of thought and feeling.

> In truth, nothing short of *a* total *change of* dynasty and moral *code*, in that
> interior kingdom, was adequate to account for the impulses now commu-
> nicated to the unfortunate and startled minister. At every step he was incited
> to do some strange, wild, wicked thing or other, with a sense that it would be
> at once involuntary and intentional; *in spite of himself*, yet growing out of a
> profounder self than that which opposed the impulse. (I:217, italics mine)

In this regard Dimmesdale typifies the Freudian subject and its determination to
write itself off.

> Now, during a conversation of some two or three moments between the
> Reverend Mr. Dimmesdale and this excellent and hoary-bearded deacon, it
> was only by the most careful self-control that the former could refrain from
> uttering certain blasphemous suggestions that rose into his mind, respecting
> the communion-supper. He absolutely trembled and turned pale as ashes, *lest*
> *his tongue should wag itself*, in utterance of these horrible matters, and plead
> his own consent for so doing, without his having fairly given it. And, even
> with this terror in his heart, he could hardly avoid laughing to imagine how
> the sanctified old patriarchal deacon would have been petrified by his minis-
> ter's impiety. (I:218, italics mine)

And to "the eldest female member of his church" (I:218), who seeks the "heaven-
breathing Gospel truth from his beloved lips" (I:219), he once again consigns
himself to this other voice:

> On this occasion, up to the moment of putting his lips to the old woman's
> ear, Mr. Dimmesdale, as the great enemy of souls would have it, could recall
> no text of Scripture, nor aught else, except a brief, pithy, and, as it then ap-
> peared to him, unanswerable argument against the immortality of the human
> soul. . . . What he really did whisper, the minister could never afterwards
> recollect. There was, perhaps, a fortunate *disorder in his utterance*, which
> failed to impart any distinct idea to the good widow's comprehension, or
> which Providence interpreted after a method of its own. (I:219, italics mine)

Once Dimmesdale finally reaches home, he is again confronted with this dis-
ordered self. His very meaning is disrupted, his significance broken:

> There was the Bible, in its rich old Hebrew, with Moses and the Prophets
> speaking to him, and God's voice through all! There, on the table, with the
> inky pen beside it, was an unfinished sermon, *with a sentence broken in the*
> *midst*, where his thoughts had ceased to gush out upon the page two days
> before. He knew that it was himself, the thin and white-cheeked minister,
> who had done and suffered these things, and written thus far into the Election
> Sermon! But he seemed to stand apart, and eye this former self with scornful,
> pitying, but half-envious curiosity. That self was gone! Another man had
> returned out of the forest. (I:223, italics mine)

Dimmesdale's dilemma echoes Hawthorne's predicament in "The Custom-House." He too experiences the chiasm of his discourse. What has been hitherto inscribed within the other, he must pen himself, expressing that authority which is his own though still repressed. Thus "flinging the already written pages of the Election Sermon into the fire, he forthwith began another, which he wrote with such an impulsive flow of thought and emotion, that he fancied himself inspired" (I:225). And with the first sign of sunrise, he yet subsists "the pen still between his fingers, and a vast, immeasurable tract of written space behind him" (I:225). What lies ahead, however, constitutes the measurable tract of his own authority. These "blank pages" which lie before him, and which have heretofore been writing into his very flesh, reveal by concealing: what is absent cannot hide—what is present can.

From the structure of repression, there emerges the lack of meaning in Pearl's existence as well. While she refuses the ideal—"I have no Heavenly Father" (I:98) —she nevertheless repeatedly invokes the name of the real father. Without this name, of course, she lacks a "history": she is a story begun, but anonymous. Until Dimmesdale's final confession, she remains a character in search of an author (Arthur): a letter takes the place of a name, an initial the place of a signature. Though she lives with Hester as her mother, she must abide the Letter in place of the father. This substitution confers upon Pearl the status of an inauthentic document. It happens as no coincidence, then, that the central character in the novel possesses the Letter as the central, though hidden, letter in her name (PeArl);[14] for so long as Dimmesdale refuses to nominate himself as the author of this work, Pearl's missing identity resides purely in the Letter. While Arthur conceals his Letter behind conventional clothes, Hester ironically wears his secret and hypocrisy as her very garment. In this respect Pearl's identification with the Letter is made all too easy: "She *is* the scarlet letter" (I:113, italics mine). Her own attire mimics this confusion, arrayed "in a certain velvet tunic, of a peculiar cut, abundantly embroidered with fantasies and flourishes of gold thread" (I:102). From birth, Pearl seeks to decipher the enigmatic significance of the Letter as that which holds the very key to her existence; she grasps it, flings flowers at it, embellishes it with burrs, and places eel-grass on her own breast in its form—"freshly green, instead of scarlet" (I:178):

> "I wonder if mother will ask me what it means!" thought Pearl.
> "My little Pearl," said Hester, after a moment's silence, "the green letter, and on thy childish bosom, has no purport. But does thou know, my child, what this letter means which thy mother is doomed to wear?"
> "Yes, mother," said the child. "It is the great letter A. Thou hast taught it me in the horn-book." (I:178)

The Letter takes the place of a denomination which demands to be announced: there is a proper name involved in its sound for which no substitution can bequeath to Pearl her meaning without the loss of significance. As Derrida remarks, "Every signified whose signifier can neither vary nor be translated into another signifier without loss of significance, suggests a proper-name effect." [15] Thus while the "A" appears in different places, different forms, and while it meaningfully inscribes itself into the existence of others, for Pearl it lacks any and all signification proper to herself. She is an unaccomplished work, missing the other letters. In relation to the other, she stands as a meaningless phoneme—although not insignificantly as the first letter both of the alphabet and of Arthur's name. Isolated as "the great letter "A" of her horn-book, she implies the missing part of a whole text and subsequently constitutes "a law unto herself, without her eccentricities being reckoned to her for a crime" (I:134–35). Not until the end, when Dimmesdale discloses his corresponding Letter and gives her his name, is Pearl at last authorized and authenticated.

At the conclusion, moreover, her substitution for the Letter confers upon *The Letter* a significant displacement—a self-reflexive and therefore bifurcated commentary. Pearl's name, in fact, is interchangeable with Hawthorne's title for the book; we might read into her various "properties," the status of the art work. Thus from America, where Pearl "became the richest heiress of her day, in the New World" (I:261)—a circumstance which "wrought a very material change in the public estimation" (I:261)—Hawthorne cleverly dispatches his "child" (*The Scarlet Letter*) to Europe, where it "grew into a legend" (I:261). The reader is invited to this "christening," permitted to witness the birth of American Art. In this beginning there is the promise that others will follow—a situation as pregnant with possibilities as Pearl herself: "And, once, Hester was seen embroidering a baby-garment" (I:262). At last, having come into her own authority, Pearl's correspondence with Hester—"Letters came" (I:262)—here parallels her correspondence with *The Letter*. Regarding both, the end of Hawthorne's story holds forth the birth of other beginnings. An author in her own right, bequeathed by Dimmesdale's confession the other letters of her full name, Pearl now initiates her correspondence with the other as one who has come into the fullness of the alphabet. Thus, to Hester, *other* "Letters came" (B, C, D, E, F, G, H, I, J, K, L, M, N, O, P, Q, R, S, T, U, V, W, X, Y, and Z?) And with her signature *The Letter* too begins its round of nomination, the proselytization of American letters in Europe: "Through the remainder of Hester's life, there were indications that the recluse of the scarlet letter was the object of love and interest with some inhabitant of another land" (I:262).

Furthermore Pearl's signature commends the Letter to its authentic assignment. Though Hester is sentenced to wear the sign of the Letter, she nevertheless redeems it by way of embroidery. Indeed, what the pen is to Hawthorne, the needle is to Hester. With it she transforms her subjectivity to discourse. By means of her needlework, Hester confers upon the existent "a fictitious value even to common or worthless things; . . . Hester really filled a gap which must otherwise have remained vacant" (I:82): she weaves herself into the status of a text. Her sentence is becoming to her: she becomes a sentence. Upon entering a church, for example, "it was often her mishap to find herself the text of the discourse" (I:85). Indeed she often fancies "that the scarlet letter had endowed her with a new *sense*" (I:86, italics mine). With her return from abroad, she is at last bequeathed a textuality of her own making on a new threshold in her story:

> But there was a more real life for Hester Prynne, here, in New England, than in that unknown region where Pearl had found a home. . . . She had returned, therefore, and resumed,—of her own free will, . . . the symbol of which we have related so dark a tale. Never afterwards did it quit her bosom. . . . the scarlet letter ceased to be a stigma . . . and became a type. . . . And, as Hester Prynne had no selfish ends . . . people brought all their sorrows and perplexities, and besought her counsel. (I:262–63)

Now given over to dialogue, the Letter thence transforms itself toward its revelation as a sacred scripture of love—a text whose very nature is destined to unknot itself "in Heaven's own time" (I:263) and is therefore doomed to remain forever undisclosed:

> Hester comforted and counselled them, as best she might. She assured them, too, of her firm belief, that, at some brighter period, when the world should have grown ripe for it, in Heaven's own time, a new truth would be revealed, in order to establish the whole relation between man and woman on a surer ground of mutual happiness. Earlier in life, Hester had vainly imagined that she herself might be the destined prophetess, but had long since recognized the impossibility. . . . The angel and apostle of the coming revelation must be a woman, indeed, but lofty, pure, and beautiful; and wise, moreover, not through dusky grief, but the ethereal medium of joy; and showing how sacred love should make us happy, by the truest test of a life successful to such an end. (I:263)

And so the harbinger of the new sexuality must be a woman—one, we might conjecture, who would dismiss the epithalamion as superfluous. In all of this there is again the ironic bifurcation of significance, for insofar as Hawthorne's own child (*The Scarlet Letter*) is female (Pearl), his book will not perpetuate his paternal name. This suggests that writing does not simply play at childbirth across the abyss of paternity alone, but rather articulates the androgynous abyss across which signs signify, the continually problematic status of being which combines the absence of the dead father with the presence of the living mother. "Writing leaps back and forth across this impossible interval, doubling, multiplying, with no escape save annihilation."[16]

Just as the Letter multiplies its meaning across the otherness of itself (adultery, angel, apostle, able, authority, authenticity, alpha, alphabet, american, art, alterity), so too with the subject: the signifier acquires its meaning from the other signifiers, resisting a transcendental signified. The otherness of the Letter always and everywhere returns its bearer to the place in which it inaugurates the subject to the responsibility for language and the inscription of the self upon the margin of another text. As Geoffrey Hartman remarks, "The word that is given up is not given up: it must inscribe itself somewhere else, as a psychosomatic or mental symptom." [17] Thus, for example, while Hester is tempted—should Pearl be taken from her—to enter the forest, where souls are consigned to the devil, and sign her name in "the Black Man's book" (I:117), she yet refuses to resign herself to another text. Rather than submit to either this or the Puritan conscription—"she will be a living sermon against sin" (I:63)—she chooses to embroider a discourse of her own. Reassigning the Letter of the Puritan law to herself, she thereby returns it to the Puritan community at the very point at which it originated, for her needlework now clothes the community in garments of her own making. By means of her embroidery, Hester rewrites their history as her story, reversing the short circuit: those who would initially write her off are finally written by her, a discourse signed, sealed, and delivered, moreover, with her very signature. It is no wonder then, that the Letter (as symptom) shows up on the blank page of the night sky to (dis)cover the entire community.

Dimmesdale, on the other hand, re( )signs himself to the "A." By its absence from consciousness, the Letter is destined to be present elsewhere. Its symptomatic manifestation inscribes itself upon his very body in the form of his psychosomatic illness. When he speaks, the Letter bespeaks him; just as his sermons represent a paranoid form of dictation, the divine writing calls him to remember a dead Letter and thereby forget himself. For Dimmesdale the Letter must be uncovered, laid bare: he must expose himself to self-aversion. Hawthorne's addiction to the truth —"Be true! Be true! Be true! Show freely to the world, if not your worst, yet some trait whereby the worst may be inferred!" (I:260)—simply underscores the sentence whereby human existence is called to express the inter-textuality of self and other, the inter-subjective dimension of being oneself. In this context truth knows nothing of fact but rather exposes the facticity of being. To be true is to express one's self as an original, to discover a voice of one's own, to fabricate a version, to rehearse the dialogic interval of existence: "To open an intercourse with the world" (IX:6). To be false, on the other hand, is to be missing a version of one's self. To repress a version constitutes the very perversion of being to which Dimmesdale is given over until the end.

Like Hester's Letter, furthermore, Dimmesdale's final revelation allows a multiplicity of versions to figure forth once again. With his disclosure, not only the Letter's significance, but its very appearance, have yet to be discerned. For some it represents his self-inflicted penance; for others it represents the impotence of Chillingworth's necromancy; for still others it represents "the ever active tooth of remorse, gnawing from the inmost heart outwardly" (I:258). A special few, moreover, who "professed never once to have removed their eyes from the Reverend Mr. Dimmesdale, denied that there was any mark whatever on his breast" (I:259). Except for this last, blind version, which obviously misses the mark, Hawthorne permits each version to stand side by side with the others: "The reader may choose among these theories" (I:259). Herein subsists that genuine conversion of consciousness which Hawthorne's oeuvre provokes, the inter-textuality of existence. As Donatello remarks to Kenyon, the problematic status of the sign invites interpretation. "'My dear friend,' exclaimed Kenyon, 'how strangely your eyes have transmuted the expression of the figure! It is divine Love, not wrath!' 'To my eyes,' said Donatello stubbornly, 'it is wrath, not Love! Each must interpret for himself' " (IV:306). With *The Letter* Hawthorne's openendedness allows us to choose and thereby releases us from the narrative authority: the reader is called upon to authorize the text in terms of its significance to self.[18] And while the narrative announces its desire, once the Letter has done its office, to "erase its deep print out of our brain" (I:259), the trace of this effacement must nonetheless remain forever upon the heart. By handing over the potential of this lack, Hawthorne entrusts the reader with the task of further inscription—that in the overabundance of this otherness, the reader would write himself all the more.[19]

In all of this there is implied the ontological status of language—"the page of life" (I:37)—and being itself, as the narrator of *The Marble Faun* observes regarding Miriam's life:

> In weaving these mystic utterances into a continuous scene, we undertake a task resembling, in its perplexity, that of gathering up and piecing together the fragments of a letter, which has been torn and scattered to the winds. Many words of deep significance—many entire sentences, and those possibly the most important ones—have flown too far, on the winged breeze, to be recovered. If we insert our own conjectural amendments, we perhaps give a purport utterly at variance with the true one. Yet, unless we attempt something in this way, there must remain an unsightly gap, and a lack of continuousness and dependence in our narrative. (IV:92–93)

Narration occupies both story and history at their points of embarkation, that locus of authorization which makes existence into a work. Meaning is born through exposition, the temporal fabrication in which existence is made to stand out. It must have a narrator. Hawthorne's pre-text ("The Custom-House"), Pearl's correspondence, Dimmesdale's confession, Hester's embroidery—each inscribes the story of the self in the context of the other to which it corresponds; each discourse makes the other its own. While Hester, for example, initially rejects her needlework as sin, she learns its joy as "*a mode of expression*, and therefore soothing, the passion of her life" (I:84, italics mine). Both Chillingworth and the Puritans in general, on the other hand, deny being its exposition. Adverse to expression, repression thus circumscribes the subject as an "impostor" (as not its own), and therefore articulates the very imposition of being. Precisely and ironically to the extent that Chillingworth, for example, entirely subscribes to or underwrites the text of Dimmesdale's life, he serves as but an annotation to the authority of another. What is the Letter, if not the cutting edge of this bifurcated, asymmetrical structure: self-other? If at its origin the self is always already written by another, it nevertheless is called upon to inaugurate the manner and meaning of its significance. In its intention to secure a beginning, the self thus authorizes its emergence into the world as an authentic work—one of its own making. With this expressive exposition, being is provoked to itself. Hawthorne's villains, however, revoke the self to the failure of being, entirely spoken for and written by the other—upon this line of resistance to the self at the insistence of another, existence is repressed. Authentic existence would yet tie this original (family) line with a significant knot of its own expression: the subject itself is always a fiction.[20]

Hawthorne's *Letter* exposes this duplicity of being within the very structure of his work. His authorial switch from the first-person "Custom-House" to the third-person "romance" enacts the abyss between self and other, subject and object, fiction and fact, individual and community, private and public. Here the personal pronoun not only reveals the reciprocity between subject and object within narration, but also its reciprocal means of being present/absent to itself. The gestalt of a consciousness articulated both within and without implies the very otherness of discourse. Insofar as existence is given over to language, to the irreducible discrepancy between signifier and signified, the subject transacts both speech and writing as separate aspects of the same phenomenon, the otherness of being itself. Each is the horizon of, though neither is ontologically prior to, the other. The narrative discourse comes from the manuscript of Surveyor Pue, although this manuscript, in turn, originates in the gossip of the age; Hester's discourse comes to her from the spoken judgment of the Puritan tribunal; Pearl's discourse comes to her from Dimmesdale's confession; Dimmesdale's discourse, on the other hand, comes to him from the unspoken name—the written mark inscribed upon his very flesh, the ghost of a divine insignia. In every case discourse is called to assume responsibility both for the discourse of the other as its own and for its own otherness. Hawthorne assumes his pen in order to write his romance; Hester utilizes her needle in order to embroider her garments; Pearl takes up her armorial seals in order to post her letters of correspondence; Dimmesdale employs his voice in order to sing the song of himself. In every case, moreover, the subject is provoked to sign the other with a discourse which encircles the (w)hole of its (in)significance.

Expression redeems the subject from the abyss of nothingness across which the signs signify and for significance itself, just as Hepzibah, for example, is "redeemed from insignificance" (II:41) by her scowl. Expression articulates the heartfelt meaning of being in its exposition—the subject's correspondence to the heart of things is the matter of discourse. Dimmesdale's voice suggests this correspondence: "It breathed passion and pathos, and emotions high or tender, in a tongue native to the human heart" (I:243). Within the logic of the head, of course, significance is purely arbitrary: Hawthorne's repetitions and signs function solely as a self-referential system, precluding any and all sense of totality (the A itself is but a fragment). Yet this is not the case within the logic of the heart. While Hawthorne "undoes meaning"[21] at the level of reason, he nonetheless secures the self to a significance which precedes it and thus occasions the very possibility of self-expression—the greatest danger imaginable to the Puritan community as a whole. Both Dimmesdale's voice and Hester's needle disrupt the communal *ratio*. As Nina Baym observes: "Disguised as a social document, the work of art secretly expresses the cry of the heart. Doing this, it covertly defies society in response to hidden but universal needs. . . . *The Scarlet Letter* makes it clear that imagination serves the self."[22] Imagination interrupts the *ratio* of reason in as much as it returns the subject to an irreducible locus of signification from which all meaning originates. Imagination bestows upon the subject the possibility of exposing what is at the very center of its existence, what inheres as its irreducible *Kern*, to use Freud's term: *a heart of nonsense*. What Hawthorne's narrator in *The Marble Faun* observes of the image in painting articulates the core of textuality in general: "*that indefinable nothing*, that inestimable something, *that constitutes the life and soul*" (IV:60, italics mine). As Lacan suggests, all discourse harbors within it this locus of the imaginary by which means the subject constructs the images both of the real world and of itself: "The *I* is not a being, it is a presupposition with respect to that which speaks."[23]

How else, in fact, are we to account for Hawthorne's final tombstone inscription which would efface its very discourse insofar as it substitutes or displaces the symbolic with the imaginary?

> All around, there were monuments carved with armorial bearings; and on this simple slab of slate—as the curious investigator may still discern, and perplex himself with the purport—there appeared the semblance of an engraved escutcheon. It bore a device, a herald's wording of which might serve for a motto and brief description of our now concluded legend; so sombre is it, and relieved only by one ever-glowing point of light gloomier than the shadow:—
> "On a Field, Sable, the Letter A, Gules." (I:264)

In one sense, of course, Hawthorne returns this final image to symbolic discourse inasmuch as he translates its significance into the language of heraldry: "On a Field, Sable, the Letter A, Gules." In another sense, however, there remains only the image itself or rather its ghost: the after-image of what can now only suggest the presence of a dead Letter. If anything, this reading of the inscription is reinforced by Hawthorne's narrative description: for here the invisible motto—the visible "A"—is "relieved only by one ever-glowing point of light gloomier than the shadow." The oxymoron expresses what in the register of the symbolic must remain forever unspeakable: existence is a dead end.

It also seems that in the lack of a verse upon the tombstone, there is once again failure in signing a name. The missing epitaph marks the point of origin of this ghost story, that most simple discontinuous space of the Freudian *fort-da* where the presence of the father-to-be—that is, the presence of the father—"playing" with the absence of the mother engenders a symbolic lack of discourse: "Writing oscillates between a name that cannot be inscribed and the dead body, a corpse-effect whose intrusion into the real is the sign and signature of this impasse. . . . the tomb is the point at which name and body are wed in their common impasse."[24] It should come as no surprise that in the failure of adequation—the signifier as that which represents a subject for another signifier—death has already taken place, has taken up its place in the end, and has done so from the beginning. This crossing of signifiers constitutes, in effect, the very locus of significance as the gap or void of being itself. As the skeleton at "The Christmas Banquet" betokens:

> And if, in their bewildered conjectures as to the purpose of earthly existence, the banqueters should throw aside the veil, and cast an inquiring glance at this

figure of death, as seeking thence the solution otherwise unattainable, the only reply would be a stare of the vacant eye-caverns, and a grin of the skeleton-jaws. Such was the response that the dead man had fancied himself to receive, when he asked of Death to solve the riddle of his life; and it was his desire to repeat it when the guests of his dismal hospitality should find themselves perplexed with the same question. (X:287)

The subject comes and goes upon its round of nomination, and reads in advance this ever-unwritten inscription: "Death . . . is an idea that cannot easily be dispensed with, in any condition between the primal innocence and that other purity and perfection, which, perchance, we are destined to attain, after travelling round the full circle" (X:393).

Here reading and writing are one and the same: for in the end, as we have seen regarding its ultimate design, the Letter which goes abroad is finally returned to its initial place. Lacan observes the same of Poe's "Purloined Letter," in which the sender receives from the receiver his own message in reverse form: "Thus it is that what the . . . 'letter in sufferance' means is that a letter always arrives at its destination."[25] Throughout its circular course, in fact, the Letter elicits the reader's response—indeed, repeats the very trauma of interpretation which inaugurates the self to meaning. As Barbara Johnson says of psychoanalysis: it is "the traumatic deferred interpretation not *of* an event, but *as* an event which never took place as such. The 'primal scene' is not a scene but an *interpretive infelicity.* . . . Psychoanalysis has content only insofar as it repeats the dis-content of what never took place." Similarly, every reader is destined to have the Letter addressed to him precisely to the extent that the Letter's destination is "wherever it is read."[26] Hawthorne's Letter assigns the reader to himself. Thus fiction simultaneously conceals and reveals its truth. This open-ended text refers us to the infinite regress of referentiality. The source of a story is always another story. Each and every discourse on/of the Letter bears the trace of another signifier, another letter, a dead letter. We are recalled to Hawthorne's pre-text in "The Custom-House," where the Letter turns up as simply one of the innumerable pieces of dead weight which clutter the House itself: the mere ghosts of men who through the repetition and redundancy of bureaucratic scribbling have come to occupy this dead letter office. It is indeed their office to repress—by means of idle chit-chat and procrastination—the very thing bureaucracy perpetually defers: the dead-line. Here it is (mis)construed, of course, that life goes on forever. How else are we to understand the overpowering lethargy that befalls Hawthorne, surrounded by these dead letters, these "beings-of-no-consequence" who because they are always talking are therefore never able to write a thing, insuring a veritable dead end which by its impotence leaves everything unfinished?

Within this House of dead letters, the subject is provoked to build, to dwell, to construct the text of himself. The Letter serves to distinguish Hawthorne from both the other(s) and himself, as he inaugurates the repetition of its various rounds within the symbolic structure of discourse. Hawthorne's writing is this House of Fiction, which constructs a passageway between self and other, and thereby opens him to intercourse with the world: "Thoughts are frozen and utterance benumbed, unless the speaker stand in some true relation with his audience" (I:4). Upon the threshold of this (Custom) House, Hawthorne's discourse initiates that homecoming of the subject to itself. As he expressed it in a letter to his publisher, James T. Fields, "'The Custom-House' is merely introductory,—an entrance-hall to the magnificent edifice which I throw open to my guests." [27] Hawthorne's prefaces are thus significant precisely to the extent that they function as various thresholds to this single house. Edgar Dryden brilliantly seizes the significance of this event when he observes that the Custom-House sketch "endows the familiar house-of-fiction metaphor with an important ontological dimension." [28] Indeed, Hawthorne's House of Fiction is nothing less than language itself. Thus he could refer to fiction as the very "kingdom of possibilities" (XII:119).

Meaning here constitutes the play of presence and absence, disclosure and concealment, whereby the ghost of substitution assumes its port of entry. Language expresses the otherwise silent correspondence between signifier and signified, subject and object, self and other. The structure of signification plays across a silent abyss in which the Letter is both cutting edge and knot. Regarding all forms of being, there is the gap, the chasm which yawns—waiting for the subject to insert itself, to uncover its meaning, its truth. Being shelters absence within the house of language itself. Discourse implies an ontology wherein both presence and absence equiprimordially obtain: the construction and repetition of a story in which the subject is at all times missing and thereby stands in need of interpretation. Interpretation returns us to Hawthorne's own obsession for masquerade, the persona of textuality—disclosure in concealment: being (exposed or unmasked) in the very face of the masked text. Herein dwells the genuine *work* of Hawthorne's world, the tangle whence emerges its na(rra)tivity. And in this fabrication, this construction, this weaving, is inscribed the magic limen—the thread of a story designed to be, yet from the outset fated to end: the very knot of being itself. When Hawthorne posts his *Letter*, it is for nothing less than this: to send being on its way, its destination—to be more than the k(not).

Notes

1. *The Scarlet Letter*, in *The Centenary Edition of the Works of Nathaniel Hawthorne*, ed. William Charvat, Roy Harvey Pearce, and Claude M. Simpson (Columbus: Ohio State University Press, 1962), I:31. Subsequent references to Hawthorne will be exclusively to this edition, hereafter parenthetically cited in the text by volume and page number only.

2. This slippage (*glissement*) of the signifier, moreover, constitutes a "fall." See Jacques Lacan, "The Subversion of the Subject and the Dialectic of Desire in the Freudian Unconscious," *Écrits*, trans. Alan Sheridan (New York: W. W. Norton, 1977), p. 303.

3. Jacques Lacan, "Tuché and Automaton," *The Four Fundamental Concepts of Psycho-Analysis*, trans. Alan Sheridan (New York: W. W. Norton, 1978), pp. 55–56.

4. Lacan, "The Subversion of the Subject and the Dialectic of Desire in the Freudian Unconscious," p. 311: "This margin being that which is opened up by demand, the appeal of which

can be unconditional only in regard to the Other, under the form of the possible defect, which need may introduce into it, of having no universal satisfaction (what is called 'anxiety')."

5. *Ibid.*, pp. 310–11: "which is what I mean when I say that no metalanguage can be spoken, or, more aphoristically, that there is no Other of the Other." In the register of the symbolic, the Letter here constitutes the very edge of the Oedipal law, the "cut" in Hawthorne's discourse, the eradication or erasure of the phallus which allows it to (re)emerge as the signifier of desire. It is this "fallen" signifier which disrupts the discourse of the manuscript (history) and confers upon Hawthorne the responsibility of authorship (fatherhood) for his story.

6. For another reading of Hawthorne's "manliness" in "The Custom-House," see John T. Irwin, *American Hieroglyphics* (New Haven: Yale University Press, 1980), pp. 276–84.

7. See Jacques Derrida, "Differance," *Speech and Phenomena*, trans. David B. Allison (Evanston: Northwestern University Press, 1973), pp. 129–30: "The verb 'to differ' (*différer*) seems to differ from itself. On the one hand, it indicates difference as distinction, inequality, or discernibility; on the other, it expresses the interposition of delay, the interval of a *spacing* and *temporalizing* that puts off until 'later' what is presently denied, the possible that is presently impossible. Sometimes the *different* and sometimes the *deferred* correspond in French to the verb 'to differ.' This correlation, however, is not simply one between act and object, cause and effect, or primordial and derived. In the one case 'to differ' signifies nonidentity; in the other case it signifies the order of the *same*. Yet there must be a common, although entirely differant (*différant*), root within the sphere that relates the two movements of differing to one another. We provisionally give the name *differance* to this *sameness* which is not *identical*: by the silent writing of its *a*, it has the desired advantage of referring to differing, *both* as spacing/temporalizing and as the movement that structures every dissociation."

See also Gayatri Spivak, "The Letter as Cutting Edge," in *Literature and Psychoanalysis: The Question of Reading, Otherwise*, ed. Shoshana Felman (Baltimore: Johns Hopkins University Press, 1982), pp. 209–10. If postponement recollects forward there being (*Dasein*) a future, premonition recollects backward the future as that which has already been. Postponement knows behind itself from out of the future; premonition knows ahead of itself from out of the past.

8. Arthur C. Danto, "Narration and Knowledge," *Philosophy and Literature* 6 (1982), p. 18.

9. Alfred H. Marks, "German Romantic Irony in Hawthorne's Tales," *Symposium* 7 (1953), p. 278.

10. See Marshall Van Deusen, "Narrative tone in 'The Custom House' and *The Scarlet Letter*," in *Nathaniel Hawthorne: A Collection of Criticism*, ed. J. Donald Crowley (New York: McGraw-Hill, 1975), pp. 53–62.

11. Authority is thus devoid of propositional logic. Insofar as no text can ever be said to supply its whole field—or even its intention—in advance of itself, as Edward Said points out, it can properly be said to begin only with a large supposition: if meaning is to be produced in writing, this beginning intention remains always and everywhere a fiction. See Edward W. Said, *Beginnings: Intention and Method* (Baltimore: Johns Hopkins University Press, 1975), pp. 59–60.

12. *Ibid.*, pp. 65–67.

13. Freud, "Moses and Monotheism," *The Standard Edition of the Complete Psychological Works of Sigmund Freud*, trans. James Strachey (London: Hogarth Press, 1964), XXIII:43. See also Said, *Beginnings: Intention and Method*, p. 59.

14. I am indebted to one of my students, Lloyd Kirk, for this observation.

15. Jacques Derrida, "Coming into One's Own," in *Psychoanalysis and the Question of the Text*, ed. Geoffrey H. Hartman (Baltimore: Johns Hopkins University Press, 1978), p. 127.

16. Daniel Sibony, "*Hamlet*: A Writing-Effect," in *Literature and Psychoanalysis: The Question of Reading, Otherwise*, p. 74.

17. Geoffrey H. Hartman, "Preface," *Psychoanalysis and the Question of the Text*, p. xviii.

18. See Richard H. Brodhead, *Hawthorne, Melville, and the Novel* (Chicago: University of Chicago Press, 1976), pp. 67–68.

19. See Philippe Sollers, "Freud's Hand," in *Literature and Psychoanalysis: The Question of*

Reading, Otherwise, p. 337, note 1: "Freud makes the following suggestion: that writing was invented by women through the weaving and braiding of their pubic hairs." In this respect, *The Letter's* "ghostly presence" now prohibits all interpretation precisely insofar as it "cuts" across it. To this extent, the narrative wish to disembody the Letter serves merely to revive the deadly trace that marks it — the disappearance of a dead-*line* which *knots the historical* (w)hole *to* the very center of a ghost *story*, the maternal cathexis (narrativity) in place of the missing phallus (nativity).

20. See Michael Ragussis, "Family Discourse and Fiction in *The Scarlet Letter*," *English Literary History* 49 (1982), p. 880.

21. Jonathan Arac, "Reading the Letter," *Diacritics* 9 (1979), p. 49: "*The Scarlet Letter* offers the most famous example of the disjunction between things and words, or meanings." Yet Arac's reading ignores the prereflective correspondence between subject and object within the logic of the heart. In Hawthorne, the thing itself occasions a matter for discourse: indeed, it is this matter, this expression.

22. Nina Baym, *The Shape of Hawthorne's Career* (Ithaca: Cornell University Press, 1976), p. 142.

23. Lacan, "From Interpretation to the Transference," *The Four Fundamental Concepts of Psycho-Analysis*, pp. 250ff. We might read into this a correlation between an original signifier or *Kern* of irreducible non-sense and the pervasive sense of an original sin in Hawthorne's oeuvre. If signification originates in a si(g)n or fortunate fall of the signifier into the de-nominator as zero, it constitutes the very possibility of value and signification, and kills all meaning. The gap or fold of the subject (as represented by a signifier for another signifier) is therefore an infinity of possibilities: $s \div o = \infty$ against the finitude of desire. This, in turn, constitutes the subject in its freedom.

24. Sibony, "*Hamlet*: A Writing-Effect," pp. 82 and 75, respectively.

25. Lacan, *Seminar on the Purloined Letter*, quoted in Barbara Johnson, "The Frame of Reference: Poe, Lacan, Derrida," in *Literature and Psychoanalysis: The Question of Reading, Otherwise*, p. 476.

26. Johnson, "The Frame of Reference: Poe, Lacan, Derrida," pp. 499 and 502, respectively.

27. Cited in James T. Fields, *Yesterdays with Authors* (Boston: James R. Osgood, 1874), p. 52.

28. Edgar A. Dryden, *Nathaniel Hawthorne: The Poetics of Enchantment* (Ithaca: Cornell University Press, 1977), p. 149.

The Disappearing Self / *Mark C. Taylor*

I beseech You, God, to show my full self to myself.

Augustine

In the life of the individual the task is to achieve an ennoblement of the successive within the simultaneous. To have been young, and then to grow older, and finally to die, is a very mediocre form of human existence; this merit belongs to every animal. But the unification of the different stages of life in simultaneity is the task set for human beings.

Søren Kierkegaard

Once I produce, once I write, it is the Text itself which (fortunately) dispossesses me of my narrative continuity.

Roland Barthes

My work, my trace, the excrement that robs *me of* my possessions after I have been *stolen from* my birth, must thus be rejected. But to reject it is not, here, to refuse it but to retain it. To keep myself, to keep my body and my speech, I must retain the work within me, conjoin myself with it so that there will be no opportunity for the Thief to come between it and me: it must be kept from falling far from my body as writing. For "writing is all trash." Thus, that which dispossesses me and makes me more remote from myself, interrupting my proximity to myself also soils me: I relinquish all that is proper to me. Proper is the name of the subject close to himself—who is what he is—and abject the name of the object, the work that has deviated from me. I have a proper name when I am proper.

Jacques Derrida

In August of 1980, the annual philosophical colloquy at Cerisy was devoted to "Les fins de l'homme à partir du travail de Jacques Derrida." The topic of the conference and the title of the book of its proceedings[1] are taken from an essay by Derrida published in *Marges de la philosophie* ("Les fins de l'homme"). Derrida explains that he wrote this essay in 1968—between April ("the weeks of the opening of the Vietnam peace talks [in Paris] and of the assassination of Martin Luther King") and May (when "the universities of Paris were invaded by the forces of order—and for the first time at the demand of a rector—and then reoccupied by the students").[2] Derrida, as well as many other leading French intellectuals, detected in the events of the spring of 1968 a significant cultural shift that exposed cracks in the foundations of Western society and culture.[3] One of the most important aspects of the cultural critique unleashed by the social unrest of the sixties was the declaration of the end of a form of Western humanism that dates back to the Renaissance and has its roots in the Judeo-Christian tradition. Only two years before Derrida wrote his essay, Michel Foucault had concluded his highly influential book *Les Mots et les choses* by declaring:

> To all those who still wish to talk about man, about his reign or his liberation, to all those who still ask themselves questions about what man is in his essence, to all those who wish to take him as their starting-point in their attempts to reach the truth . . . to all these warped and twisted forms of reflection we can answer only with a philosophical laugh—which means, to a certain extent, a silent one.[4]

Though he consistently resists the label of "structuralist," Foucault seems to agree with Lévi-Strauss's claim that "the goal of the human sciences is not to constitute man, but to dissolve him."[5]

It would, however, be a mistake to insist that the end of man or the disappearance of the self is first thematized by French philosophers in the 1960s. More than a century earlier, Kierkegaard foresaw the erasure of the individual in the emergence of the modern industrial state. As Heidegger has suggested, Kierkegaard's vision has become a reality in twentieth-century technological society. This reality has been given graphic expression in contemporary art and literature. For example, the anonymous canvases of a Barnett Newman and the characterless texts of a Robbe-Grillet bespeak an absence that seems to spell the closure of humanism.

Derrida is unusually sensitive to these social and cultural currents. For this reason, he describes the *ends* rather than *an* or *the end* of man. Unlike many interpreters of modernity, Derrida does not view the dissolution of the subject as a catastrophic event that befalls an integral tradition from without. To the contrary, the centered self was not "there" in the first place. According to Derrida, the subject is never present but is "always already" absent. From this point of view, it becomes possible to understand the history of Western philosophy and metaphysics as a prolonged effort to deny or repress the impossibility of total self-presence and complete self-identity. Derrida develops his argument by radicalizing Heidegger's interpretation of the relation between being and time. He acknowledges the persuasiveness of Heidegger's account of the "ontotheological" tradition in which being is experienced as presence. But Heidegger does not go far enough in his critique of this tradition. Derrida insists that Heidegger remains caught in "an entire metaphorics of proximity, of simple and immediate presence, a metaphorics associating the proximity of Being with the values of neighboring, shelter, house, service, guard, voice, and listening."[6] Over against Heidegger, Derrida argues that it is precisely the identification of being and presence that has become (or more precisely, has always been) problematic. In the last section of "The Ends of Man," he writes:

> Is not this security of the near what is trembling today, that is, the co-belonging and co-propriety of the name of man and the name of Being, such as this co-propriety inhabits, and is inhabited by, the language of the West, such as it is buried in its *oikonomia*, such as it is inscribed and forgotten according to the history of metaphysics, and such as it is awakened also by the destruction of ontotheology? But this trembling—which can only come from a certain outside—was already requisite within the very structure that it solicits. Its margin was marked by its own (*propre*) body. In the thinking of the language of Being, the end of man has been prescribed since always, and this prescription has never done anything but modulate the equivocality of the *end*, in the play of *telos* and death. In the reading of this play, one may take the following sequence in all its senses: the end of man is the thinking of Being, man, is the end of the thinking of Being, the end of man is the end of the thinking of Being. Man, since always, is his proper end, that is, the end of his proper. Being, since always, is its proper end, that is, the end of its proper.[7]

In the following pages, I attempt to situate recent discussions of the end(s) of man by examining distinctive features of human subjectivity that have emerged in the course of Western philosophy and theology. The epoch of selfhood, I argue, spans a period that extends roughly from Augustine's *Confessions* to Hegel's *Phenomenology of Spirit*. A reconsideration of this tradition in the context of current debate enables us to understand more fully the shape of selfhood that seems to be disappearing. The careful examination of the arguments of formative figures like Augustine and Hegel lends considerable support to Derrida's claim that "in the thinking of the language of Being, the end of man has been prescribed since always." This end, as we shall see, has something to do with time—the time of selfhood that is always already past.

Image, Identity, Imitation

Throughout the history of the West, to be a self is to possess and to be possessed by a name. For every self, the primal scene is that of nomination—that of naming and being named. A name awakens identity by calling forth, setting apart, and establishing difference. Nomination is a vocation, a call that is both a blessing and a curse. Since this vocation poses the task of a lifetime, the identity bestowed by naming opens rather than closes the drama of selfhood. By marking a paradoxical coincidence of freedom and fate, the name focuses the subject's struggle for self-definition.

Within the Western *theological* tradition, the "original" scene of nomination involves God and man. The relation between God and self is thoroughly specular;

one mirrors the other—man is made in the image of God. This *imago* is a copy, likeness, similitude, representation, or shadow of divinity. The *imago dei* confers upon man an identity establishing a vocation that can be fulfilled only through the process of imitation. The specularity of the God-self relation forges an inseparable bond between the name of God and the name of man.

While the roots of the distinctively Western interpretation of subjectivity lie in the Letters of Paul, it is Augustine who must be credited with the discovery of personal subjectivity.[8] Augustine's relentless self-reflection leads to the creation of a new literary genre—autobiography. In the course of presenting what eventually becomes the dominant view of God in the West, the *Confessions* elaborates a genuinely new vision of personal identity. In the centuries following Augustine's death, Christian thinkers repeatedly returned to his writings for guidance in expressing beliefs and formulating arguments. For medieval Catholic theologians as well as for Protestant reformers, it was Augustine who effectively defined the bounds of faith. The influence of Augustine is not, however, limited to early periods in the history of Christianity. His innovative analysis of human selfhood is in many ways peculiarly modern. The far-reaching implications of Augustine's recognition of the interplay between theology and anthropology do not become explicit until the nineteenth century. Hegel fills in the self-portrait initially sketched by Augustine. But Hegel's completion and fulfillment of the subject surpass and sublate Augustine's insights. In the *Phenomenology of Spirit* Hegel actually joins the *Confessions* and the *City of God* to form an all-inclusive *Bildungsroman* that simultaneously recapitulates the emergence of individual identity on both a personal and a cultural scale and inscribes the end of self-consciousness. By so doing, the *Phenomenology* concludes the epoch of selfhood and marks the end of man. It is this closure that created a seminal opening.

In order to chart the coordinates of the trajectory that leads from Augustine through Hegel to the debates of contemporary philosophers and critics, it is necessary to begin by examining the most significant attributes traditionally predicated of God. A consideration of the complex interplay of God's being, eternity, transcendence, unity, identity, substantiality, essence, and subjectivity points to characteristics that eventually become definitive of human selfhood.[9]

In the Judeo-Christian tradition, God is above all else the supreme Creator who brings the world into being and providentially directs its course. As Heidegger, and, following him, Derrida stress, this divine source, ground, and cause of all things is virtually indistinguishable from the power of Being or Being-itself. To the extent that Being is interpreted as presence, God is viewed as absolutely present and thus totally self-present. Insofar as Being is associated with the present, God is regarded as always present and hence eternal. God, who is the original source, groundless ground, and uncaused cause, is both spatially and temporally omnipresent. In most cases the identification of God with Being and presence does not lead to belief in divine immanence. To the contrary, God is consistently regarded as radically transcendent; the Creator is other than, and separate from, the creation over which He exercises omnipotent rule. Because of this transcendence, divinity remains, in some sense, inaccessible to humanity. Though completely self-present, the Creator is never totally present to the creature or in the created order. God possesses a hidden inwardness or unapproachable interiority that never becomes outward or exterior. Revelation, therefore, is necessarily incomplete and forever partial. Despite divine omnipresence, the mysterious God always manages to escape one's grasp.

This transcendent God is not only the supreme Creator; He is the sole Creator. From its earliest days, Christian, as well as Jewish, theology rejected the polytheism that was typical of both many ancient Near Eastern religions and Roman paganism and refused to accept the principle of divine hierarchy that characterized various forms of Gnosticism and informed Neoplatonic speculation. For Jew and Christian, God is one. To claim that God is one is to suggest that God is centered in Himself and is the center of everything else. This self-centered center that is inwardly unified forms the founding principle of all cosmic and personal unity. When early Christian theologians attempted to articulate the nature of divine unity, they tended to insist that God's oneness is indissociable from His eternity and immutability.[10] Since plurality is always subject to change, the immutable cannot be many and must be one. It is important to note in this connection that God's unchangeability requires His omniscience. Unable to suffer any change whatsoever, God's knowledge cannot develop and therefore must always be perfect or complete. The divine eye views everything *sub specie aeternitatis.*

The transcendent unity of God points toward the identity of the divine. Identity, which derives from the Latin *idem,* means "the quality or condition of being the same in substance, composition, nature, properties, or in particular qualities under consideration." Identity can also refer to "the sameness of a person or thing at all times or in all circumstances; the condition or fact that a person or thing is itself and not something else; individuality, personality."[11] In sum, identity includes two closely related elements: self-sameness at a particular time and continuity through time. In the eternal life of divinity, these dual aspects of identity join to form a structure of absolute self-relation. It is important to realize that such self-relation does not involve a simple equality-with-self. As Hegel points out, absolute self-relation establishes a self-identity that

> is in its self-sameness different from itself and self-contradictory, and that in its difference, in its contradiction, is self-identical, and is in its own self this movement of transition of one of these categories into the other. . . . In other words, identity is the reflection-into-self that is identity only as internal repulsion, and is this repulsion as reflection-into-self, repulsion which immediately takes itself back into itself. Thus it is the identity as difference that is identical with itself.[12]

This understanding of God's complex self-identity suggests why so many theologians have found the category of substance particularly useful for interpreting the life of the divine. Substance (*substantia: sub,* under + *stare,* to stand) traditionally has been associated with the Greek conception of *ousia* or essence. The notion of substance designates what underlies phenomena and forms the permanent foundation of things. While never itself a mode, substance is that in which accidents inhere and of which they are modifications. This abiding substratum constitutes an essence that is always present. The omnipresence of substance is implied in the verbal link between *Wesen* (substance or essence) and *Anwesenheit* (presence; *Anwesen*, property). Essential substance or substantial essence is always present—both to itself and in its own other. Otherness, therefore, is merely apparent; it is only illusory being. The recognition of appearance as appearance is at the same time the discovery of essence. Through a process of double negation, essence first negates itself in appearance and then negates this negation by reappropriating appearance as its own self-manifestation.

When substance is grasped as essential and essence is viewed in terms of double negation, substantiality appears to be indistinguishable from subjectivity. As Derrida points out, "The concept of a (conscious or unconscious) subject necessarily refers to the concept of substance—and thus of presence—out of which it is born." [13] This notion of subjectivity both grows out of and takes up into itself each of the divine predicates previously considered. Hegel provides a concise description of the interpretation of subjectivity to which our analysis has led when he explains that the subject "*relates itself to itself* and is *determinate*, is *other-being* and *being-for-self*, and in this determinateness, or in its self-externality, abides within itself; in other words, it is *in and for itself*." [14] In different terms, the structure of subjectivity is essentially reflexive. Throughout the course of Christian theology, this reflexivity has been repeatedly illustrated by two primary examples: love and knowledge or, more precisely, auto-affection and self-consciousness. From this point of view, divine subjectivity comes to completion in loving and knowing itself.

It was Augustine who first recognized and defined the principle of subjectivity. Plagued by doubt and uncertainty not unlike that which Luther and Descartes would suffer centuries later, Augustine turned inward and reflected upon his own personality. The world within proved to be as perplexing as the puzzling world without. Rather than being able to identify a simple individual or singular substance, Augustine found the self to be complex and inwardly divided. In an effort to interpret the insights derived from his self-analysis, Augustine argues that since man is created in the image of God, the structure of selfhood must mirror the structure of the divine. From the time of the early church councils, Christian orthodoxy had insisted that though God is one, He is triune. Augustine's genius lay in interpreting the doctrine of the trinity in terms of subjectivity. By means of this important theological innovation, Augustine provides what seems to be a reasonable account of the relationship between God and self. Inasmuch as it is a reflection of the divine subject, human subjectivity is triune. Augustine argues:

> We both exist, and know that we exist, and rejoice in this existence and this knowledge. In these three, when the mind knows and loves itself, there may be seen a trinity, mind, love, knowledge; not to be confounded by any inter-

mixture, although each exists in itself, and all mutually in all, or each in the other two, or the other two in each.[15]

Although Augustine's account of the specular relation between God and the self was highly influential throughout the tradition, its full implications were not realized until Hegel formulated his speculative philosophy. By drawing directly and indirectly on Augustine's insights, Hegel developed a reinterpretation of the concept of subjectivity that proved to be nothing less than revolutionary. In order to grasp the distinctive features of Hegel's analysis, it is necessary to recognize its relation to certain theological and epistemological principles. As will become increasingly evident, Hegel's account of reflexive subjectivity forms a significant chapter in the appearance and disappearance of the self.

According to Hegel, the notions of self-love and self-consciousness combine to form the identity of God. For the Christian, God is love. The speculative significance of this claim, Hegel argues, emerges with the recognition that

love implies a differentiation between two who are, however, not merely different from one another. Love is this feeling of being outside myself, the feeling and consciousness of this identity. I have my self-consciousness not in myself, but in another in whom alone I am satisfied and am at peace with myself—and I am only insofar as I am at peace with myself, for if I do not have this, I am the contradiction that sunders itself.[16]

The love relation provides a representation (*Vorstellung*) of God that points toward the more complete expression of divine subjectivity disclosed in the structure of self-consciousness. God's self-love is, of course, impossible apart from His self-knowledge. The self-consciousness of God involves an act of self-differentiation that maintains identity even in difference. God beholds Himself in what apparently is different from, and other than Himself. For this reason, His relation to otherness is mediated self-relation. In order to understand the nature of the self-relation involved in auto-affection and self-consciousness, it is necessary to distinguish cognition, reflection, and reflexion. It has long been recognized that consciousness is always consciousness *of* something and hence is invariably related *to* an object. Cognition, reflection, and reflexion are defined by contrasting interpretations of objectivity. In the movement from cognition through reflection to reflexion, subject and object become ever more closely united.

The gaze of the cognitive subject is directed outward, toward an object that appears to be other than the knowing self. The aim of cognition is knowledge of the external object. The reflective subject, by contrast, turns inward. The object of reflection is, in fact, cognition. In reflection, the subject thinks about itself thinking about an object that seems to be different from itself. Reflexion deepens this inwardness by taking reflection as its object. The reflexive subject thinks about thinking about thinking. The relation of cognition, reflection, and reflexion can be summarized as follows:

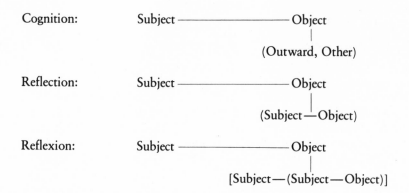

The coincidence of subject and object in reflexive subjectivity defines the structure of absolute self-relation. Thoroughly reflexive and completely self-related, the divine subject is fully self-sufficient, totally self-present, and absolutely self-conscious.

Created in the image of God, the human subject reflects divine subjectivity. The self, therefore, can be defined in terms of self-relation. The activity of self-relation culminates in the reflexivity of self-consciousness. The self-conscious individual mirrors the self-conscious God. Such self-consciousness is not, of course, immediately given. It poses a task that constitutes the self's vocation. *Imago* (which is related to the same root as *imitari*) invites *imitatio*. The image that the self is called upon to imitate is not at all obvious. The transcendent God who can never be fully known in Himself must be known indirectly through a mediator. For the Christian, the divine Logos, Christ, effects this mediation. By representing the presence of God to humanity, the Logos reveals the self to itself. Christ, who is the perfect image of God, is also the figure of complete human being. To actualize selfhood fully, every person must, according to the biblical injunction, attain "to the measure of the stature of the fullness of Christ" (Ephesians 4:13). In this way, the self transforms itself into the very image of Christ.

Since the Christian subject's full realization of the *imago dei* necessarily entails the *imitatio Christi*, the self is actually an image of an image, an imitation of an imitation, a representation of a representation, and a sign of a sign. In this paradoxical way, the self becomes *itself*. In struggling to relate itself to itself, the human subject attempts to enact a complex movement of repetition in which it becomes what in some sense it already is. The aim of such imitative repetition is self-appropriation. By means of the activity of self-relation, the subject seeks to take possession of itself and to secure its identity. The interplay of image, imitation, and identity reveals that the stages on life's way that comprise the believer's journey to selfhood repeat the stations of the cross marked by Christ.

Naming: Propriety, Property, Possession

To be a self, I have suggested, is to possess and to be possessed by a name. Not just any name will do. The self-identity of the subject presupposes that one possess a *proper* name. The self in search of identity is forced to confess: "I have a proper name when I am proper." The relation of naming, propriety, property and possession raises many questions: What does it mean to be proper? What constitutes propriety? Is propriety appropriate or inappropriate? What is possession? What are possessions? Are possessions possessed or do they possess? Are properties possessions or are possessions properties? What exactly *does* it mean to possess (or be possessed by) a (proper [or improper]) name?

Proper derives from the Latin *proprius*, which specifies that which is one's own, special, particular, peculiar, not held in common with others. Accordingly, proper means "Belonging to oneself or itself; (one's or its) own, owned as property; that is the, or a, property or quality of the thing itself, intrinsic, inherent; distinctive; characteristic; opposed to common; private possession, private property, something belonging to oneself." Proper can also mean "excellent, admirable, commendable, capital, fine, goodly, of high quality; of good character, or standing; honest, respectable, worthy; adapted to some purpose or requirement, fit, apt, suitable, appropriate to circumstances or conditions; what it should be, or what is required; such as one ought to do, have, use; right, in conformity with social ethics or with the demands and usage of polite society; respectable." In French, *propre* means not only own, very, same, selfsame, proper, peculiar, appropriate, fitted, suitable, good, right and correct, but also denotes neat, tidy, and clean. The German *eigentlich* is cognate with *eigen* (proper, inherent, own, characteristic, specific, peculiar, individual), and can be defined as proper, true, real. But *eigentlich* also means authentic.

A proper name, therefore, is peculiar, characteristic, and individual. It is one's own, a private possession or property. One who has a proper name is not common, but is distinctive, correct, of high quality and good character . . . respectable, never soiled, stained, or blemished, always neat, tidy, and clean. To have a proper name is to be true, real, authentic.

Possession of a proper name is not only the aim of sojourning subjects; it is also, according to Derrida, the goal of Western philosophy and theology: "A name is proper when it has only one sense. Or rather, it is only in this case that it is properly a name. To be univocal is the essence, or rather the *telos*, of language. This Aristotelian ideal has never been rejected by any philosophy as such. It is philosophy." [17] When one moves from philosophy to theology, it becomes clear that monotheism extends beyond the narrow confines of religion "proper" to encompass selves and the uni–verse as a whole. From a monotheistic perspective, to be is to be one. In order to be one, the subject cannot err and must always remain proper. By following the straight and narrow course, the self hopes to gain its most precious possession—itself. Norman O. Brown suggests the inseparability of questions of propriety, property, and possession when he writes:

I am what is mine. Personality is the original personal property. . . . "By property I must be understood here, as in other places, to mean that property which men have in their persons as well as goods." Here is the psychological root of private property. Every man has a "property" in his own person.[18]

The property of personality suggests that owning is oneing and oneing is owning. The interplay of oneness and ownness implies the inextricable relation between propriety and proximity. Propriety requires ownership of private propert(y)ies. To own something is to possess, appropriate, seize, or lay claim to it. Ownership draws near (*proximare*), and by so doing establishes propriety. Since propriety presupposes proximity, proper subjectivity requires self-proximity. Propriety in other words, is impossible apart from self-presence.

Far from being lost in the past, the scene of nomination is always (the) present. Naming realizes *parousia* by manifesting a presence that entails self-proximity and presupposes the property of own-ness. The self-presence embodied in the proper name is most fully realized in self-consciousness. By becoming conscious of itself, the self becomes present to itself. The subject's self-presentation effects an adequation of subject and object in reflexive subjectivity that erases error and inscribes proper knowledge, i.e., ideas that are clear and distinct or that are univocal rather than equivocal. With this self-awareness, the self is freed from the anxiety of uncertainty and for the enjoyment of certainty. When understood in this way, the self-presence of the self-conscious subject reflects the self-presence of absolute subjectivity.

Such self-presence is possible, of course, only in the present. In self-consciousness, the subject is totally present to itself in the fullness of the present moment. The recognition of the interrelation of propriety and presence implies an interpretation of time that in effect absolutizes the present. In order to speak

> of the present, as the absolute form of experience, one *already* must understand *what time is*, must understand the *ens of the praes-ens*, and the proximity of the *Being of this ens*. The present of presence and the presence of the present suppose the horizon, the precomprehending anticipation of Being as time. If the meaning of Being has always been determined by philosophy as presence, then the *question of* Being, posed on the basis of the transcendental horizon of time . . . is the first tremor of philosophical security, as it is of self-confident presence.[19]

Throughout the Western ontotheological tradition, there has been an awareness of the essential relation between subjectivity and time. Within this framework, however, time has been consistently understood in terms of the present. Since only the present is, whatever is must be present. Being and presence are, therefore, one. Moreover any thing that is present is, in principle, nominal. Proper names indicate what is by specifying substantives that represent both objects and subjects. Insofar as presence and the present are indissoluble, the subject cannot appear apart from the verb. The verbal form of the subject is always the present tense. In order to appreciate the significance of the bond joining subjectivity and presence, it is necessary to examine more carefully the intricate relation between time and the self.

In a variety of ways Western philosophy and theology have repeatedly, even if usually implicitly, expressed the importance of time for being. It was not, however, until Augustine's penetrating analysis of the self that the full scope of the problem of time was realized. It would not be too much to say that Augustine's discovery of the subject would have been impossible apart from his recognition of the subjectivity of time. In the course of his confession, Augustine asks:

> What then is time? I know what it is if no one asks me what it is; but if I want to explain it to someone who has asked me, I find that I do not know. Nevertheless, I can confidently assert that I know this: that if nothing passed away there would be no past time, and if nothing were coming there would be no future time, and if nothing were now there would be no present time.[20]

Further reflection discloses deeper complexities. In a certain sense, neither the past nor the future exists. Since the past is no longer and the future is not yet, Augustine concludes that the present alone is actual. He recognizes, however, that while only the present is, the present is not simple. Augustine insists that it is

> perfectly clear that neither the future nor the past are [sic] in existence, and that it is incorrect to say that there are three times—past, present and future. Though one might perhaps say: "There are three times—a present of things past, a present of things present, and a present of things future." For these three do exist in the mind, and I do not see them anywhere else: the present of things past is memory; the present of things present is sight; the present of things future is expectation. If we are allowed to use words in this way, then I see that there are three times and I admit that there are.[21]

Contrary to common sense, time is not made up of three separate tenses or three discrete moments. There is but one tense of time, the present, which is comprised of three inseparable modalities.

The complexity of the present complicates the presence of the self. The self-conscious subject is not immediately present to itself but must become self-present through the process of self-presentation. In different terms, the identity of the self is synthetic rather than simple. Although the self is one, it is at the same time triune—a unity that is a trinity. The activity of self-presentation constitutes a process of self-appropriation through which the subject comes into possession of itself. By relating itself to itself, the subject realizes itself as self-present subjectivity. Only with this self-presence does the subject assume its proper name.

Due to the internal distention of the present, the realization of the self's full presence to itself necessarily involves a process of remembering or recollection. Augustine already recognized the close connection between *cogo* (to drive together to one point, collect, compress, crowd, bring or urge together, assemble, gather together) and *cogito*. Building on his Platonic and Neoplatonic heritage, Augustine goes so far as to argue that to know is to re-collect. In the act of knowing, the subject re-members or re-collects what previously had been dismembered or dispersed. Insofar as the object of consciousness is the self itself, self-knowledge inevitably entails self-recollection. Such recollection must not be confused with the simple act of recalling. As the words in German (*Erinnerung*) and Danish (*Erindring*) imply, a recollection and inwardness are closely related. Recollection involves a process of interiorization or internalization that draws sustenance from memory. Instead of merely retrieving "facts" that have been stored in the "belly of the mind," recollection interiorizes the diversity of experience. Sequential succession gives way to coherent interrelation. Apart from or prior to recollection, events and/or things seem fragmented and unrelated. Recollection joins what apparently is disjoined and connects what seems to be disconnected. When thought turns on itself, recollection enables the self to become present to itself by comprehending, gathering together, and unifying the three modalities of the present. The complex self-presence that results from self-recollection mirrors the intricacy of the present itself. Self, as well as time, is one substance with three modes.

The necessary interplay of self-appropriation and recollection points to the importance of autobiography for self-realization. Recollection graphs the self or plots the stages of the subject's journey to selfhood. The activity of remembering re-presents the story of its own becoming to the self-conscious subject. The aim of autobiography is the establishment of personal identity through the integration of the personality. To achieve this coherence, it is necessary to relate the multiple experiences the self has undergone in such a way that they constitute a comprehensive and comprehensible totality. The meaning of any particular event or experience is a function of its place within the total life of the individual. Since the meaningful totality for which the autobiographer searches is not immediately given, it must be constructed. By means of the synthetic power of the imagination, the subject attempts to weave the various strands of experience into a unified whole. Rather than merely chronicling experience, the autobiographer narrates the story of the self becoming itself. As Paul Ricoeur explains:

> Every narrative combines two dimensions in various proportions, one chronological and the other nonchronological. The first may be called the episodic dimension, which characterizes the story as made out of events. The second is the configurational dimension, according to which the plot construes significant wholes out of scattered events.[22]

The relationship between narrativity and meaning is so close as to suggest that absence of the former leads to lack of the latter. Conversely, meaning emerges when episodes are narrated so as to form a plot. The coherence of any plot requires an identifiable center to provide the organizing focus of the narrative.

In Augustine's autobiography, for example, the conversion experience serves as such a meaningful center. Reflecting on this pivotal episode in his life, Augustine becomes convinced that it is, in H. Richard Niebuhr's terms, the "intelligible event which makes all other events intelligible."[23] Prior to this experience, he is a sick soul or an unhappy consciousness who suffers interminable conflict brought by inward dismemberment. With self set against self, Augustine is unable to find the peace and rest for which he longs. But all of this changes suddenly when he hears a voice in the garden, which calls: "Take it and read it. Take it and read it." Augustine reports what followed:

> I snatched up the book, opened it, and read in silence the passage upon which my eyes first fell: *Not in rioting and drunkenness, not in chambering and wantonness, not in strife and envying: but put ye on the Lord Jesus Christ, and make not provision for the flesh in concupiscence.* I had no wish to read further; there was no need to. For immediately I had reached the end of this sentence it was as though my heart was filled with a light of confidence and all the shadows of my doubt were swept away.[24]

This experience in the garden is, in effect, Augustine's scene of nomination. It constitutes nothing less than a revelation that illuminates his entire inner history. After years of apparently pointless erring, Augustine at last responds to his vocation. Following in the footsteps of the prodigal son, he finally comes home—home to himself. But homecoming remains incomplete until the sojourner offers a narration of his travels. In order to be a self in the "proper" sense of the word, every subject must tell and retell its tale. But to whom is this story addressed?[25]

Augustine's autobiography offers a possible answer to this important question. The *Confessions* is actually a confession. Augustine presents himself to himself by presenting himself to the omnipresent God. As the sovereign Creator, God is the ground and source of all presence. From Augustine to Hegel, "God is the name of the element of what makes possible an absolutely self-present self-knowledge."[26] The self becomes present to itself only in the presence of God. Since God is the name of names, the subject cannot name itself without at the same time naming God. For Augustine, the full presence of God to self, self to God, and self to itself is actualized in speech or voice. His confession, therefore, takes the form of an extended prayer that is spoken to God. The spoken word permits the self to become transparent to itself by becoming visible to God. Speech, in other words, is the element of self-presence, the medium in which presence becomes fully present.

The interplay of speech, presence, divinity, and subjectivity that informs Augustine's confession is, as Derrida has demonstrated, typical of the ontotheological tradition. Until recently, Western thinkers have privileged speech over writing. In a variety of subtle and not-so-subtle ways, writing has been debased because it seems to disrupt the self-presence that is both the *arche* and *telos* of Western history. In a passage that serves as one of the epigrams for this essay, Derrida explains:

> For "writing is all trash." Thus, that which dispossesses me and makes me more remote from myself, interrupting my proximity to myself also soils me: I relinquish all that is proper to me. Proper is the name of the subject close to himself—who is what he is—and abject the name of the object, the work that has deviated from me.[27]

The simple opposition of speech and writing in terms of presence and absence is, however, misleading. If Derrida is right, presence always harbors the absence it seeks to deny or repress. There is a premonition of the inseparability of speech and writing in Augustine's own work. His confession is, after all, also the *Confessions*. The prayer is not only spoken; it is also written. In its written form, the confession constitutes a book that is an auto-bio-*graphy*, i.e., writing about the life of the self. The Derridean reading of writing suggests that writing subverts the intentions of an author like Augustine. Rather than securing personal identity, writing erases the proper name by disclosing the uncanniness of both presence and the present. More than the work of a single author is, of course, at stake in Derrida's analysis. The critique of the metaphysics, and I would add the theology, of presence strikes at the very foundations of Western society and culture.

Uncanniness of Presence: Representation and Repetition

In order to glimpse the improper space of writing, it is necessary to return to the work of the person in whom ontotheology reaches its closure: Hegel. By drawing attention to aspects of Hegel's argument usually overlooked, Derrida's interpretation of Western philosophy suggests that by insinuating itself at the very heart of Hegel's analysis, writing subverts his entire system. Hegel inadvertently demonstrates the impossibility of totally present self-consciousness and fully realized subjectivity. In other words, Hegel writes the opposite of what he wants to say.

Hegel begins his account of the experience of consciousness in the *Phenomenology* by considering what he takes to be the least complicated example of naming, i.e., the denomination of something that is present here and now. Contrary to expectation, the presence of the *hic et nunc* disappears in the very effort to establish it. To the question "What is Now?", Hegel replies, "Now is Night." Then in a move whose full implications he fails to notice, Hegel proposes to test this claim by writing it down. "A truth," he insists, "cannot lose anything through our preserving it. If *now, this noon*, we look again at the written truth we shall have to say that it has become stale. The Now that is Night is *preserved*, i.e., it is treated as what it professes to be, as something that *is*; but it proves itself to be, on the contrary, something that is *not*." [28] The same analysis, of course, applies to every "Here" that seems to be present. Through an unexpected twist, Hegel's writing experiment shows that here and now are never really present or are "present" only as always already absent. It is important to stress that Hegel's argument carries significant implications not only for named objects but also for naming subjects. This becomes obvious when the correlative notions of representation and repetition are examined.

Hegel's analysis of the *hic et nunc* suggests that nomination is not a simple act of presentation; it is, instead, the complex activity of representation. Always hurrying to grasp the fleeting here and now, representation can only re-present a presence/present that never is and never can be fully realized. Since representation invariably opens the gap it seeks to close, it necessarily entails a certain spacing. The space opened by representation marks an irreducible exteriority—an outside that can never by interiorized and an absence that cannot be presented. Inasmuch as all presentation is representation, the subject's struggle to secure identity and establish a proper name inevitably fails. As Derrida points out, "We are disposed of the longed for presence in the gesture of language by which we attempt to seize it."[29] Like Alice gazing into the looking glass, the reflective/reflexive subject discovers an uncanny hole through with it disappears.

We have seen that though the self is made in the image of God, the *imago* presents the task of *imitatio*. Through imitation of the image, the self seeks to achieve identity or to become what it is. In order to come into possession of the property of a proper name, the subject must become present to itself by presenting itself to itself. Since presentation is actually re-presentation, there is no identity without repetition. Though usually not noticed, such repetition is the condition of both the possibility and impossibility of identity. For something to possess identity, it must be capable of being repeated. This necessary repetition, however, introduces a difference that cannot be reduced to identity. The doubling presupposed by identity creates a space that fissures identity as such. In different terms, nothing is ever simple; everything is always duplicitous. The acknowledgement of the inescapability of duplicity marks the transition from the identical to the same.

Identity, I have noted, is usually defined in terms of same, and same in terms of identity. But this direct identification of the two proves misleading. Identity encompasses a synchronic element (identity at any particular moment) and a diachronic factor (continuity over time). While it is tempting to view the former component as spatial identity and the latter as temporal identity, this would obscure the space within time and the time of space. The notion of the same captures the play of time and space by pointing to the representative character of all presence and every present and by underscoring the repetitiousness of all identity. The same is not a simple identity; it is a structure of iterability that includes both identity and difference. The self that becomes what it is, becomes the same. In becoming the same, however, the self does not merely become itself but simultaneously becomes other. The repetition involved in self-becoming embodies iterability, which joins identity and difference. Instead of establishing propriety and assuring purity, naming marks or inscribes the end of all identity that is only itself. Thomas J. J. Altizer correctly insists that "we can evoke an actual or real identity only by embodying difference, a real and actual difference, a difference making identity manifest, and making it manifest as itself. Only the presence of difference calls identity forth, and calls it forth in its difference from itself."[30] Here lies the duplicity involved in all self-presentation. There is always difference within identity and absence within presence. Through an unanticipated inversion, repetition and re-presentation turn out to involve a de-presentation that disrupts presence and dislocates the present. Contrary to common sense, the interior doubling through which presence and the present appear also makes them disappear. Presence/present and identity are forever fugitive—they disappear in the very act of appearing. If, however, something can appear only by disappearing, it would seem to be undeniably temporal and unquestionably mortal.

I have emphasized that throughout the Western tradition there has been a very close relationship between being and time. Being has been consistently interpreted as presence and hence constantly regarded in terms of the present. While apparently establishing the essentiality of time, this customary view of the relation between being and time actually serves to repress the inevitable temporality of selfhood. This repression becomes evident when one recognizes some of the hidden implications of Augustine's extraordinarily influential interpretation of time and self. While Augustine's self-analysis leads to the related discoveries of the subject and the subjectivity of time, his argument remains bound to the traditional identification of being and presence. For this reason, he insists that, since the present alone exists, the self is only to the extent that it is (or becomes) present to itself. To be is to be present, and to exist fully is to be present totally. Unlike his predecessors, however, Augustine recognizes that the present is complex and not simple. Instead of being an isolated point or a punctual Now, the present is constituted by three modes, which, though distinguishable, are, nonetheless, all present. This is the basis of his conviction that the present consists of a present of things past, a present of things present, and a present of things future.

Viewed from a slightly different angle, Augustine's provocative examination of time leads to significantly different conclusions. The "omnipresence" of past and future within the present uncovers an "original" nonpresence at the very heart of the present. Past and future are not modalities of the present but signify irreducible absence. Just as identity possesses and is possessed by difference, presence necessarily involves absence. As a matter of fact, "only the alterity of past and future presents permits the absolute identity of the living present as the self-identity of non-self identity." [31] Elsewhere Derrida underlines an important inference that can be drawn from this insight:

> One then sees quickly that the presence of the perceived present can appear as such only inasmuch as it is *continuously compounded* with a nonpresence and nonperception, with primary memory and expectation (retention and protention). These nonperceptions are neither added to, nor do they *occasionally* accompany, the actually perceived now; they are essentially and indispensably involved in its possibility. [32]

This conclusion recalls our earlier discovery of the inseparability of Now and not-Now. The absence of presence opens the gap through which the space of time appears. Time not only transpires "in" space; space "indwells" time. The spacing of time creates a hole that can never be completely filled and engenders a desire for presence that cannot be totally satisfied.

Due to the everlasting interplay of identity and difference, and of presence and absence, the present is never totally present but appears as what Derrida labels a "trace." Rather than a *nunc stans*, time is ceaseless transition, perpetual motion, and constant movement (*momentum*). So understood, temporality is an endless passage that is irreducibly transitional and hence irrevocably liminal. As Derrida maintains, the radical temporality of the trace escapes traditional Western notions of time:

The concepts of *present*, *past*, and *future*, everything in the concepts of time and history which implies evidence of them—the metaphysical concept of time in general—cannot adequately describe the structure of the trace. And deconstructing the simplicity of presence does not amount only to accounting for the horizons of potential presence, indeed of a "dialectic" of pretention and retention that one would install in the heart of the present instead of surrounding it with it. It is not a matter of complicating the structure of time while conserving its homogeneity and its fundamental successivity, by demonstrating for example that the past present and future present constitute originarily, by dividing it, the form of the living present.[33]

Unmasterable by logic of identity and noncontradiction, the trace marks the place where identity and difference, presence and absence, constantly cross.

Inasmuch as time and selfhood are inextricably related, the self remains nailed to this cross. While Augustine discerned the subjectivity of temporality, his reduction of the absence of past and future to the presence of the present obscures the temporality of subjectivity. Thus he failed to recognize the radical, indeed revolutionary, implications of his insight. The thoroughgoing temporality of subjectivity effectively erases the presence of the self.

Upon the basis of our examination of the epoch of selfhood extending at least from Augustine to Hegel, it is possible to conclude that in the very effort to secure its identity and establish its presence, the self discovers its unavoidable difference and irrepressible absence. The search for self-presence in self-consciousness leads to the discovery of the absence of the self. Apparent self-affirmation is actual self-negation. The ever-elusive trace registers this shattering of the subject. Within the play of writing, presence can never be fully present. The absence that is always "present," the outside that is always "inside" is death itself. The search for selfhood is the struggle to deny death. Death, however, will not be denied. The death of the self is the uncanniness that haunts presence. Within the space of the trace is inscribed a cross that marks the site where the self is forever disappearing. The impossible interval marked by this cross opens aw(e)ful possibilities that we are only beginning to suspect.

Notes

1. *Les fins de l'homme à partir du travail de Jacques Derrida* (Paris: Editions Galilée, 1981).

2. Jacques Derrida, *Margins of Philosophy*, trans. Alan Bass (Chicago: University of Chicago Press, 1982), p. 114.

3. I am persuaded that one of the chief reasons for the extraordinary response of so many Americans to contemporary French philosophy and criticism is that leading French thinkers have given serious consideration to the significance and implications of what took place in Europe and America during the 1960s.

4. Michel Foucault, *The Order of Things: An Archaeology of the Human Sciences* (New York: Random House, 1973), pp. 342–43.

5. Claude Lévi-Strauss, *La Pensée sauvage* (Paris: Plon, 1962), p. 326.

6. Derrida, *Margins of Philosophy*, p. 130.

7. *Ibid.*, pp. 133–34.

8. The distinguished historian Charles Norris Cochrane goes so far as to credit Augustine with "the discovery of the personality." He explains and defends this claim in his outstanding book: *Christianity and Classical Culture* (New York: Oxford University Press, 1957). See especially chapter 11. It is important to stress that the interpretation of Augustine has undergone noteworthy changes in recent years. This is largely the result of the revisionary scholarship of Peter Brown. In *Augustine of Hippo: A Biography* (Berkeley: University of California Press, 1969), Brown demonstrates the intricate relation between Augustine's life and thought and the complex Mediterranean culture of his day. By so doing, Brown has brought attention to elements in Augustine's writings that too often have been overlooked. In particular, Brown stresses the importance of movements like Neoplatonism, Gnosticism, and Manichaeism and stresses the social force of certain esoteric mystery cults. While acknowledging the significance of this rereading of Augustine, my interest in this context is somewhat different from Brown's. I am concerned with identifying those aspects of Augustine's thought that have contributed to typical Western understandings of human selfhood.

9. Any such list of qualities is, of course, incomplete. In the argument that follows, I shall attempt to justify my selection of these particular attributes of God.

10. The insistence on divine immutability points to the increasing importance of Greek philosophy for Christian theology. Well before Augustine, Greek thought had influenced Christian interpretations of God. For very helpful accounts of these developments, see Harry Wolfson, *The Philosophy of the Church Fathers* (Cambridge: Harvard University Press, 1956) and George Prestige, *God in Patristic Thought* (London: S.P.C.K., 1969).

11. Throughout the essay, I have taken definitions from *The Oxford English Dictionary* (New York: Oxford University Press, 1972).

12. G. W. F. Hegel, *Science of Logic*, trans. A. V. Miller (New York: Humanities Press, 1969), pp. 412–13.

13. Jacques Derrida, *Writing and Difference*, trans. Alan Bass (Chicago: University of Chicago Press, 1978), p. 229.

14. G. W. F. Hegel, *Phenomenology of Spirit*, trans. A. V. Miller (New York: Oxford University Press, 1977), p. 14.

15. Augustine, quoted in Cochrane, *Christianity and Classical Culture*, p. 403.

16. G. W. F. Hegel, *Lectures on the Philosophy of Religion*, vol. 3, trans. E. S. Haldane (New York: Humanities Press, 1968), pp. 10–11.

17. Jacques Derrida, "White Mythology: Metaphor in the Text of Philosophy," *New Literary History* 6/1 (1974), p. 48.

18. Norman O. Brown, *Love's Body* (New York: Random House, 1968), p. 214.

19. Jacques Derrida, *Writing and Difference*, p. 134.

20. Augustine, *Confessions*, trans. Rex Warner (New York: Mentor-Omega Books, 1963), p. 267.

21. *Ibid.*, p. 273.

22. Paul Ricoeur, "Narrative Time," *Critical Inquiry* 7 (1980), p. 178.

23. H. Richard Niebuhr, *The Meaning of Revelation* (New York: Macmillan Co., 1967), p. 39.

24. Augustine, *Confessions*, p. 182.

25. The necessary role of narration in the correlative processes of self-presentation and self-realization carries significant implications for the notion of the self. In view of the imaginative coherence of autobiography, the centered self appears to be more of a literary creation than a literal fact. "The 'subject,'" in Nietzsche's words, "is not something given, it is something added and invented and projected behind what is there" (*The Will to Power*, trans. Walter Kaufmann [New York: Random House, 1967], p. 267). As the product of the literary imagination, the self assumes the form of a fictive text. From this perspective, "the 'subject' is only a fiction" (*ibid.*, p. 199). The inversion of this insight further clarifies human selfhood. Insofar as the self is a function of narrative,

it can also be understood as a narrative function. The self is present to itself as a character, usually the leading character, in a story. Autobiography, therefore, is really the subject's auto-graph.

26. Jacques Derrida, *Of Grammatology*, trans. Gayatri Spivak (Baltimore: Johns Hopkins University Press, 1976), p. 98.

27. Derrida, *Writing and Difference*, pp. 182–83.

28. Hegel, *Phenomenology of Spirit*, p. 60.

29. Derrida, *Of Grammatology*, p. 141.

30. Thomas J. J. Altizer, *The Self-Embodiment of God* (New York: Harper and Row, 1977), p. 37.

31. Derrida, *Writing and Difference*, p. 132.

32. Jacques Derrida, *Speech and Phenomena and Other Essays on Husserl's Theory of Signs*, trans. David Allison (Evanston: Northwestern University Press, 1973), p. 64.

33. Derrida, *Of Grammatology*, p. 67.

"What's in a Name?": A Critical Look at Onomastics in the French Novel / Eugène Nicole

There is a tradition of literary onomastics which is to the study of the textual function of proper names what onomastics is to the theory of the name. This tradition is characterized by relatively dispersed and limited observations which attempt, mainly through etymology, to bring to light the semantic "value" of character or place names in works whose authors are apt to choose these signs with particular sensitivity. Such is the case of Henry James or of Kafka who are well represented in the American journal *Names*, a publication specializing in what American scholars call literary onomastics. Often presented as an intriguing aside to the study of literary texts, this kind of research tends to limit itself to the unveiling of a signifier's motivations or to the discovery of certain "keys."

Literary onomastics of this kind have been scarce in France. But since the sixties a new sort of interest in onomastical problems has appeared within the framework of the new French critical trends. It now marks the proper name's accession to the semiotic study of the text, particularly in the novel. Already present in the works of the Russian formalists as well as in Saussure's studies of the *Nibelungen*, the proper name is currently considered a central element not only in the semiotics of characterization but also in narrative typology. As Roland Barthes wrote in 1970, "One can say that the essential property of narrative is not the event, but the character as proper name." At about the same time, in attempting to elaborate a theory of the novelistic text and what he sees as its "modes of producing interest," Charles Grivel devoted an important section of the same essay to the name. Jacques Derrida, after having set forth in his *Grammatology* an innovative reflection on the metaphor and the name, stresses the importance of the writer's signature. "A text exists, resists, consists, represses, can be read or written, only if the illegibility of a proper name is at work in it." Just as have other branches of contemporary literary criticism, the study of the proper name has both permeated and taken advantage of approaches linked to various fields in the human sciences including sociology, anthropology, logic, linguistics, semiology, and psychoanalysis.

Such interdisciplinary relations are only natural. The use of proper names in the text of a novel is obviously related to their use in the society the novelist is representing and to the linguistic code he uses. This is evident first and foremost in the identification process recognized as the name's primordial function (although there are novels which are devoid of proper names). Many of the hypotheses made in the analysis or observation of the name's social functions are transferable to the thus enlarged realm of literary onomastics. Grivel, for example, in his study of their function in the novel, consistently makes use of a theory of names as the system of "classification" presented by Lévi-Strauss in *The Savage Mind*. Inversely, a traditional problem in analytical philosophy such as that Kripke presents when opposing definite descriptions to proper names (only the latter, according to him, capable of referring to an individual regardless of the transformations he may undergo) is also a theme thoroughly developed in the Proustian novel. Its illustration in *The Remembrance of Things Past* could furnish the logician with quotations, undoubtedly "fictive," but surely as pertinent as laboratory samples. The literary proper name, rather than being restricted to a self-contained realm, may actually become part of the general idiom, creating both a new concept and a new word. A "Don Juan," a "Pollyanna," are examples of words which originate in the literary text but which have gradually entered into everyday language on the same footing as common nouns. These literary neologisms, known in rhetorics as *antonomasia*, come into being largely because of the semantic content associated with the characters named, and partially, perhaps, because of the expressiveness inherent in the signifier. (This is made quite clear by the fact that such nouns not only lose their associations with a person, real or fictive, but also lose the capital letter which originally identified them as proper names. There are examples such as *silhouette*, but also those such as *gavroche, tartufferie*.)

However, literary onomastics cannot be solely defined within the boundaries established by the social theories of the name. It is generally recognized that the social use of the name coexists with a poetic use which forms exceptions to the fundamental assumptions on which social theories are based. This holds above all in the case of linguistics, especially for the dominant tradition of John Stuart Mill, which denies the proper name any connotation, viewing it as a mere label "whose entire meaning is contained in its phonetic substance."[1] This may explain the ambiguity of the Jakobsonian position. On the one hand, in *Essais de Linguistique Generale* he limits the proper name's meaning to the designation of the bearer, in contrast with the common noun which signifies a set of properties. On the other hand, he demonstrates in *Closing Statements: Linguistics and Poetics* how the poet is apt to integrate the onomastic signifier with its semantic environment, as in Wallace Stevens' poem "An Ordinary Evening in New Haven":

> The dry eucalyptus seeks god in the rainy cloud.
> Professor Eucalyptus of New Haven seeks him in New Haven . . .
> . . . . . .
> The instinct for heaven had its counterpart:
> The instinct for earth, for New Haven, for his room . . .[2]

Finally in *The Sound Shape of Language*, Jakobson links the frequency of play on proper names to their unique status in vocabulary.

Analytical philosophy also draws a line between the poetic and social use of the name. Here we systematically find that names are defined uniquely as signs or expressions which "actually" denote an individual. Fiction would thus by definition have to be considered a space void of proper names. But Gottlieb Frege makes the following qualification:

In literature, aside from the beauty of sounds, only the meaning of various textual propositions and the images or feelings brought forth by these meanings captivate the reader. Thought remains identical whether or not Ulysses' name has a denotation. Therefore it is of little import to know whether this name, for example, has a denotation as long as we perceive the poem as a work of art.[3]

It is obvious then that while literary onomastics derives some of its theoretical background from a diversified body of thought constituting a general semiology of the name, it must elaborate on the specific parameters of its own field. Aside from its crucial contribution to the general theory of the text, one can hope that this endeavour will help to further elucidate our more general understanding of, and relation to, a sign which is deeply impressed upon every aspect of our social lives.

In order to illustrate the specificity of the literary use of the name, and while classifying the various phenomena brought forth in its analysis, we may ask how the three recognized functions of proper names—identification, classification, signification—present themselves in the novelistic text. In so doing I will try to give a better account of the influences and innovations that can be linked to the new French critical interest in the name.

1

It is obvious that proper names in the novel, as is the case for any group of individuals, are used primarily in order to identify the members of the group and to insure the continuity of such identification throughout the narrative. An index of proper names like that in the Pléiade edition of *The Remembrance of Things Past* crystallizes the property which was in motion both in the reading and writing of the text. The index entries present an uninterrupted list of the characteristics and situations which, in the text, were only gradually attributed to the name/individual in question. Beyond this canonical function, however, the identification conveyed by the proper name in the novel (or rather, by the novel's system of identification) presents unique features.

Naming in the novel is the starting point of a semantic process fundamental to the grammar of the narrative. Through this process, and under specific conditions, the character as such is constituted. Barthes describes this process in *S/Z*: "When identical traits repeatedly intersect with the same name and come to dwell within it, a character is born."[4] In the classical novel this relationship is crucial; as Grivel writes, "a nameless character is unthinkable."[5]

From a more strictly narrative point of view, identification by name conjoined with the aforementioned semantic traits (and even at times the mere repetition of a name) not only marks the foundation of narrative but also orients the reader toward the expectation of a forthcoming individual destiny. In this respect the name frequently acts as a focus. Such is true of the beginning of Emile Zola's saga of the *Rougon-Macquart* in which, after a brief sociological introduction, one reads:

> It was until 1841, in this peculiar social milieu, that an obscure family vegetated . . . whose head, Pierre Rougon, was later to play an important role. . . . Pierre Rougon was the son of peasants. . . .

The identification of the character in the novel's population has to be viewed in relation to the specific structures of the underlying "syntagma" of the story. It is at this level that the extraordinarily powerful property inherent in the repetition of a single name is most evident. Narration and name are inextricably linked by anaphora. The "classical" novel undoubtedly grows out of such reiteration although this may not always be apparent at the outset even to the novelist himself. We know for example that Honoré de Balzac first conceived of the gigantic cycle of *The Human Comedy* when he retrospectively discovered the power to be gained from "the return to the same names" from volume to volume. The expression is Proust's, who saw therein "Balzac's most genial idea" while noting that it had been, so to speak, *imposed* on him at some advanced stage in the composition of his masterpiece. Within a novel of which we have numerous drafts, such as Proust's *Remembrance*, we can observe how a name chosen at some point in the writing process is retrospectively given to characters who previously had other names or had remained designated by descriptive phrases—and who are placed under the new sign in the obvious goal of creating a tighter chain of associations. Identification by name would appear in this instance to be one of the constitutive modes of the "novel's interest," to use Grivel's terms, inasmuch as the novel can be read as a chain made up of the reiteration of proper names. A kind of "echo" is created around the name which becomes in turn the symbol of a given quality or a sign repeatedly associated with a specific concept. This is an important phenomenon in the Proustian novel, one illustrated by the frequency of forms such as "a Vinteuil," "an Elstir," "a Bergotte."

The modern novelist may want to disrupt the cohesive quality of the name's function as anaphora. In a relatively classic tradition, the onomastic chain may have been carefully perturbed or broken. Critics have often pointed out the efficiency of this technique in the *Remembrance*. A name (Mme de Saint-Loup, for example), strategically introduced in the first pages of the text, will appear much later to have concealed within it other names which the reader comes to know only gradually. One will also discover that the "Princesse de Guermantes" who appears in the final reception is none other than Mme Verdurin, although the author initially takes pains to conceal her marriage to the prince when he reintroduces the characters in the novel's final sequence. More insidiously maybe, Faulkner chose to give the same name to two central characters in *The Sound and the Fury*.

But precisely if the reader is thus deceived—for the sake of a greater subsequent delight—it is not only because such practices contradict the norms of identification but also because the function of anaphora is particularly potent in the novel. Its very power commences with the selection of a given number of characters and places which will eventually exhaust the possibilities of the fictive space. From which it follows that the basic rules of identification by name can be manipulated or even completely left aside by a novelistic technique whose aim is to disorient the passive reader too prone to habit.

As a case in point, we may recall several features often found in the French "New Novel": the total absence of names, or alternately, a plethora of ever-changing signifiers. The denial or systematic destabilization of traditional identification are central to the ideology of the "New Novel" which obliterates the traditional concept of character, but which retains, in one form or another, the constraints and effects of the narrative process. What we witness in some of these works (particularly in those of Robert Pinget) is the eminently playful role of names, profoundly subversive of their identificatory function although subversion is linked to the disappointed expectation of their normal use.

We may then understand why at the very time that narratology and textual semiotics were coming up with models for the classical function of the name, Barthes was able to write: "What is outdated today, is not the novel, but the name," a formula which paradoxically confronts us with the importance of the onomastic sign as a symptom of the radical change the novel has undergone.

2

In giving names to his characters the novelist already classifies, creating a dichotomy essential to most novels by opposing those who have names to those who have not. Properly speaking the character, as already stated, belongs to the first category. This original distinction requires that we compare literary onomastics with appellations in the broader sense, were it only to acknowledge specific exceptions to this initial repartition. One of the most striking features of the system of appellation in Proust's *Remembrance*, for instance, is precisely the meticulous erasure of reference to the omnipresent narrator-hero's name. Keeping this fundamental dichotomy in mind, what specific features can we assign to the appellative systems in the novel? In answering this question I will draw from the anthropological thesis which must currently form the basis for any reflection concerning the classificatory functions and properties of the name.

In *The Savage Mind* Lévi-Strauss deciphers, despite the complexity and variety apparent in the systems of denomination in use in totemic societies, a single intention which includes even the individual (or what is perceived as such) in the vast classification of the real world enacted by all societal institutions. This intention is simultaneously revealed by the onomastic mobility and by the formal structure of the name, ideally composed of terms implying or referring to common nouns. Strictly speaking this situation only applies in our modern Western societies to those subsystems of nomination in which the particular is felt to be part of a universal (for example, in the botanical realm the scientific name is typically composed of three common nouns). To which might be added those appellations encoding a relation to the other: the "Widow" So-and-so (Mme veuve Untel), for example, which remind Lévi-Strauss of "totemic" practices, foreign to us only in appearance, which occur on the death of a close relative. What we call a proper name is less a matter of linguistics than of anthropology insofar as it depends on a threshold of classification which varies according to historical eras and societies. "In our civilization," writes Lévi-Strauss, "it is as if each individual took his personality for a totem. It is the signifier of his signified being."[6]

Moreover, proper names are always experienced as, or rather situated within, a paradigm, resulting from their marginal status in language. This is true even of "Vercingetorix," says Lévi-Strauss, a name which, according to those attached to tenets of the "purely denotative" function, would be a proper name in the strictest sense of the word—what A. H. Gardiner calls a "disembodied name," merely a "distinctive sound." Countering this view Lévi-Strauss writes:

> Without hypothesizing on the place of Vercingetorix in the Gallic nominative system, it is clear that for us it designates an ancient warrior endowed with a name exclusive to him and peculiar in sound, who is neither Attila, nor Genseric, nor Jugurtha, nor Gengis Khan. . . . As for Popocatepetl, another example dear to Gardiner, every schoolchild, even those innocent of geography, knows that this name refers to a class which also includes Titicaca. One classifies as one can, but one classifies.[7]

Applying these observations to our own field, we note in the first place that names in the modern novel appear, as Grivel puts it, as "the practice of a practice." The name in the text acquires meaning because naming in general obligatorily represents insertion into a system whose function is to identify, classify, socially define. From this point of view, on top of a narrative function that designates the character as such and which identifies him by encapsulating his traits in a single unit, the name "bases the novel in the truth" by transferring to it the apparent "propriety" which is always the name's in everyday use. For Grivel this is a quasi-automatic function of the name in the text. But I would say that this function is dependent on a very diversified use of linguistic components belonging to the morphophonological level of language. This is precisely what allows some names to be more convincing than others. Although Grivel states that the novelist has the right, and even the duty, to insure the renovation of the social code, he notes that the basic condition for the name's efficiency consists in the application of this code to the fictional world. This position concurs with the "theory" of the text that he establishes for the time period 1870–80 from which his examples are drawn. But we know that the degree of verisimilitude between the social code of naming and the novelistic code of naming is one of the characteristics accounting for the emergence of the realist novel as a genre. In France this trend appears to originate about the time of Mme de Lafayette and is indeed primarily evidenced by a use of names more consistent with the morphophonology of the French language.

Furthermore, the novelist has at his disposal not only the general semantic connotations present in the lexicon, but also more cultural ones such as those often associated with first names. These connotations will be recognized by all speakers of a common language. But the foreign reader will only recognize such names as designators. The fictive name can even attempt to reproduce a "real" name by modifying it. It is well known that Tolstoy attributed to some of his characters in *War and Peace* the patronyms of famous aristocratic Russian families, names slightly varied, but still eminently familiar to his readers.[8]

This novelistic use of various onomastic codes needs to be analyzed in monographic studies which will have to take into account the semantic structure of the fictive names under scrutiny. This analysis must also be sensitive to the relative freedom of the fictive codes as well as to their specific values as components of the unique textual systems. The classificatory function stressed by Lévi-Strauss materializes in the novel under the twofold guise of constraint and playfulness— typical of the relation between social names and their fictive counterparts.

It goes without saying that such analysis would be insufficient were it not pursued at the level of the onomastic paradigms each text develops or within smaller textual contexts in which names may exhibit semantic or phonological relations to other words around them. Before clarifying and illustrating this methodologically important distinction, let me note that the descriptions of structural forms of nomination, such as those brought to light by anthropological studies, confirm that any inquiry must be expanded to include all linguistic forms through which a character can be designated in the narrative discourse, particularly those which project on the appellation a vast connotative system. In their frequency and multiplicity such forms constitute a system unequaled in everyday language and obviously inseparable from literary narrative.

Along with the proper name the novelistic text naturally makes use of all the resources available in the appellative system: certain common nouns, titles, terms of kinship or social relations. These forms, besides the social meaning they imply, are specifically pertinent to narrative analysis because they provide a more exact inscription of the character's designation (and thus of the character himself) within the textual system at hand. A given social appellation signifies because it is systematically and exclusively used by the author. In Stendhal's *The Red and the Black*, Madame de Renal's first name (Louise) appears once (during her husband's soliloquy) and only once in the novel. Although she is Julien's lover, she will never be designated by her first name outside of her relation to her husband. We might say, using Lévi-Strauss' terminology, that she has no "autonymic appellation." Borrowed from the social code, the form in use (Madame de Renal) *does* signify in this case insofar as it reveals a careful erasure of all possible appellative substitutes. Conversely, we find in the *Remembrance* a complete apparatus of techniques whose purpose is to guarantee the anonymity of the narrator-hero. But on closer analysis a coherent network of appellative phrases punctuates the vacuousness of the pronominal designation to which he confines himself and consistently connotes his relation to others. Quoting Madame de Guermantes somewhat at random we find such appellations as "this poor little one," "the young man," "my poor little one," "the little one," "that little one," "my little one."

It must be noted finally that the "socialized" appellative forms which parallel the use of the proper name in everyday language belong to relatively limited sets (i.e., "the little boy," "the girl") and are above all relatively restricted in use. The situation is entirely different in the text of the novel which, as we witness in the New Novel, systematically substitutes the individual appellation by the generic one. Alain Robbe-Grillet's *In The Labyrinth* makes exclusive use of the generic name, both the protagonists being referred to only as "the soldier," "the boy." This systematic choice of a token denomination originates in the ideological refusal of a traditionally individualized character. It simultaneously enforces the semantic ambiguity which is characteristic of that kind of novel. (Is it always the same "soldier" or the same "boy?") In this instance the choice is also limited to only two "lexical" appellations. One may wonder however if, from the point of view of semantic structure, the use of this type of signs doesn't have an antecedent in the classical novel, in which an appellative subclass appears in the numerous judgments made by the narrator-author in the presentation of his characters. More flexible to contextual factors, these locutions, which have been analyzed as one of the forms of the author's "interference" in the narrative, go far beyond the appellation's lexical sphere. In *The Remembrance of Things Past*, and again somewhat at random, we find examples such as "the illustrious Norwegian philosopher," "the charming apostolic chauffeur," "the arborescent bell-hop." Far more than in everyday speech, the systems of denomination in fictive discourse have a propensity to use what Lévi-Strauss in *The Savage Mind* called "abstract" categories of appellation.

3

Is is obvious that the classificatory function accomplished by appellations in the text (and eminently among them proper name) is also in the broader sense a signifying function. For some writers these two concepts are even equivalent: "To signify, in the case of the proper name, means inserting the bearer into hierarchies and inscribing him in the place where he belongs."[9]

Let me add that this function may be hypothetically considered all the more potent in that the novel, given its limited set of names, puts each one in conjunction with the others. This explains what enables us to perceive the celebrated dichotomy between noble and plebeian names which Barthes discovered in Proust's *Remembrance* based on microscopic features in the names themselves. I might add to Barthes' opposition the evidence of other contrasts in nominative systems: those which divide the French and the foreign, the Gentile and the Jewish populations. In the latter case, not only are the forms of the Jewish names of interest, but they also give birth to a varied series of incidents and commentaries within the text itself.

This recognition of the signifying function of proper names would still be very incomplete if thought of merely as an effect directly transferred from the onomastic codes of language. We must take into account all phenomena associated with the presence of the very peculiar signs names are in the novelistic text, were it only because, unlike any other words in the text, these can be "created" by the novelist. At this level, turning to the onomastic signifier, we must consider simultaneously the genesis and the poetics of the novelistic name. Both are consistent with a point of view which would place them in a field particularly open to the iconic interpretation of language, as in the thesis advanced by Rigolot in his work on Renaissance poetry: "The natural opaqueness of the name makes it an excellent candidate for symbolic remotivation." In his article entitled "Proust and Names," which reintroduced the Platonic reference to Cratylus to critical discourse, Roland Barthes writes in an almost prescriptive tone, "The novelist has a duty to create names that conform to their bearers." Although it would be an error to consider that the proper name is the only unit of the text that can benefit from the motivation process, the novelist enjoys relative freedom when it comes to naming.[10]

If, as Karl Bühler demonstrated in his *Essays on Language*, the inclination towards a "mimetic use of linguistic sounds" is hindered in the everyday use of language by three interlocking limitations: the first on the syntactical level (the language assigns a set order to words); the second on the phonological level, and the third on the lexical level (by preventing the individual invention of expressive words)—one sees that, at least in the case of the name, the third prohibition does not apply.

Many novelists have devoted particular attention to the question of names in their works. The *Notebooks of Henry James*, essentially made up of anecdotes which might form the nucleus of stories or novels, also contains abundant lists of names for potential use in the elaboration of such plots. As James makes clear in a letter dating from 1896:

> Fiction-mongers collect proper names, surnames, etc.—make notes and lists of any odd or unusual, as handsome or ugly ones they see or hear—in newspapers (columns of births, deaths, marriages, etc.) or in directories and signs of shops or elsewhere; fishing out of these memoranda in time of need the one that strikes them as good for a particular case.[11]

Such selective appropriation is presumably frequent among writers of all descriptions. Although it is difficult to generalize, this is nonetheless indicative of an inclination which renders appreciable the role of names in the genesis of the novel.[12]

We might more generally speaking note that the relationship between a name and its textual content can be traced back either to internal or external factors. In the first case, the role of the name appears so fundamental to the text that it can only have been contemporary with its original conception or at least with its first drafts. A classical example is the case of the transparent name like "Candide." A more contemporary case might be that of "Bleston," the name of the city in Michel Butor's *L'Emploi du Temps*, which is so intrinsically linked by the incantatory repetition of its syllables to the very essence of the narrator's voice that, independent of any semantic connotations it may have, it becomes one of the most cogent words of the narrative. As for examples of the external relation between the name and the making of a text, these are most interesting when they also exemplify a direct semantic relation of some sort. Nathalie Sarraute is known to have said that the name of "Martereau" came to represent for her the existence of a "mono-lothic" character.

This genetic relationship between the name and the semantic content (as well as with other textual structures) had already been put forth in Saussure's studies on the *Nibelungen*:

> It is with this in mind that I will undertake the study of any problem in legend because each character is a symbol, in which exactly as for the rune, there is variation in a) the name, b) the relation to others, c) the temperament, d) the function, the deeds. If a *name* is transformed, it may be that some of the actions follow suit, and vice versa, or that the entire dramatic set of events is changed by an accident of this kind.[13]

Furthermore, there is Aristotle's evidence concerning what he called the *topos onomatos* (*Poetics* 1400b) which consists of the novelist's reading into the name. One of the most striking examples, recently commented on by various scholars, is to be found in the opening lines of "Z Marcas," a short story by Balzac:

> I never saw anyone, not even among the most remarkable men of the day, whose appearance was as striking as his; the study of his countenance first gave me a feeling of great melancholy and then an almost painful sensation. There was a certain harmony between the man and his name. The Z. preced-ing Marcas, to be seen on his letterhead and which he never omitted from his signature, as the last letter of the alphabet, seemed to contain the notion of fatality.

> Marcas! Repeat this two-syllable name to yourself, doesn't it sound as if it had a sinister meaning? Doesn't it seem to you that its owner must be doomed to martyrdom? Though foreign, savage, the name has a right to be handed down to posterity; it is well constructed, easily pronounced, and has the brevity necessary for fame. Isn't it pleasant as well as peculiar? But doesn't it sound unfinished? I would not want to take it upon myself to assert that names have no influence on the destiny of men. There is a certain secret and inexplicable concord or a visible discord between the events of a man's life and his name which is truly surprising; often some remote but very real correlation is revealed. Our globe is round: everything is linked to everything else. Perhaps there will one day be a return to the occult sciences.

> Do you not discern the appearance of contraries in the letter Z? Doesn't it seem to prefigure the wayward and fantastic zigzag of a tormented life? What wind has blown on the letter, which, in any language, begins no more than fifty words? Marcas' first name was Zephirin; Saint Zephirin is highly revered in Brittany and Marcas was a Breton.

> Study the name once more: Z. Marcas! The man's whole life is to be found in the juxtaposition of these seven letters. Seven! The most meaningful of all

cabalistic numbers. And he died at thirty-five so his life extended over seven lusters. Marcas! Does it not hint of some precious object broken by a fall, with or without a crash?

In such a passage it is obvious that the choice of a name goes hand in hand with the argument which is none other than that of the short story itself—an argument to be found in embryo, so to speak, in this extravagant reading into the name of Z. Marcas. Beyond its aesthetic and cabalistic considerations, or even the visible ingenuousness with which the sign is forced into an alliterative or metaphorical pattern (Marcas: martyr; Marcas: crash), the entire passage seems to claim for the name an exceptional stance: that of name as a sign of text's motivation, as the very source of the narrative, as the nucleus of a remarkable fate. Here such a thread can be traced back to the opening lines which in their interpretation of the name call on every possible level of language (including the graphic strata when the Z is said to "prefigure the wayward and fantastic zigzag of a tormented life"). In other works the name's power is sometimes anagramatically inscribed within a pattern corresponding to the internal universe of the text. In the first chapters of *The Red and the Black*, when Julien Sorel stops for a visit at the church in Verrières, he finds a scrap of newspaper describing the execution of a certain Louis Jenrel. Encoded within this anagram is the hero's own fate, as Stendhal, in a play on words, will have Julien quite literally observe: "Who could have left this paper here? said Julien. The poor unfortunate, he added with a sigh, his name ends just as mine does."

4

A more contemporary example, the Proustian text has been a privileged field of critical inquiry for scholars interested in the function of the name. There are intrinsic reasons for this fascination since the wealth of onomastic patterns in the Proustian text pertains to every level of the novel's structures, thus constituting an ideal framework for the detailed illustration of the name's permeation of the text.

Invoked by the famous reveries on names to which the young hero of the *Remembrance* abandons himself, the main question tackled by these studies (inaugurated by Barthes' article in 1967 and continued from various angles by Genette 1969/1976, Gaubert 1971, Butor 1972, Milly 1974, Quémar 1977, and Lelong 1981) concerns the poetic function of proper names, that is to say in the final analysis, the form of the signifier. In the case of Lelong's psychoanalytical approach, this linguistic dimension is acknowledged by his recognition of the affective and stylistic contrast encoded in noble and bourgeois names. The former typically have "long or elongated sonorities"; the latter are "dry, slightly ridiculous, without class." [14]

Outlined by Barthes, who was the first to identify an opposition between the noble and plebian name encoded in the phonological structure of the final syllable

("Guermantes," long ending vs. "Brichot," short ending), and recognized by Genette in a note pointing out that such opposition invariably occurs as a result of the novelist's intervention in the arbitrary character of language (and thus stands in contrast with the "shortcomings" of real names), the various kinds of onomastic motivation in the *Remembrance* remain to be explored in full. Reading Milly one realizes that this motivation is indirectly linked to the context of the name and perhaps more often to be found at a metaphoric level than at that of phonetic alliterations—although these, because of the "syneasthesia" invoked by the young hero—are more visible at a first reading. One can even, in scrutinizing the first drafts published by Quémar, reconstitute the diachronic process of such associations or at least those to be found on the famous pages devoted to Norman and Breton names. The name "Pont-Aven," "the white and pink wing of a coiffe . . . which trembles on the wind [vent] and is reflected in the greenish waters of its river," was spelled "Ponta Ven" in one of Proust's manuscripts. This would seem to confirm the reading which, invalidating any etymological interpretation, introduces in its imaginary and poetic meaning the common word *vent* through the homophonic filiation [vã]: making of the city, literally, "a bridge [*pont*] on a river swept by the winds [*vent*]."

There are thus, methodologically speaking, at least two aspects to be distinguished in these studies: the relation between the sign and its context and the structure of the sign itself. The evidence of a Proustian "poetics" of the name which can be defined either as play with the onomastic signifier (as Quémar views it) or as the "anchoring of the name in the text" (as Milly prefers to describe it) poses the stylistic problem of perceiving its effects within the context or, and this is of a critical nature, the reconstruction of the associative mechanisms on which they are based. Since every word, from this point of view, can be associated with the general poetic function described by Jakobson as the projection of "the principle of equivalence from the axis of selection into the axis of combination," it would appear to be a matter of questioning how aptly the proper name enters into this poetic use, obligatorily linked to context.[15]

I am more interested here in the specific modalities of this use than in its frequency. If the latter is high in some passages of the Proustian novel, it is because these passages (they can be found not only in the onomastic reveries proper but also in their subsequent negation) directly expose the young narrator's belief in a motivation of the name. His belief becomes the quasi-exclusive fuel for his linguistic imagination and his reveries are good illustrations of his particular semiotic sensitivity. Although severely criticized by the mature narrator in the *Remembrance*, Jakobson assures us in *The Sound Shape of Language* that such sensitivity is very common.

It is because of a sort of internal redundancy specific to the Proustian text that the poetic function of the proper name is also in many instances an illustration of its power and lyricism. But there are many passages where this quality fades before the much more dubious social game, consisting of pejorative associations between the name and its bearer (i.e. the puns on the name of the Verdurins: Verdurin/

ordure, literally Verdurin/trash). The function of the fictive proper name is not limited to the poetic structures in which it is mainly to be found. On some occasions it merely comments on the importance the name carries in social life. It also appears to be the potential field for a narrative encoding like that observed in Balzac's "Z. Marcas" since the Balzacian "maneuvering" with the "meaning" of the name announces the story to follow.

To the extent that it is embedded in the context, the novelistic use of the name can already be conceived as a gamut of textual effects extending from what Jakobson called "the poetics of sounds" to the semantic figure of remotivation. At the very least, the presence of a name may signify through a metonymic relation to its context. In book 1 of *The Red and the Black*, during the scene in which Julien overcomes his shyness and takes Madame de Renal's hand, Stendhal introduces an apparently offhand remark, which however one cannot fail to relate to his obsession with cowardice in these pages: "The tree under which this scene takes place has been according to local tradition planted by Charles the Bold."

It remains obvious that it is within the poetic function proper that we find most of the procedures in which a relation between the sign and the context takes place, either in order to motivate the latter by a name which will be sufficiently transparent, or (and this appears to be more frequent) in order to motivate the name itself. In this process I see, as Rigolot does, a desire to reduce the name's "natural opaqueness," a desire that can also be placed within the broader framework of the novel's economy where motivation works on all levels of the text.

Gerard Genette has shown in *Mimologiques* that the search for an accord between the name's designation and its meaning has, since the *Cratylus*, been a frequent practice taking the indirect shape of what is called *eponymy*:

> The function of eponomy is to give a meaning to a name which is not thought of as having any, that is to say to find in it one or two hidden nouns, by definition endowed with meaning.[16]

This is the technique, if not the only function, of the operation bringing together sound and meaning which induces Proust to see in the name Pont-Aven, for example, a "city swept by the winds," or to portray Swann's anger by having him call the Verdurins "trash." Necessarily one with the act of writing, this process constitutes a localized exploitation of the virtual semantic power of a given proper name as contained within a signifier hypothetically devoid of meaning, but which can always be poetically integrated in the word chain of common nouns. This process also applies when the proper name is itself a kind of eponymy, as demonstrated in the ancient example of Tristan's cycle.

This name appears with all the characteristics of a descriptive surname in the Thomas version of the legend:

> Because of the torments and the pain, the sadness and the sorrows, because of the anguish, because of the terrible misfortune which struck us at his birth, it seems fit to name this child Tristan. In this name, "trist" means sad, "an" means "one."[17]

Whereas the same name in two manuscripts of the so-called Folie Tristan is either transformed:

> Chaunges his name, makes hymself hatte Tantris . . .
>
> (Folie de Berne) [18]

or becomes part of a paronomasia:

> Tristan sojournes in his aune contray
> Doelful, mourneful, triste and pensyf . . .
>
> (Folie Tristan d'Oxford) [19]

Although linked by definition with the formal structure of the sign, all these poetical uses of the name must not be confused with what Genette calls the expressive structure of the signifier—which one should be able to perceive in the sign itself independent of any reference to its context. Confronted nowadays with names in the novel which are almost invariably "opaque" in meaning, the problem for criticism is to explain the more or less hidden "connotations" which correspond to the greater or lesser degree of "rightness" felt in the name.

The very notion of rightness may include rather diverse concepts, often quite foreign to the lexical coincidence found at the level of the name in its entirety in the exceptional case of an eponymy such as "Candide" or even that of "Baron Thaler" in *The Red and the Black*. In the latter example the motivation of the sign veils itself behind a foreign language, a relatively frequent occurrence, and only one of the forms of what we might call the *latent motivation of the sign*. It can be found in part of the word (based on a more or less recognizable morpheme) or can be traced back through the process of translation or etymology. Theoretically and practically this line of research seems based on linguistic findings demonstrating the extreme subtlety of a speaker's competence in the very fine articulation of the lexical structures of language.

Traditionally the hypothesis concerning the motivation found on a smaller scale than that of the morpheme has been privileged by research on "sound symbolism." Experimentally demonstrated, this phenomenon seems more prevalent in the comparison of pairs of sounds (e:o :: light: somber) than in the relation between a sound and a perceived quality. Its effect may contribute to the name's expressiveness although to a lesser degree than that created by an explicit lexical association (as is the case in contextual eponymies) or by an implicit one (since there is a strong inclination to associate names with other names or words more or less similar in form).

Sound symbolism is at work in Barthes' reading of proper names in the *Remembrance* since he relies on the existence of a phonetic opposition between the noble and bourgeois name. In so doing he draws a diagrammatical structure binarily relating long and short endings with a class dichotomy. Furthermore, Barthes adds to his argument a point which no longer applies exclusively to the phonetic stratum:

> Long and short endings are used here not as strictly phonetical terms, but in
> the broad sense they have in everyday use partially because of their written

form. The French, because their culture is essentially written, are apt to perceive a tyrannical opposition between masculine and feminine rhymes, the first felt to be short, the second to be long.[20]

This more complex and diversified analysis of the effect produced on the user of language by the name is confirmed by those rare studies which have attempted to describe the "general semantic connotation" or the "level of admissibility" of a name. It is at this level that we can practically verify, through individual and microscopic analysis, that as a creator of names, the novelist works with possibilities intrinsic to his idiom, possibilities which the great writer alone reveals.

To create a name is an operation which relies on the relations existing in the phonological and morphological levels structured by different rules in every language. Although they are often at a low level of phonological admissibility (a characteristic they share with archaisms and neologisms), proper names are nonetheless bound to deep lexical structures. If they belong to a class of words to which the native speaker has the strongest aesthetic reactions, be they positive or negative, it seems that these reactions can be traced to linguistic microstructures within a given name. It is on this basis that we can attempt the analysis of onomastic variants found in the various drafts of a manuscript. This hypothesis can also be illustrated in a pragmatic manner when the form of a name modified by a writer to create a class connotation (In Dickens' *Doctor Marigold's Prescriptions*, "Willum" for William) must be translated into a foreign language. In Valesio's "Levels of Phonological Admissibility," we are shown how the corresponding variant of the first name thus modified can be "constructed," taking into account structural relations to be found in the other language, and that in this respect the various possibilities the translator considers differ in quality. This approach may also explain why some words sound more poetical than others. In Italian, for example, the first name Isotta, although linked to prestigious cultural associations, "does not work well as a poetic name." [21] D'Annunzio avoids it, preferring Isáotta, which he creates, or Isolda.

Valesio's analysis shows that the very low admissibility of Isotta has to do with its homophony with the diminutive (and pejorative) suffix -ott-, which occurs in a large number of lexical items, and/or with a suffix ending with -tt-, and whose stressed vowel is not [e]. The first constraint to the poetic value of the name disappears with Isáotta since the change in stress eliminates the homophony with the suffix -ott-. But the second constraint remains. Furthermore, the cluster /áo/ is very rare in Italian. Both disadvantages are overcome in the name Isolda.[22]

Theoretically important, the practical applications of these analyses would undoubtedly lead the search for the modalities of the proper name's motivation in the direction of the phonemic, graphemic, and morphophonological structures whose pertinence had already been hinted at from the very beginning of modern phonology in the works of Troubetzkoy. Whatever the case, it is under a twofold perspective that we must approach the analysis of the signifier. In naming, the novelist, consciously or not, either makes use of complex structures existing in the lexicon of his language or he exploits phonetic traits contained in the name within a given context. In theory these two levels are independent of one another. At times they complement each other. In Zola's *La Curée* the whole process is staged in the narrative itself. The protagonist, Aristide Rougon, is choosing a name suitable to the ambitious enterprises of which he dreams. From his wife's name "Sicardot," suggested by his brother, discarded because it sounds "stupid" and "smells of bankruptcy," they proceed to "Siccard," eliminated because it "sounds a little too light." Masking Zola himself, Rougon finally gets enthusiastic about "Saccard," "with a double c . . . mind you! There's money in that name, you'd think you were counting dollars." His brother concludes: "Yes, it's a name that would end you up in jail or make you millions."

5

Having distinguished between the encoding of the name as it relates to general structures of the lexicon and the associations with the close context, we must remember that these two levels between them do not make up the entire realm of functions associated with the name as signifier in the novel. Another level is present in the paradigms of the text. In the case of the *Remembrance*, to quote but one well-known example, the resemblance between Morel's first name (Charlie) and the name of Charlus is obviously not haphazard. It was incidently the result of a very late correction on Proust's part. The curious frequency of the syllable /bER/ in the proper names of the text has also been noted and hypothetically linked to the name of Proust's grandmother, Adele Berncastel, or more interestingly perhaps to the Merovingian names Proust came across in his reading of Augustin Thierry.

In a strange critical reversal, the proliferation of hypotheses concerned with the analysis of the onomastic signifier has recently made of the proper name a key to many levels of the text, sometimes even to an entire literary oeuvre. Barthes had suggested that as the "linguistic equivalent of memory," the name, whose entire system, he conjectured, had been constituted as early as 1907–8, marked the decisive acquisition which had allowed Proust to write *The Remembrance of Things Past* after the unsuccessful attempts of *Jean Santeuil* and *Contre Sainte-Beuve*. In his *Les Sept Femmes de Gilbert le Mauvais*, Butor indulges in a kind of lexical daydream about the name Guermantes. Although he expresses some skepticism about its theoretical underpinnings, his writing illustrates quite well what might be called a new phantasm in literary criticism: that of the proper name as the ultimate secret of the text. What is striking about Butor's analytical maneuvering is its mixture of plausible and extravagant elements. He begins by reading into the name Guermantes the words "germain"/"germanique" (first cousin/germanic). These associations are plausible because the Guermantes are indeed a large and extended family and because their name is contained in the geographic label "Guermantes-Bavière." More extravagant is the reading which sees in Guermantes a signified "germe" (seed) and "naissance" (birth), words which allow Butor to link the Guermantes with the family central to Jean Santeuil (the *Remembrance*'s seminal predecessor). This family's name is "Reveillon," the Christmas feast with an obvious metonymical proximity to "Noël." In the last step of this progression, Butor claims that the provincial pronunciation of "Noël" would reveal it to be none other than the modified name of Anna de Noailles, a name thus hidden on virtually every page of the *Remembrance* and inscribed in the mysterious nucleus of its genesis.

The process is labyrinthine and would be tortuous in relation to its revelation, if it did not illustrate in its own way a very ancient ambiguity. In his *Rhetoric* Aristotle places the name among the *topoi* on which one can base a valid argument and then contradictorily excludes it from this place, relegating it to the list of dubious ways of reasoning. On the critical level such an ambiguity might seem to be a search for a formula. Considering the gamut of phenomena mentioned above I would rather say it manifests itself as a set of diversified functions. This is the function of a sign obviously essential to the economy of the classical novel, to the mere designation of its characters and places. In some privileged cases, among which we must certainly include *The Remembrance of Things Past*, the name's function is remarkably varied. Not only is it essential to the very existence of the characters it structures, but also, because it is never completely detached from reference to the real world, the name is reappropriated by the novelist at all levels of writing and textual imagination. It may even figure in some cases as the sign most proper to textual strategy.

Notes

1. The phrase is Jean Molino's in his summary of Mill's, Funke's, and Gardiner's theses. See Molino, "Le nom propre dans la langue," *Langages*, 66, pp. 5–20. All translations from the French, unless otherwise indicated, are mine.

2. Roman Jakobson, "Closing Statements: Linguistics and Poetics," in *Style in Language*, ed. Sebeok (Cambridge: MIT Press, 1960), p. 377.

3. Gottlieb Frege, "Sens et Denotation," in *Ecrits logiques et philosophiques* (Paris: Edition du Seuil, 1971), p. 108.

4. Roland Barthes, *S/Z* (Paris: Seuil, 1970), p. 74.

5. Charles Grivel, *Production de l'intérêt romanesque: un état du texte (1870–80); Un essai de constitution de la théorie* (The Hague and Paris: Mouton, 1973), p. 132.

6. Claude Lévi-Strauss, *La Pensée sauvage* (Paris: Plon, 1962), p. 284.

7. *Ibid.*, p. 285.

8. See Roman Jakobson and Linda Waugh, *La Charpente phonique du langage* (Paris: Editions de Minuit, 1980), pp. 34–35.

9. Grivel, *Production de l'intérêt romanesque*, p. 130.

10. François Rigolot, *Poétique et Onomastique: l'exemple de la Renaissance* (Geneva: Droz, 1977); Roland Barthes, "Proust et les noms," in *To Honor Roman Jakobson* (Paris: Mouton, 1967), vol. 1, p. 283.

11. *The Notebooks of Henry James*, ed. F. O. Matthiessen and K. B. Murdock (New York: Oxford University Press, 1961), p. 63.

12. Eugène Nicole, "Personnage et rhétorique du Nom," *Poétique* 46, pp. 200–17.

13. See Jean Starobinski, *Les Mots sous les mots: les anagrammes de Ferdinand de Saussure* (Paris: Gallimard, 1971), p. 16.

14. Yves Lelong, "Marcel Proust: roture et métaphore," *Poétique* 46, p. 217.

15. Jakobson, "Closing Statements," p. 358.

16. Gerard Genette, *Mimologiques* (Paris: Seuil, 1976), p. 25.

17. *Le Roman de Tristan par Thomas: poème du XIIeme siècle publié par Joseph Bedier* (Paris: Firmin Didot, 1907).

18. *Les deux poemes de la folie Tristan*, ed. Joseph Bedier (Paris: Firmin Didot, 1907), v. 126–27. Translation from the French by Sarah Sanderlin.

19. *Ibid.*, v. 1–2.

20. Barthes, "Proust et les noms," pp. 150–58.

21. Paolo Valesio, "Levels of Phonological Admissibility," *Linguistics* 106, p. 44.

22. *Ibid.*, p. 50.

Same Difference: The French *Physiologies,* 1840–1842 / *Richard Sieburth*

Several years ago, a relatively obscure New York publishing firm brought out *The Official Preppy Handbook*, a humorous vade mecum to the manners and mores of the American WASP. Illustrated with specimen photographs and drawings of the typical Preppy, and accompanied by charts, statistics, and lists detailing the characteristic habitats and distinguishing foibles of this social species, *The Official Preppy Handbook* fell somewhere between an instruction manual and a satiric ethnography of America's ruling class. The book was an instant success: 55 weeks on the Best Seller list, 26 printings, sales of 1,305,000 copies. As was inevitable, it spawned a slew of sequels and imitations among rival publishers eager to cash in on the fad (e.g., *The Official JAP Handbook, The Official Lawyer's Handbook, Real Men Don't Eat Quiche*, etc.).

The recent boom in America of manuals and "how to" books satirizing social and ethnic types recalls a similar episode in the history of nineteenth-century French publishing, namely, the craze that swept Paris in the early 1840s for a series of small illustrated volumes marketed under the generic title of *physiologies*. Some 120 different *physiologies* were issued by various Parisian publishers between 1840 and 1842 (ranging alphabetically from the *Physiologie de l'amant de coeur* to the *Physiologie du voyageur*), and it is estimated that approximately half a million copies of these pocket-sized books were printed during this same two-year span. Even admitting the possibility that this figure is somewhat inflated (the population of Paris during the period numbered little more than a million, only half of whom could read), the extraordinary success of these pseudo-scientific portraits of social types is attested by many contemporary authors.[1] Balzac, for example, describes the phenomenon in his *Monographie de la presse parisienne*:

> La Physiologie était autrefois la science exclusivement occupée à nous raconter le mécanisme du coccyx, les progrès du foetus ou ceux du ver solitaire, matières peu propres à former le coeur et l'esprit des jeunes femmes et des enfants. Aujourd'hui, la Physiologie est l'art de parler et d'écrire incorrectement de n'importe quoi sous la forme d'un petit livre bleu ou jaune qui soutire vingt sous au passant sous prétexte de le faire rire et qui lui décroche les mâchoires. . . . Le XVIIe siècle a eu la mode des Carlins, aujourd'hui nous avons celle des physiologies. Les Physiologies sont comme les moutons de Panurge, elles courent les unes après les autres. Paris se les arrache, et on vous y donne pour vingt sous plus d'esprit que n'en a dans son mois un homme d'esprit.[2]

[Physiology was once a science solely concerned with explaining the mechanism of the coccyx, the development of a foetus or a tapeworm, all subjects hardly suited to mold the hearts and minds of young women and children. Today, physiology has become the art of speaking and writing incorrectly about anything in the shape of a small blue or yellow book which sells for one franc under the pretense of offering amusement to split the readers' sides. . . . The fad of the seventeenth century was lapdogs, today it's physiologies. *Physiologies* are like Panurge's sheep, one chasing after another. Paris fights over them and one franc buys you more wit than our wittiest minds manage in a month.]

As Balzac notes, the very term *physiologie* has its roots in the scientific discourse of the late eighteenth and early nineteenth centuries. Although certain genealogists of the genre trace its origins as far back as the medieval *physiologus* or *speculum*, or the encyclopedic anatomies of the Renaissance, most historians tend to link the notion of *physiologie* to a materialist current in post-Enlightenment thought often associated with the *idéologues*. They cite such influential medical titles as Cabanis's *Traité du Physique et du moral de l'homme* (1798–99), Bichat's *Recherches physiologiques sur la vie et la mort* (1800), Richarand's *Traité de physiologie* (1802), and Demangeon's *Physiologie intellectuelle* (1808), to which might be added the names of the paleontologist Cuvier, the zoologist Saint-Hilaire, the phrenologist Gall, and, perhaps most important, the physiognomist Lavater, whose impact on the development of literary portraiture in the nineteenth century cannot be overestimated.[3]

If the very title of the *physiologies* evokes a tradition of confident scientific materialism (or, in the case of Lavater and Gall, a firm belief that man's exterior features are the infallible signs of his inner being), the inventory of contemporary social types found in these little books would seem rather to derive from the various *études de moeurs* which were quite popular with the growing urban reading public of the late eighteenth and early nineteenth centuries. Most frequently cited among the precursors of the *physiologies* are such prerevolutionary works as Naugaret's *Les Astuces de Paris* (1775) and his *Les Sottises et les folies parisiennes* (1781), as well as Mercier's twelve-volume *Tableau de Paris* (1781–88). Mossé's *Chronique de Paris ou le spectateur moderne* (1812) and Jouy's five-volume *L'Hermite de la Chausée-d'Antin* (1813–14) reinvigorated the genre under the Empire, and new sequels to their remarkably successful formula appeared throughout the 1820s and 1830s, in competition with such newer arrivals as Balisson de Rougemont's six-volume *Le Rôdeur français ou les moeurs du jour* (1816–27) or the fifteen-volume *Paris ou le Livre des Cent-et-un* (1831–34), a collectively authored encyclopedia of urban vignettes selected to suit the *juste milieu* tastes of the July Monarchy. The thirst of the Parisian public for images of itself and its city, however, was not entirely slaked by the more or less documentary scope of these *études de moeurs*. Next to these early examples of urban ethnography (whose *rôdeurs* and *hermites* prefigure the *flâneur*) there also flourished a sizeable market for popular *romans de moeurs* whose most mawkish best-sellers are associated with the names of August Picard, Paul de Kock, and Frederic Soulié.[4]

The more specifically comic appeal of the *physiologies* is related to the increasing popularity of vaudeville and of *comédies de moeurs* among the early nineteenth-century public (Lemaître's *Robert Macaire*, for example, would become an eloquent vehicle for Daumier's satire of the thirties), as well as to the corresponding vitality of such satiric journals as *La Silhouette*, *La Caricature*, and *Le Charivari*. Charles Philipon, the mastermind behind all three of these newspapers and influential editor at the Maison Aubert, was perhaps more responsible than any other individual for engineering the success of the *physiologies* in the 1840s. Shrewd businessman that he was, Philipon seized on a title whose commercial viability had already been proved by Brillat-Savarin's *Physiologie du goût* (1826) and Balzac's *Physiologie du mariage* (first published in 1830, but conceived as early as 1824–26). Balzac had originally considered entitling this work *Code marital ou L'Art de rendre sa femme fidèle*—a title that alluded to a series of books cooked up by his fellow journalist Horace Raisson and known as *Les Codes littéraires*. Balzac himself published a *Codes des gens honnêtes ou L'Art de ne pas être dupe des fripons* in 1825, and the popularity of such titles as *Le Code gourmand*, *Le Code de la conversation*, *Le Code des boudoirs*, *Code Parisien ou Manuel complet du provincial et de l'étranger à Paris* was such in the late twenties and thirties that Raisson brought out a series of sequels: *L'Art de mettre sa cravate*, *L'Art de faire des dettes et de fair promener les créanciers*, *L'Art de donner à dîner*, etc.[5]

Hybrid blends of the etiquette book, the instruction manual, and the tourist guide, and early examples of modern "self-help" books, these various *Codes* and *Arts de* served a purpose that was both descriptive and prescriptive, both parodic and didactic. The same tone is found in the *physiologies*, as is the emphasis on the codification of contemporary custom into a system of formulas and conventions as rigorous as those governing any language or semiotic system (as is nicely brought out by an 1827 title, *Grammaire conjugale, ou principes généraux à l'aide desquels on peut dresser la femme, la faire marcher au doigt et à l'oeil et la rendre aussi douce qu'un mouton, par un petit cousin de Lovelace*). Like many of the pulp humor books of the period, these *Codes* were the creations of that newly emerging cadre of journalists and hack writers evoked by Balzac in *Illusions perdues*, and the *physiologies* of the forties have similar affiliations with the press, particularly with the publishers, writers, and artists associated with satirical illustrated newspapers. *La Silhouette* published a *Galerie physiologique* as early as 1830, and its successor, *La Caricature* (also directed by Philipon, with Balzac, Grandville, and Daumier among its collaborators), regularly featured satirical physiological vignettes, the most celebrated being Philipon's *portrait-charge* of Louis-Philippe in the shape of a pear, which in turn inspired Peytel's *Physiologie de la poire* (1832), often cited as the first example of the genre that was to become so successful a decade later.

Philipon and his collaborators at *La Caricature* and *Le Charivari* perfected the basic format which was to distinguish the *physiologies* from the earlier *Codes* and *études de moeurs*, a format based on the witty interaction of image and text, drawing and caption, seeing and reading. Baudelaire, for one, saw this reduplication of the verbal and the visual as a characteristic flaw of the caricaturists associated with Philipon and later with the *physiologies*, and he contrasted their work with the more purely iconic power of Daumier: "Daumier's talent is frank and direct. Take away the captions and his drawings will speak just as loudly and clearly. With Gavarni, it's another story; his talent is double: first take the drawing and then the caption. And note how the best things are always in the caption, his drawings being unable to articulate as much." [6] Though Baudelaire may have found their work too discursive, too redundant, it was perhaps for this very reason that the publishers of the late thirties and forties were quick to recruit such artists as Grandville, Monnier, Gavarni, and Traviès to contribute to the growing number of illustrated volumes depicting contemporary Parisian life.

Byproducts of the recent technological advances in printing and paper manufacturing which had made illustrated books more commercially feasible and analagous to the various dioramas and panoramas which enjoyed a considerable popularity during the period, these illustrated anthologies of urban sites and mores catered to the public's desire to see its social space as a stage or gallery whose intelligibility was guaranteed both by its visibility as image and its legibility as text. The titles of these various albums of city life are in themselves indicative of their panoptic or encyclopedic ambitions: *Paris au XIXe siècle, Recueil de scènes de la vie parisienne* (1838); *Le Museum Parisien, Histoire physiologique, pittoresque, philosophique et grotesque de toutes les bêtes curieuses de Paris et de la banlieue* (1841); *Le Prisme, encyclopédie morale du XIXe siècle* (1841); *Les Français peints par eux-mêmes* (1840–42); *La Grande Ville, nouveau tableau de Paris, comique, critique, et philosophique* (1842–43); *Le Diable à Paris, Paris et les parisiens* (1845–46). Lavishly illustrated, filled with anecdotes, vignettes, and descriptive essays by journalists and literary *boulevardiers*, these omnibus volumes were presumably intended for exhibit in the drawing rooms of the more affluent bourgeoisie—both the book and the city represented between its covers thus becoming equivalent objects on display.[7]

The *physiologies* are a subgenus of this vast "panorama literature" of the forties. But whereas such deluxe albums as Curmer's *Les Français peints par eux-mêmes* were designed to take their place within the cozy confines of the bourgeois *intérieur* (where, as Walter Benjamin remarks, they served to reduce the potentially threatening exteriority of the city to the more domesticated dimensions of the coffee table book), the *physiologies* were aimed instead at the buyer off the street.[8] Sold at one franc apiece when the going price of a book was three francs fifty, the *physiologies* were clearly conceived with a mass audience in mind. One of their most salient features was their standardized paperback format and their marketing as a uniform collection or series. To sample the varied gallery of contemporary social stereotypes, one had merely to pluck the requisite volume from the booksellers's shelf, as if consulting an entry in a reference work or as if selecting items exhibited in a shopwindow, each one different, yet all reassuringly alike—as is illustrated by the following list of *physiologies* drawn from the first letters of the alphabet:

Physiologie de l'amant de coeur	[Physiology of the adoring lover]
Physiologie des amoureux	[Physiology of the lovers]

Physiologie de l'anglais à Paris	[Physiology of the Englishman in Paris]
Physiologie de l'argent par un débiteur	[Physiology of money by a retailer]
Physiologie des bals de Paris	[Physiology of Parisian balls]
Physiologie du bas-bleu	[Physiology of the blue-stocking]
Physiologie du blagueur	[Physiology of the prankster]
Physiologie du Bourbonnais	[Physiology of the Bourbonnais]
Physiologie du bourgeois	[Physiology of the bourgeois]
Physiologie du buveur	[Physiology of the drinker]
Physiologie du célibataire et de la vielle fille	[Physiology of the bachelor and the spinster]
Physiologie du chasseur	[Physiology of the hunter]
Physiologie du cocu	[Physiology of the cuckold]
Physiologie du créancier et du débiteur	[Physiology of the creditor and the retailer]
Physiologie du curé du campagne	[Physiology of the country priest]
Physiologie du débardeur	[Physiology of the stevedore]
Physiologie des demoiselles de magasin	[Physiology of the salesgirl]
Physiologie du deputé, etc.	[Physiology of the deputy, etc.]

The very uniformity of the *physiologies* not only defined the distinctive gimmick or trademark that set them off from competing collections (such as, say, Alphonse Karr's *Guêpes*), but doubtless also facilitated their "packaging" and distribution as commodities destined for mass consumption. The *physiologies* provide a nearly perfect example of that transformation of book into commodity which Balzac chronicles in *Illusions perdues* and Lukács analyzes in *Studies in European Realism*. Quickly produced and marketed, consumed and discarded, only to be repurchased under a slightly different title, the *physiologies* (like the sensational tabloids or *canards* hawked on Parisian streetcorners of the period) are early instances of the cheap, throwaway "instant book" whose appeal lies in its very topicality and ephemerality. The authors of the *physiologies*, far from trying to disguise this fact, often allude to the new marketplace conditions which have transformed the author into producer and the reader into consumer. Peytel, for example, observes in his early *Physiologie de la poire* (1832):

> Les longs ouvrages font peur maintenant au public. Nous en sommes arrivés à la politique en pamphlets, à la littérature en satires hébdomadaires, à la science en resumés. La rage de tout abréger a fait irruption partout. Le monde n'est plein, au moment où nous parlons, que de lecteurs pressants et d'écrivains pressés. . . .[9]

> > [Today's public is afraid of long books. That's why politics has been reduced to pamphlets, literature to satiric weeklies, and science to formulas. The urge to abridge is everywhere. Today's world seems to be made exclusively of hurried readers and harried writers. . . .]

In his *Physiologie du floueur*, Charles Philipon humorously alludes to his exploitation as author by the publisher Aubert (whose house brought out the majority of

Figure 1

the *physiologies*). As if to emphasize the connection between publishing and other forms of capitalist speculation, the following dialogue is preceded by a drawing of various stock certificates arranged *en éventail* (figure 1):

—Doucement! doucement s'écriait tout-à-l'heure le célèbre Aubert, vous me donnez de la matière pour dix *Physiologies*.

En style d'imprimeur et d'éditeur, le manuscrit, fût-il de Chateaubriand, de lord Byron ou de Trissotin, c'est de la *matière*, rien que de la matière.

Lancez donc votre génie dans le ciel de la poésie,—creusez-vous donc la cervelle pour produire laborieusement un chef-d'oeuvre, votre éditeur n'y verra toujours que de la matière!

Tenez, Aubert, voici un chapitre que nous allongerons d'une lieue, si cela est nécessaire, —un chapitre que vous couperez, comme une ficelle, tout juste à l'endroit où finiront vos cent vingt et une pages.

C'est un chapitre de faits détachés. —J'en ai dans mon sac autant qu'il faudrait pour remplir les vingt-cinq Physiologies de votre collection. —Vous n'avez qu'à parler.

> [—Slow down! Slow down! the famous Aubert was pleading just a while ago. —You are providing me with enough matter for ten *Physiologies*.
>
> In the jargon of printers and publishers, a manuscript, whether Chateaubriand's, Lord Byron's or Trissotin's, is *matter*, nothing but matter.
>
> You may as well cast your talent into the heavens of poetry, or dig deep into your brain to extract, after immense toil and trouble, a worthy masterpiece, and yet, according to your publisher, you have produced only matter!
>
> —Look here, Aubert, here is a chapter that could easily be made a mile longer, if necessary—a chapter that you can cut, like a string, the moment you have reached your one hundred and twenty-one pages.

Figure 2

It's a chapter made of disconnected facts.—I have a bag full of them, enough to fill out the twenty-five *Physiologies* in your collection. —All you have to do is ask.]

There follows a drawing (figure 2) of a figure standing in a landscape holding an enormous ribbon of paper covered with various hieroglyphic images—presumably the "material" which will be cut up and assembled into yet another *physiologie*.

The anonymous *Physiologie des physiologies*, a more or less parodic spoof of the entire genre published at the height of the fad by Desloges in 1841, outlines "Les Ingrédients qui composent une Physiologie," as if to underscore the fact that these volumes are merely mass-produced *articles de série* generated by variations on a single formula:

Prenez une pincée de Labruyere; —une cuillerée de *Lettres persannes*. [*sic*]
Faites infuser les *Guêpes*;
Les *Papillons noirs*;
Les *Lettres Cochinchinoises*;
La *Revue Parisienne*;
Les *Nouveautés à la Main*;
Mettez à contribution les feuilletons du *Corsaire* et du *Charivari*.
Ou il y'a à prendre, prenez; ne vous gênez pas.
Remuez bien le tout; pétrissez, —amincissez, —amolissez, —alongez, —re-

trécissez, —aplatissez; —enveloppez le tout dans une feuille des *Français,* inventés par M. Curmer, et servez chaud.

Ça n'est pas plus malin que cela.

[A pinch of Labruyere; a tablespoon of the *Lettres persannes.* [*sic*] Macerate, in the same container:

Les Guêpes
Les Papillons noirs
Les Lettres Cochinchinoises
La Revue Parisienne
Les Nouveautés à la Main

To all this add the feuilletons of the *Corsaire* and the *Charivari.*

Season to taste with whatever is handy; anything will do. Then, mix well—knead —pull—soften—stretch—squeeze—cut to size—flatten—wrap it all up in a sheet of M. Curmer's *Français* [*peint par eux-mêmes*], and serve hot.

It's as simple as that.]

Although this recipe might suggest the Dada cut-ups of a Tristan Tzara, it more accurately describes the slapdash *bricolage* of the average *physiologie.* As long as he adhered to the standard formula (i.e., the description and classification of a given social type or milieu via a blend of La Bruyere and Buffon), as long as he observed the standard format (120 or so pages, interspersed with 30 to 60 illustrations), the *physiologiste* was free to throw his book together from the recycled detritus of *feuilleton* journalism—anecdotes, warmed over jokes, squibs, vignettes, portraits, descriptions, digressions. His only obligation was to supply the reader with a prescribed dose of easy entertainment and to make sure that the humor never went beyond the bounds of utter innocuousness.

As Walter Benjamin was the first to point out, the innocuousness (*Harmlosigkeit*) and perfect *bonhomie* of the satire contained in the *physiologies* mark them as a basically petit bourgeois genre, virtually devoid of genuine social insight —typical examples, to use Baudelaire's distinction, of the French taste for "le comique significatif" which, unlike "le grotesque comique absolu" of British or German humor, merely reinforces, rather than radically disorients, our most conventional assumptions regarding human nature and society.[10] Benjamin cites the pioneer historian of caricature, Eduard Fuchs, to explain the emergence of this particularly bland mode of satire in France of the thirties and forties. Fuchs sees the rise of the *physiologies* (as well as other examples of panorama literature such as *Les Français peints par eux-mêmes*) as a direct consequence of the political censorship of the theater and press instituted by the Laws of September of 1835.[11] The impact of censorship on the shape of contemporary humor was immediate and dramatic, as is graphically reflected by the suddenness with which the fierce political satire of Philipon's *Caricature* gave way to the milder social mockery featured in his *Charivari.* Baudelaire interprets the depolitization of Philipon's and Daumier's *Robert Macaire* series in the wake of 1835 as emblematic of this transformation: "*Robert Macaire* marks the official beginning of the caricature of customs. The great political battles had subsided a bit . . . the pamphlet gave way to comedy. . . . It's at this point that caricature assumed a different aspect and ceased to be specifically political. It be-came broad social satire. It moved onto the novel's turf." [12]

Following Baudelaire's lead, many historians of literature have linked the *cari-cature de moeurs* of the late thirties and forties, particularly the inventory of social types found in the *physiologies*, to the rise of the realist novel. Maynial's *L'Epoque réaliste* (1931) provides a classic instance of this line of analysis:

> Nulle part les prétentions scientifiques qui sont à la base de la doctrine réaliste, comme on les retrouve plus tard à l'origine du naturalisme, nulle part cette assimilation arbitraire entre l'art de l'écrivain,—celui du romancier en parti-culier,—et la méthode du savant, n'apparaissent mieux que dans ces petites monographies littéraires qui pullulent en France de 1840 à 1850, sous le nom de *Physiologies*. Elles procèdent de deux idées systématiques: les espèces sociales sont, commes les espèces animales, le produit du milieu ou elles se développent; les passions humaines sont, commes les maladies, des cas orga-niques. Derrière cette physiologie, il y a déjà une pathologie. . . .[13]

> > [Nowhere do the scientific pretensions at the basis of the realist doctrine, such as we will find them again at the origins of naturalism, nowhere does this arbi-trary fusion of the writer's art—the novelist's in particular—and the scientist's method appear more clearly than in these small literary monographs which swarm all over France between 1840 and 1850 under the name of *Physiologies*. They stem from two systematic notions: social species are, like their animal counter-parts, the product of their environment; and human passions are, like any illness, physical "cases." Behind this form of physiology one can already detect a certain pathology. . . .]

Although it is certainly no mere coincidence that the *Avant-Propos* to the *Comédie humaine*, which contains Balzac's most ambitious statements on the novelist as taxonomist of "les espèces sociales," was composed at the very height of the *physiologie* vogue (1840–42), and although Balzac himself contributed a *Physio-logie de l'employé* and a *Physiologie du rentier* to the series, it would be misleading to equate Balzac's "scientific" theory of the novel with the taxonomic project of the *physiologies*. Their humorous recourse to the language or method of Buffon, Linneaeus, or Cuvier merely serves to create what Barthes might have termed an *effect de science* whose humor lies in the obvious disproportion between the rarefied scientific technicality of the description and the utter banality of the social species in question.

Balzac is a master of this kind of humor, as in his celebrated *Monographie du rentier*:

> Rentier. Anthropomorphe selon Linné, Mammifère selon Cuvier, Genre de l'Order des Parisiens, Famille des Actionnaires, Tribu des Ganaches, le *Civis inermis* des anciens, découvert par l'abbé Terray, observé par Silhouette, maintenu par Turgot et Necker, définitivement établi aux dépense des Pro-ducteurs de Saint-Simon par le Grand-Livre. Voici les caractères de cette Tribu remarquable adoptée aujourd'hui par les micrographes les plus distingués, de

la France et de L'Etranger. Le Rentier s'élève entre cinq à six pieds de hauteur, ses mouvements sont généralement lents, mais la Nature attentive à la con-servation des espèces frêles, l'a pourvu d'Omnibus à l'aide desquels la plupart des Rentiers se transportent d'un point à l'autre de l'atmosphère parisienne, au delà de laquelle ils ne vivent pas. Transplanté hors de la Banlieue, le Rentier dépérit et meurt.[14]

> [Rentier. Anthropomorphous according to Linnaeus, mammiferous according to Cuvier, Genus of the Parisian Order, Family of the Stockholders, Tribe of the Blockheads, the *Civis inermis* of the ancients, discovered by Father Terray, ob-served by Silhouette, supported by Turgot and Necker, definitely established, at the expense of Saint-Simon's Producers, by public debt. These are the characteris-tics of this remarkable tribe adopted by today's most distinguished micrographers, both in France and abroad. The Rentier stands anywhere between five and six feet tall, his movements are generally slow, but Nature, which tends to preserve the weaker species, has provided him with the Omnibus, by means of which most Rentiers can move from one point to the other within the Parisian atmosphere, outside of which they cannot survive. Transplanted beyond the outskirts of the city, the Rentier wastes away and dies.]

This can no more be read as a "realistic" description than any of the other portraits included in the gallery of the *physiologies*. The discourse of science is merely de-ployed as an intertextual model to be comically subjected to rewriting. Natural science is not appropriated for its method, but merely for the *code* it affords the writer: Balzac's semiotic play with the system of taxonomic description (or historical allusion) is so explicitly foregrounded as to completely overshadow any mimetic relation this text might bear to an actual *rentier*. Although the *physiologies* might therefore seem to be parodying, and thereby devaluing, the classificatory enterprise of the natural sciences, there is nothing even vaguely subversive about their humor. Far from carnivalizing (in Bakhtin's sense of the term) scientific discourse, they merely parasitically echo its formulas, for beyond providing a ready-made descrip-tive system or *poncif*, the discourse (*logos*) of a Buffon or Cuvier allows the social to be read as reassuringly natural (*physis*) — as natural, say, as the automatic repeti-tion of a *lieu commun* or cliché.[15]

One should oppose Maynial's rather misleading assimilation of the *physiologies* to realism to Walter Benjamin's more penetrating analysis of these works as an expression of a petit bourgeois ideology which has less to do with the "realistic" or "scientific" depiction of social reality than with its systematic occultation into what Benjamin terms "l'univers d'une fantasmagorie." In "Paris, Capitale du XIXe siècle," an essay composed in French in 1939 as an introduction to his un-finished masterpiece of surrealist historiography, *Das Passagen-Werk*, Benjamin sketches the major emblems of this modern urban phantasmagoria: the *passages*, the *expositions universelles*, the *flâneur*, the collector, and the typological represen-tation of society found in the *physiologies*.[16] If Benjamin was the first historian to analyze the ideological significance of the *physiologies* (and to dissociate them from the various *idées reçues* about the rise of realism), it was because he was above all fascinated with the transformation of Paris into a "cité pleine de rêves" (Baudelaire) or an "Unreal City" (T. S. Eliot), that is, its metamorphosis under capitalism into a ghost town populated by phantom figures and phantom desires, an uncanny marketplace in which all objects, all human relations have been transformed into commodities, into reproducible signs or fetishes, each an identical copy of the other.

The phantasmagoria of repetition is closely associated with the *Zertrümmerung der Aura* ("decay of the aura") which Benjamin describes in his seminal essay "The Work of Art in the Age of Mechanical Reproduction."

> The contemporary decay of the aura . . . rests on two circumstances, both of which are related to the increasing significance of the masses in contemporary life. Namely, the desire of contemporary masses to bring things "closer" spatially and humanly, which is just as ardent as their bent toward overcoming the uniqueness of every reality by accepting its reproduction. Every day the urge grows stronger to get hold of an object at very close range by way of its likeness, its reproduction. . . . To pry an object from its shell, to destroy its aura, is the mark of a perception whose "sense of the universal equality of things" has increased to such a degree that it extracts it even from a unique object by means of reproduction.[17]

The *physiologies* may be taken as manifestation of this decay of the aura, since they are reproductions or copies in several senses of the term. First, as commodities produced for mass consumption, their commercial value obviously lay in their cheap reproducibility and in the sheer quantity of copies sold—at a time when the average printing of a book was 1,000 to 2,000 copies, a number of *physiologies* reached editions of 10,000 copies or more. But the *physiologies* were copies in another sense as well: inasmuch as they pretended to be accurate (albeit satiric) representations of contemporary social types, they functioned as latter-day versions of the *speculum consuetudinis*, that is, they provided a reproduction (both in image and text) of familiar models drawn from modern life, designed to render the full range of social diversity more visible, more legible, and more accessible to their readership. This purported mimesis of current *moeurs*, however, is entirely subordinate to their (comic) imitation or rewriting of the codes of scientific or journalistic discourse: if they imitate anything, then, it is not contemporary social life, but rather the immense fund of the *déjà-écrit* and *déjà-lu* which Barthes identifies with *la doxa*. More often than not, moreover, the *physiologies* simply imitate each other, each publisher trying to get in on the fad and accusing the others of plagiarism, as in the following notice inserted in the *Physiologies du Gamin de Paris, du Poète, de la Presse*, and *du Viveur*:

> Il est important de ne pas confondre notre série avec tous ces mauvais petits livres que notre succès a fait naître, et qui n'ont pris le titre de *Physiologie* que pour profiter de la vogue dont jouit notre Collection.

[It is important not to confuse our series with all those nasty little books conceived in the wake of our success, which have assumed the title of *Physiologies* only to profit from the vogue that our Collection has been enjoying.]

As Benjamin reminds us, it is not the least of the paradoxes of the Age of Mechanical Reproduction that every copy, every imitation, every commodity, should aspire to the auratic status of the original, the unique, the "one and only."

So it is with the procession of figures represented in the *physiologies*: each type (or each volume) is singular, different, individual, and yet each one, filtered through the same taxonomic lens, and encapsulated in the same package, is virtually identical. In this respect, the gallery of Parisian life placed on display in the *physiologies* serves a "myth" not unlike the one analyzed by Barthes in his discussion of the photographic exhibit, *The Family of Man*:

This myth functions in two stages: first, one affirms the difference between human morphologies, one overdoes exoticism, one parades the infinite variations of the species, the diversity of skins, skulls, and customs, one babelizes the image of the world as one pleases. Then, out of this pluralism, one magically plucks a unity: man is born, works, laughs, and dies the same way everywhere; and if among all these activities there still remain any ethnic particularities, one at least implies that at the basis of each there exists an identical "nature," that their diversity is merely a question of form which in no way denies the existence of a common matrix. This obviously amounts to postulating a human essence, and thus God is reintroduced into our Exhibit.[18]

While the *physiologies* are of course less concerned with exotic ethnic or cultural images than with contemporary social or professional classifications, they nevertheless homogenize difference in very much the way Barthes describes: the order of culture is equated with the order of nature (hence the recourse to the vocabulary of the natural sciences), and social idiosyncrasies are in turn shown to be nothing more than a manifestation of a common "human essence" — or perhaps one should say a common French, and more specifically, a common *Parisian* essence — over which the *physiologiste* casts his bemused and God-like glance.

"Transplanted beyond the outskirts of the city, the Rentier wastes away and dies" — Balzac's insistence on the thoroughly Parisian habitat of this *espèce sociale* is typical of the way in which each *physiologie* stresses the Parisianness of the type or phenomenon it describes, and no doubt the deliberately topical, local color of these little books contributed considerably to their commercial success. The Parisianness they celebrate is grounded in a fundamental strategy of exclusion: provincial life (with few exceptions) is omitted from the field of representation, as is the world of the upper classes and the aristocracy. As for the *classes laborieuses*, or *le peuple*, or the homeless lumpen proletariat of Paris, they barely exist.[19] The social world portrayed in the *physiologies* is a universe at once full and empty — full to the extent that it conjures up an illusory panorama of human diversity, but empty to the extent that this wealth of urban portraiture, based as it is on the

Figure 3

systematic exclusion of the non-bourgeois, of the other, does little more than repeat, in different versions, the recurrence of the same.

Commenting on the tendency of the *physiologies* to represent the population of Paris as a petit bourgeois assemblage of amusing oddballs and harmless eccentrics, Walter Benjamin observes: "Such a view of one's fellow man was so remote from experience that there were bound to be uncommonly weighty motives for it." [20] Among the motives he adduces is the particular uneasiness associated with the emergence of the modern urban crowd. If the *physiologies* and panorama literature in general were so popular, he suggests, it was because they served to reduce the crowd's massive alterity to proportions more familiar, to transform its radical anonymity into a lexicon of nameable stereotypes, thereby providing their readers with the comforting illusion that the faceless conglomerations of the modern city could after all be read—and hence mastered—as a legible system of differences. Armed with the appropriate *physiologie*, the Parisian citizen could be reassured that the anonymous *passante* (figure 3) glimpsed in the crowd was not (to choose from a few titles in the series) a specimen of *La Femme Honnête* or *La femme la plus malheureuse du monde* or *La Fille sans nom* or *La Grisette* or *Le Bas-bleu*, but rather that she was a representative member of the species known as *La Lorette*. Consulting his *Physiologie de la lorette* (text by Maurice Alhoy, vignettes by Gavarni), he might further discover the etymology of the name of the species (from

Notre-Dame-de-la-Lorette), its characteristic foibles (a weakness for hats, an inability to spell), its favorite activities (dancing), its feeding habits (chocolates, *marrons glacés*), its means of survival (usually provided by a gentleman generically known as an "Arthur"), and a detailed nomenclature of its various subspecies:

> La Lorette échappe à la définition.
> On l'explique pas, on l'analyse, on la classe.
> . . . .
> Nous avons promis une nomenclature. Nous pensons qu'on peut fractionner ainsi la grande famille des Lorettes.
> Première grande division du genre:
> 1. La Lorette sous puissance de père et mère.
> 2. La Lorette émancipée.
> Division de l'espèce qui peut s'allier à la classification du genre.
> 1. La Lorette plébéienne.
> 2. La Lorette avec aieux.
> 3. La Lorette à parents anonymes.
> 4. La Lorette exotique.

> > [The Lorette eludes all definition.
> > She cannot be explained, she can only be analyzed, classified.
> > . . . .
> > We have promised a nomenclature. This is how we may break down the large family of Lorettes.
> > First major division of the genus:
> > 1. The Lorette under parental sway.
> > 2. The emancipated Lorette.
> > Division of the species which can be added to the classification of the genus:
> > 1. The plebian Lorette.
> > 2. The Lorette with a lineage.
> > 3. The Lorette with anonymous parents.
> > 4. The exotic Lorette.]

This is merely one example among many of the way in which the *physiologies* tend to bagatellize (the verb is Benjamin's) difference. By multiplying taxonomic categorizations and classificatory discriminations borrowed from the natural sciences, the *physiologies* produce a system of differences whose primary purpose would seem to lie in the *reduction* of alterity, or in the masking of those genuine social antagonisms or class conflicts which might otherwise imperil the nervous complacency of their readers.[21]

The taxonomy of *La Lorette* quoted above is drawn from a chapter entitled "Classement des spécialités." The latter term is frequently employed in the *physiologies* and alludes not only to the distinguishing features of a given social species, but also carries definite commercial overtones. Huart's *Physiologie du tailleur*, for example, comments on the recent "mode de la spécialité" among Parisian merchants and shoppers:

En quelques mois nous avons vu s'établir des pharmaciens spéciaux ne vendant qu'une espèce de drogue, soit pour les dents, soit pour les yeux; ou des chapelleries spéciales, où l'on ne vend que des chapeaux sur lesquels on doit s'asseoir lorsqu'on va en société; ou des boulangeries spéciales, où l'on ne vend que des petites tartes aux cérises, etc. etc.

> [In the last few months we have seen the establishment of special pharmacists who sell only one type of drug, whether for the teeth or for the eyes; or special hatters who only sell hats to be sat on when paying social calls; or special bakeries, where they only sell small cherry tarts, etc. etc.]

The *Physiologies des physiologies* in turn seizes on "la spécialité" as a phenomenon which, more than any other, defines the particular originality or *cachet* of the nineteenth century:

Or savez-vous quelle est cette spécialité de notre siécle? Cette spécialité, Messieurs, n'est autre chose que la spécialisation. Spécialisez-vous! Spécialisez-vous! La science universelle, aujourd'hui, crève de faim; le génie a des bas troués et des fonds de culottes: la spécialité prospère.

> [Now, do you happen to know what this century's specialty is? Our century's specialty, Ladies and Gentlemen, is none other than specialization. Specialize! Specialize! Universal knowledge is starving these days, genius has holes in its stockings and patched pants, but specialization thrives.]

The *physiologies* themselves, the anonymous author continues, are merely another instance of the specialization of every sphere of contemporary activity:

Aussi, voyez—tout se divise et se subdivise. M. A. . . . a la spécialité des petits pâtés et M. B. . . . celles des tartes.—M. C. . . . celles des pantalons et M. D. . . . celle des gilets.—Chacun sa partie, comme on dit, chacun son talent. Dans le Journal du Hanneton litteraire, M. J. . . . a la spécialité du feuilleton-nouvelles, M. K. . . . celles des revues de théâtre. M. O. . . . celle des canards, M. V. . . . celles des premiers-Paris, etc. etc. etc.
Or, voici une nouvelle spécialisation non moins admirable que celle des petits pâtés, non moins lumineuse que celles des allumettes chimiques—les physiologies.

> [So, you see, everything can be divided and subdivided. Mr. A. . . . specializes in meat pies and Mr. B. . . . in tarts. Mr. C. . . . specializes in trousers and Mr. D. . . . in vests. To each his lot, as the saying goes, to each his talent. In the *Journal of the Literary May-bug*, Mr. J. . . . specializes in feuilleton news, Mr. K. . . . in theatrical reviews, Mr. O. . . . in scandal columns, Mr. V. . . . in society pages, etc. etc. etc.
> And now we have a new specialization, at least as admirable as meat pies and as luminous as sulphur matches: the *Physiologies*.]

The notion of *spécialité* thus links the classificatory enterprise of the *physiologies* to a concrete economic and professional context. Not only was each book the

Figure 4

product of a specialized division of labor between author and illustrator, but the various contributors to the series tended to gravitate toward their own areas of expertise: Monnier, for example specialized in the Bourgeois (aka Joseph Prud-homme), Gavarni's specialty was the Grisette or Lorette, Huart's forte was the vignette drawn from street life, etc. The marketing of the *physiologies* by such firms as Aubert (36 titles) and Desloges (17 titles) further reflects the transformation of publishing companies and bookstores into purveyors of *spécialités*. A drawing that reoccurs in several of the *physiologies* represents a crowd of curious observers loitering in front of the shop windows of the Maison Aubert in the Galerie Véro-Dodat, eager to glimpse the latest caricatures of the *Charivari* or the most recent addition to the *physiologies*. The drawing (figure 4) nicely captures the public's narcissistic fascination with images of itself, while underscoring the fact that both the books and the social types they illustrate are *spécialités* on display—*la société en vitrine*.

To view the city as an assemblage of different *spécialités* on exhibit is to reduce its population to the status of merchandise; Benjamin accordingly emphasized the close connection between the vogue for panorama literature and the rising popularity of the trade fairs or *expositions universelles* of the period. "The world expositions construct a world made up of specialities," he notes,"[they] idealize the exchange-value of commodities. They create a framework in which use-value re-

Figure 5

cedes into the background." [22] The privileging of exchange-value over use-value creates that particular kind of commodity which Jean Baudrillard terms *l'objet-signe*, an object not only divorced from functionality, but also from any human reciprocity of exchange: "the object-as-sign no longer derives its meaning from the concrete relation between two people, it derives its meaning from its differential relation to other signs." [23] One might argue that the *physiologies* similarly transform the Parisian world into a universe of human *objet-signes* whose meaning no longer lies in their social interactions but rather in their differential relation to other signs in the series (i.e., the *physiologies*) of which they are part. The *homme-affiche* (figure 5) or sandwichman was for Benjamin the ultimate expression of this process of reification. A walking advertisement (like Baudelaire's dandy), his function is merely to signify, to circulate through the streets of Paris as a mobile sign. He is, in Benjamin's more baroque sense of the term, a peripatetic allegory, since both allegory and commodity entail a ghostly and peculiarly modern surplus of signification: "To the singular degradation of things by their signification, which is characteristic of seventeenth-century allegory, corresponds the singular degradation of things by their price as commodities." [24]

As Baudrillard remarks, however, it is not the object in isolation that exercises its fascination on the reader or consumer, but rather its diacritic or differential relation to other signs. For the classic Marxist definition of commodity fetishism, Baudrillard accordingly substitutes the more linguistic concept of the "fetishism of the signifier, that is, the enmeshment of the subject in those aspects of the object which are factitious, differential, codified, systematized. In fetishism, it is not the passion for substances that speaks . . . it is the *passion for code* which by regulating and by subordinating both object and subject offers them over to abstract manipulation." [25] If, according to Freud, the function of the fetish is to signify and systematize difference in order to deny the reality of sexual difference (or of castration, of lack), so the *physiologies* might be said to transform the social world into an utterly predictable, utterly interpretable system of signs or marks which suppresses all problematic social alterity through a standardized code of signification whose attraction lies not in *what* it signifies but rather in the absolute *systematicity* of its signs. Profession, dress, gait, posture, gesture, facial features, manner of speech—all enter into a rigorously determined grammar whose rules, when properly mastered, render the parsing of any social syntagm virtually infallible.

Benjamin liked to quote Balzac's assertion that "la plupart des observateurs de la nature sociale et parisienne peuvent dire la profession d'un passant en le voyant venir." While the authors of the *physiologies* may have shared Balzac's manic confidence in the legibility of the city, they utterly lacked his equally strong intuition of its hidden unintelligibilities. The Paris of the *physiologies*, by contrast, is a universe so codified, so thoroughly textualized as to be completely devoid of ambiguity or enigma. Indeed, it is precisely *because* they rendered the city so readable, so transparent, so reproducible that the *physiologies*, according to Benjamin, paradoxically fostered the urban phantasmagoria which Baudelaire's work would later register. In "Paris, Capitale du XIXe siècle," Benjamin analyzes how this hypertrophy of legibility converts into its exact opposite, and how difference reveals itself as a mere replication of the same. This little-known portion of the essay, first published in *Passagen-Werk* in 1982, is worth quoting in extenso:

The *flâneur* scouts out the marketplace. And in this capacity he is at the same time the explorer of the crowd. The crowd creates a kind of inebriation in the man who abandons himself to it, and this drunkenness is accompanied by very curious illusions, so that upon seeing a passer-by swept up by the crowd, he deludes himself into believing that, on the basis of exterior features alone, he has actually managed to classify and recognize the passing stranger in all the hidden recesses of his soul. The *physiologies* of the period amply document this singular assumption. The typical characteristics recognized in passers-by are so striking to the senses that one is hardly surprised that they should stimulate a curiosity to go beyond them and to seize upon the special singularity of the subject. But the nightmare which corresponds to the illusory perspicacity of the aforementioned physiognomist involves seeing these distinctive traits which are particular to the subject in turn reveal themselves to be nothing but the constitutive elements of a new type; so that even the most sharply defined individuality turns out merely to be a specific instance of a given type. An alarming phantasmagoria thus manifests itself at the very core of *flânerie*. Baudelaire pursues this phantasmagoria most eloquently in "Les Sept Vieillards." This poem deals with an old man of repugnant aspect who reappears seven times in a row. This individual who is presented as one and the same throughout: his various multiplications testify to the anxiety which the city-dweller feels when he is no longer able to break the magic circle of type despite the most eccentric singularities brought into play. Baudelaire characterizes the appearance of this procession as infernal. But the "new" that Baudelaire lay in wait for all his life consists of nothing else but this phantasmagoria of "eternal sameness." [26]

The nightmare of "Les Sept Vieillards"—in which differences vertiginously proliferate in the shape of the same, and in which the identical is uncannily repeated as something other than itself, at once utterly familiar and utterly strange—defines a hallucinatory, surreal experience of Paris which Baudelaire shares with the Flaubert of *L'Education sentimentale*. Significantly enough in Flaubert's case this universe of pandemic stereotype and cliché finds its earliest expression in one of the first texts he ever published—his 1837 "Leçon d'histoire naturelle: Genre Commis," a *physiologie* of (what else?) *le copiste*, anticipating the slapstick phantasmagoria of *Bouvard et Pecuchet* by some forty years.[27]

This phantasmagoria of repetition, as Benjamin also points out, is closely connected to a particularly modern logic of fashion which produces the illusion of the new (*das Immer-Wieder-Neue*) through the manipulation of a closed system of variables which enforce the reiteration of the same (*das Immer-Wieder-Gleiche*). Themselves the product of a short-lived fad, and presumably purchased as "novelty items," the *physiologies* return again and again to the subject of *la mode*—to the classification of hairstyles, hats, gloves, umbrellas, canes. This rhetoric of fashion often takes the form of universal precepts or axioms:

Une jolie femme en parapluie est comme un joli vers faux.

Les provinciales se vêtent; la Parisienne s'habille.
En province, on se couvre; à Paris, on se coiffe.

(*Physiologie de la parisienne*)

Dites-moi, brune rêveuse, comment vous vous gantez, et je vous dirai qui vous êtes.

(*Physiologie du gant*)

[A pretty woman with an umbrella is like a pretty melody just slightly out of tune.

Provincial women dress; Parisian women dress up. In the province they put their hats on; in Paris they wear them.

(*Physiology of the Parisienne*)

Dreamy brunette, tell me how you are gloved and I'll tell you who you are.

(*Physiology of the glove*)]

This last apothegm is of course a variation on one of the *aphorismes du professeur* prefacing Brillat-Savarin's *Physiologie du goût* ("Dis-moi ce que tu manges, je te dirai ce que tu es")—the act of quotation (or the refurbishing of threadbare cliché) underlies both the discourse of the *physiologies* and the codes of fashion to which

Figure 6   *Figure 7*

they so frequently allude. Both are grounded in repetition-as-difference, as the *Physiologie du tailleur* openly admits:

> Or notez que la manière de procéder est toujours la même: on saute d'un extrême à l'autre. . . . Pendant ces derniers temps, les pantalons semblaient n'être confectionnés que pour servir d'étui à parapluies [see figure 6]; c'était gênant, horrible; aujourd'hui on retombe, sans transition, dans les pantalons cosaques [see figure 7] d'il y a quatre ans . . . innovation. Au mois d'octobre prochain, vous pouvez être certain qu'on reviendra au genre fourneau de parapluie qui, alors, sera reçus comme création excessivement nouvelle.

> > [Note how fashion always evolves along the same lines: it jumps from one extreme to the other. . . . Lately, trousers seemed to have been tailored to sheathe umbrellas; they were embarrassing, awful; today we have fallen back, without transition, onto the Cossack pants that were in vogue four years ago . . . an innovation. By next October, you can be sure that we'll be back to the umbrella sheath, which will then be greeted as an exceedingly new creation.]

The tone of observation here is typical of many of the *physiologies*: although the author would seem to be satirically denigrating the inanity of the phenomenon in question, the bemused posture of the social critic more often than not translates into a knowledgeable complicity with the ephemeral vagaries of current fashion, or

Figure 8

into a self-congratulatory celebration of all those trifles, all those nothings which constitute, as it were, the very essence of Parisianness—which is why Balzac could label this kind of writing *rienologie*[28] (see figure 8).

To make the new out of nothing, to create difference out of the same—this according to Benjamin is the most seductive lure of fashion: "The *new* is a quality independent of the commodity's use-value. It is at the origin of that illusion whose indefatigable purveyor is fashion."[29] Benjamin's insight is echoed by Barthes at the conclusion of his *Système de la Mode*:

> Fashion is no doubt part and parcel of all those occurrences of *neomania* which probably first appeared in our civilization with the birth of capitalism: the "new," in a totally institutionalized manner, is a value one purchases. But the "new" of Fashion seems to fulfill a well-defined anthropological function in our society, a function which has to do with its ambiguity: at once unpredictable and systematic, regular and unknown, aleatory and structured, the "new" fantastically links the intelligibility without which man could not live to the unpredictability associated with the myth of life.[30]

Barthes' semiology of fashion, and in particular his analysis of its systems of classification, could be fruitfully applied to the *physiologies* as a whole. Like fashion, they produce the mirage of the new, of the different, by multiplying the *signifiés* of the same *signifiant*, or, inversely, by generating synonyms from a single *signifié*. Their economy, like that of fashion, is therefore based on the reduction of the semantic to the semiological. Or to follow Baudrillard, both the system of fashion and the *physiologies* strip things of their use value in order to insert them into the perfectly closed (and narcissistic) space of a *collection*.[31]

One of the major selling points of the *physiologies*, as we have seen, had to do with their marketing as a collection—a concept shared, significantly enough, by both the world of fashion (as advertisements of the 1840s already indicate) and the world of publishing.[32] Not only is each book defined as an item whose identity (or value) is solely determined by its relation to other volumes in the same series, but each social type treated by the *physiologies* tends to be described in terms of a collection. Often this takes the form of an inventory of metonymic attributes, as in the following collection of items which, according to the *Physiologie de l'homme à bonnes fortunes*, characterize the perfect Don Juan:

—Un tailleur,
—De la pomade pour les lèvres,
—Un bottier,
—De la pomade pour les cheveux,
—Un coiffeur,
—De la pomade pour la peau,
—Un chapelier,
—De la pomade pour les yeux,
—Quelques paires des gants,
—De la pomade pour n'importe où,
—Et un père, etc.

> [—A tailor, —A pomade for the lips, —A shoemaker, —A pomade for the hair, —A hairdresser, —A pomade for the skin, —A hatter, —A pomade for the eyes, —A few pairs of gloves, —A pomade for everywhere, —And a father, etc.]

A similar technique is applied in the *Physiologie du flâneur* (text by Huart, vignettes by Alophe, Daumier, and Maurisset)—although here the species is not so much defined by the enumeration of its attributes or belongings as by its opposition or juxtaposition to other specimens within the same class. Collection here functions as an expanded form of definition, or as the predication of a given subject or name by a series of synonyms or antonyms. Chapter 1 rehearses the difficulty of defining the type (citing the obligatory tag from La Fontaine, "Nothing more common than the name, nothing rarer than the thing"), and then goes on to assemble a series of examples which mark the *flâneur* off (either by contrast or by contiguity) from other occupants of the same semantic field. Chapter 2, entitled "Can anyone be a *flâneur*?" lists the classes of those unfortunates who are excluded from the activity ("hunchbacks," "the lame," "the fat," "the rich," "the indebted"). Chapter 3, in turn, proceeds through a catalogue of "All the people who falsely call themselves *flâneurs*" ("little old rentiers," "the sedentary," "all the Sunday *flâneurs* around Montmartre"). The following chapters go on to discriminate between the *flâneur* and a series of nearly (but not entirely) synonymous types: *Le Musard*, *Le Badaud étranger* (or tourist), *Le Batteur de pavé*, whose family includes "le tireur" (or pickpocket), "le bonjourien" (or burglar), "l'américain" (or con man, figure 9),

Figure 9

Figure 10

Figure 11

and *Le Chiffonnier* (figure 10).[33] It is only at chapter 8 that this taxonomic pere-grination finally arrives at a definition of *Le Parfait Flâneur* (figure 11) in all his pedestrian splendor—divided into three classes ("poets," "artists," "minor bureau-crats"), and close cousin to two other street types, *Le Flâneur militaire* and *Le Gamin de Paris.*

The *Physiologie du flâneur*, like most of the volumes in the series, is organized like a family album. We pass from item to item (or from image to image) witnessing the various declensions of a common theme or name. The sequential order of the elements placed on display is more or less arbitrary. We do not so much follow the progressive unfolding of a story as stroll our way, like the *flâneur*, through a medley of anecdotal and taxonomic digressions. Visually the text is broken into short, often fragmentary sentences, paragraphs, and chapters, and punctuated by the frequent incursion of illustrations. The narrative dimension of the text, in other words, is relatively unimportant; the emphasis lies rather on the organization of its elements into a descriptive system or collection. As Philippe Hamon observes, the most fundamental conventions of literary description—whether they involve the *ekphrasis* of the Greeks, the *blasons* of the Renaissance, or the portraiture of a Balzac or Flaubert—derive from the procedures of collection, inventory, enumeration, classification.[34] It is not at all coincidental that the *physiologies* should so thoroughly conflate description with collection: both practices (as Hamon notes) are governed by the principle of "Qui s'assemble se ressemble;" that is, both tend to convert metonymy into metaphor or, in more Jakobsonian terms, to project the axis of selection onto the axis of combination. For all their numbing banality, the *physiologies* are, curiously enough, closer to the structure of poetry than to the discourse of "realist" prose. They remove social types from the order of narrative and, more crucially, from the order of history. Through the basic device of description or collection, the *physiologies* establish a paradigmatic system of equivalences by ringing changes on the same.

The figure of the *flâneur* is the perfect vehicle for the conversion of the city into collection, since he himself embodies the dominant traits of the collector or *curieux*.[35] "It's true, the *flâneur* produces very little but amasses a great deal," notes the entry in *Les Français peints par eux-mêmes*. Like the collector, his activity is essentially useless, unproductive, superfluous, its economy based not in labor but in leisure, in killing time. The capital he amasses in the course of his peregrinations is entirely immaterial, yet ever in need of replenishment and renewal, consisting as it does of the ephemeral images, fashions, and impressions of daily city life:

> Le flâneur est un être essentiellement complexe, il n'a pas de goût particulier, il a tous les goûts. . . . Il est dilettante, peintre, poète, antiquaire, bibliophile; il déguste en connaisseur un opéra de Meyerbeer, un tableau d'Ingres, une ode de Hugo; il flaire l'Elzivir, hante les baladins et court sus à la grisette. Il a des admirations pour mademoiselle Rachel et des tendresses pour Odry. Vous le rencontrez partout, dans les promenades, aux Bouffes, aux concerts, au sermon, aux Funambules, dans les salons, à la guinguette, au boulevard de Gand et dans la rue de la Grande-Truanderie. Il pose devant les carreaux de Susse, stationné tour à tour au pied de Notre-Dame et près de l'étalage d'un bouquiniste. Ile est curieux, presque indiscret.[36]
>
> [The *flâneur* is an essentially complex organism, he has no specific taste, he has a taste for everything. . . . He is a dilettante, a painter, a poet, an antiquarian, a

bibliophile; he appreciates a Meyerbeer opera, an Ingres painting and a Hugo ode like a connoisseur; he has a nose for Elzivirs, he frequents mountebanks and chases *grisettes*. He admires Mlle Rachel and is fond of Odry. One meets him everywhere, on the promenades, at the Bouffes, at concerts, in church, at the Funambules, in salons, at refreshment stands, on the Boulevard de Gand, and on rue de la Grande Truanderis. He poses in front of the windows of Susse's statuary store, and stations himself at the foot of Notre Dame or in front of booksellers' stalls. He is curious, almost indiscreet.]

The *flâneur's spécialité*, in short, is to be a specialist in everything—and nothing (although he is not to be confused with the gaping *badaud* or *musard*: "There is as much difference between a dawdler and a *flâneur* as between a glutton and an epicure"). The *passages* are his preferred habitat, for it is here, in a space that joins the open bustle of the street with the enclosed security of the *intérieur*, that he can indulge in his favorite pastime, botanizing the crowd, window shopping on the world:

> Le voyez-vous mon flâneur, le parapluie sous le bras, les mains croisées derrière le dos; comme il s'avance librement au milieu de cette foule dont il est le centre, et qui ne s'en doute pas! Tout, autour de lui, ne paraît marcher, courir, se croiser, que pour occuper ses yeux, provoquer ses reflexions, animer son existence de ce mouvement loin duquel sa pensée languit. Rien n'échappe à son regard investigateur: une nouvelle disposition dans l'étalage de ce magasin somptueux, une lithographie qui se produit pour la première fois en public . . . tout est pour lui un texte d'observations.[37]

> [Do you see him, my *flâneur*, an umbrella tucked under his arm, his hands crossed behind his back; see how he moves freely in the middle of this crowd who doesn't even suspect he is its center! Everything around him seems to walk, run, criss-cross, only to catch his eye, provoke his thoughts, animate his existence with the movement without which his mind languishes. Nothing eludes his inquisitive gaze: a new display in the window of this luxury store, a lithograph exhibited for the first time . . . everything to him is a text for observation.]

A mobile mirror at the vortex of the crowd, the *flâneur* provides the perfect perspective from which the city may be seized as a spectacle which surrounds its observer like a diorama, its images ranged around a vacant center like so many items in a shopwindow beckoning the observer into reverie.

"Everything to him is a text for observation"—what the *flâneur* collects is the text of the city, or the city as text. Illustrations frequently represent him not only as an onlooker, but more specifically as a reader. The monograph on the *flâneur* included in *Les Français peints par eux-mêmes*, for example, opens with a *tête de page* by Traviès depicting a *flâneur* holding a newspaper, observing an audience at a puppet show (figure 12). The decorative initial, functioning as a transition between illustration and text, depicts a capital C covered with posters which a *flâneur*, hands clasped behind his back, is in the process of reading. Through the opening in the C we glimpse another *flâneur* observing a man fishing off a bridge over the

Figure 12

Seine (figure 13). If the letter becomes part of the very cityscape it describes, so the *flâneur* is pulled out of that cityscape to become a linguistic inscription, a *signifiant* perfectly suited to his *signifié*: "Do you know of a sign more appropriate to its idea, of a word more exclusively French for designating a completely French personification? *Le flâneur!*"

Huart's *Physiologie du flâneur* similarly portrays him as a consumer or collector of signs. Its *tête de page* shows him in a crowd in front of the display windows of the Maison Aubert in the Passage Véro-Dodat, craning his neck to catch a look at the latest caricatures and *physiologies*, while the decorative initial represents the interior of a printing establishment, as if to underscore the fact that his relation to Paris is purely textual:

Figure 13

Figure 14

Le parfait flâneur . . . doit savoir par coeur toutes les affiches de la capitale, celle des docteurs Albert et Giraudeau, médecins brevetés pour les traitements sans mercure et sans guérison; —celles de M. Leperdriel, breveté pour les taffetas et les petits pois; —celles de M. Darbo, nourrisseur, breveté pour sa tétine, etc., etc. Il doit connaître tout cela et bien d'autres choses encores, car il devient polyglotte par la seule pratique de la flânerie: à force de lire sur les carreaux des marchands

ENGLISH SPOKEN HERE

ou bien

QUI SI PARLA ITALIANO,

il prend une teinture de l'anglais et de l'italien. . . .

> [The perfect *flâneur* must know all the posters of the city by heart: that of the Doctors Albert and Giraudeau, M.D.s specializing in treatments without mercury and without recovery; those of M. Leperdriel, with his certified taffeta and polka-dots; those of M. Darbo, baby-bottle maker, with his certified nipples, etc. etc. He must know all this and much, much more, for the practicing *flâneur* cannot help becoming a polyglot: he acquires English, or Italian inflections just by reading, time after time and on innumerable shop-windows,
>
> ENGLISH SPOKEN HERE
>
> or
>
> QUI SE PARLA ITALIANO.]

The various illustrations interspersed throughout the *Physiologie du flâneur* further emphasize the experience of the city as a site inscribed with codes or traces (e.g., figure 14)—advertisements, posters, shop signs, menus posted in front of restaurants, *canards* hawked on streetcorners, books along the *quais*, graffiti scrawled on walls by schoolchildren.

Linguist, collector, expert in trivia, man of the crowd and slightly eccentric "original," the *flâneur* becomes a metaphor for the *physiologiste* himself or for the *littérateur* in general:

> La flânerie est le caractère distinctif du véritable homme de lettres. Le talent n'existe, dans l'espèce, que comme conséquence; l'instinct de la flânerie est la cause première. C'est le cas de dire avec une légère variante: littérateurs parce que flâneurs.[38]

> > [*Flânerie* is the distinctive characteristic of the real man of letters. Talent does not exist in this species except as consequence of this primary cause: the instinct to be a *flâneur*. Slightly modifying the stock phrase, one could say: *flâneur* first, literary man second.]

If the equation were not clear enough, the article devoted to the *flâneur* in *Les Français peints par eux-mêmes* concludes:

> Qui de nous ne sentira pas dans son coeur quelque secrète sympathie pour cet être si bon, si facile, si inoffensif et si gai qu'on appelle le flâneur? Qui de nous, en interrogeant sa conscience, osera se proclamer assez pur du péché de flânerie pour jeter au flâneur la première pierre? Qui êtes-vous enfin, vous qui lisez ces lignes? Et qui suis-je qui les écris? Un flâneur.

> > [Who among us can help feeling, deep in his heart, some secret fondness for this good, easy, harmless, happy being commonly known as the *flâneur*? Who among us after duly examining his heart, will dare proclaim himself so clear of the sin of *flânerie* as to throw the first stone at the *flâneur*? Who are you, in fact, you, the reader of these lines? And who am I, their writer? A *flâneur*.]

To purchase a *physiologie*, then, is to gain vicarious access to all the prerogatives of *flânerie*: idleness, curiosity, ubiquity, and above all the confidence that the city can be known and mastered as a predetermined play of signs whose elements of chance and difference have virtually been eliminated—for there is finally nothing more predictable than the *imprévu* which the *flâneur* courts in his seemingly aleatory wanderings.

The fantasy of *flânerie* purveyed by the *physiologies* is, as should be evident, fundamentally narcissistic, since to imagine oneself as a *flâneur* is not only to conceive oneself at the center of things, but also to see and admire oneself as an observer, to watch oneself in the act of watching and being watched—all of which is nicely caught by the specular title of *Les Français peints par eux-mêmes* (figure 15). The texts of *physiologies*, filled with chatty intrusions and blatant pokes in the reader's ribs, enact a similar self-reflexive fantasy: forever reminded that he is reading, flattered into complicity with his *physiologiste cicerone*, the reader never risks losing sight of himself in the mirror of the page. The illustrations of the *physiologies* further reinforce this narcissistic relation of observer to observed. Daumier is perhaps the master of the interdynamics of the glance, but nearly every

Figure 15

volume in the series contains numerous drawings whose theme is simply that of people in the act of looking—at themselves, at each other, at the reader—constantly aware of their image in the eye of their beholder. To lack such awareness is immediately to become an object of ridicule or *dupe*. To cite only two drawings (both rich in implications): the *badaud* at the shopwindow of the Maison Aubert (figure 16), so absorbed by the images on display that he is utterly oblivious to the

Figure 16

Figure 17

Figure 18

pickpocket at his side, and the "Provincial à Paris," visiting the Louvre with *livret* in hand, so engrossed in his incomprehension of painting that the art students in the gallery cease copying the masterpieces of the past in order to sketch his caricature (figures 17 and 18).

More frequently, however, the act of observation represented in the *physiologies* is outright voyeuristic (figures 19, 20, 21, and 22)—gentlemen lodgers leering through the keyhole of a *lorette* combing her hair before the mirror, a dandy training his lorgnette on a theater crowd, a woman at a window with a telescope. This titillating confusion of observation with voyeurism reaches at least as far back as Le Sage's *Le Diable boiteux* (1707): his devil Asmodée, who possesses the power to raise the roofs of houses and peer in, reappears in the title of one of the immediate successors to the *physiologie* series, *Le Diable à Paris* (1845–46). The voyeurist appeal of much of the panorama literature of the period is doubtless linked to the security of seeing without being seen. A similar fantasy of invulnerability or invisibility underlies the comforting mechanism of satire in the *physiologies*, for it enables their readers to enjoy the (diabolic, as Baudelaire would say) superiority of laughter without themselves being implicated as targets of ridicule:

> Chacun croit y reconnaître le portrait de son voisin, et en rit. S'il se reconnaissait lui-même, il crierait au scandale. Voilà pourquoi chacun attend avec impatience sa Physiologie, c'est à dire: Le médecin, celle du charlatan; l'avocat, celle du plaideur; le deputé, celle du floueur; le ministre, celle de l'escamoteur; le comédien, celle du saltimbanque.
>
> (*Physiologies des physiologies*)

> [Everybody recognizes in it the portrait of his neighbor, and laughs. If, by any chance, he happened to recognize himself, he would be horrified. That's why everybody is waiting impatiently for his own *Physiology*, that is to say: the doctor is waiting for that of the quack; the lawyer for that of the litigant; the deputy for that of the con man; the minister for that of the conjuror; the actor for that of the buffoon.]

Oscar Wilde quipped in the preface to *The Picture of Dorian Gray*: "The nineteenth century dislike of Realism is the rage of Caliban seeing his own face in a glass. The nineteenth century dislike of Romanticism is the rage of Caliban not seeing his own face in a glass." Something of the same paradox informs the *physiologies*: while they clearly catered to the public's desire to see itself dominate the space of representation, they also flattered the public's illusion that it in no way resembled the caricatural image reflected in the mirror. As Alain Buisine has argued, the *physiologies* encouraged the most characteristic form of petty bourgeois alienation: to misrecognize oneself as other.[39]

There is a more ominous side, however, to the voyeuristic humor of the *physiologies*. Quoting Baudelaire's comment in *Le Peintre de la vie moderne* to the effect that "the observer is a prince who everywhere enjoys his incognito," Benjamin astutely drew the parallel between the *flâneur* (or *physiologiste*) and the detective sleuthing his prey through the urban crowd.[40] In a contemporary review of *Les Français peints par eux-mêmes*, Nerval had similar recourse to a criminological metaphor in describing its authors as a vast network of spies or informers: "It is a police force larger than Fouché's and the *conseil des Dix*. It is an invisible freemasonry that lurks in the darkest corners of our society; it is a conspiracy against our strengths and our weaknesses, it is a thousand hands and a thousand eyes

Figure 19

Figure 20

Figure 21

Figure 22

that watch and write at every minute."[41] Nerval's description rhymes almost perfectly with Foucault's account of panoptism: "And, in order to be effective, this power must avail itself of a constant, exhaustive, ubiquitous surveillance, capable of making everything visible, while itself remaining invisible. It must be like a faceless gaze which transforms the social body into a field of perception: a thousand eyes stationed everywhere, restless and forever alert."[42] To choose only one example among many, a passage from the *Physiologie du voyageur* concerning passports brings into sharp focus the close connection between physiological classification and those procedures of social and political control (or *fichage*) analyzed at length by Foucault in *Surveiller et punir*:

> La meilleure preuve que le passe-port ne ressemble à personne et que personne ne ressemble à son passe-port, c'est l'embarras qu'éprouve le gendarme quand il faut rendre à chacun ses papiers; le gendarme se noie dans cette forêt de cheveux, dans ces faisceaux de nez moyens et de mentons ronds; il finit par inviter chacun à se reconnaître soi-même.
>
> Il y aurait un moyen ingénieux de remplacer les passe-ports, ce serait de donner à chaque brigade de maréchaussée un daguerréotype: au moment où l'on peserait la diligence, tous les voyageurs pourraient être instantanément croqués.
>
> Chaque préfet ferait collection de ces tables artistiques; et si un nez signalé s'avisait de faire des frédaines politiques, on le suivrait dans toutes ces courses. [See figure 23].

> > [The best proof that no passport resembles its bearer and no bearer resembles his passport is the embarrassment of the policeman when he must return a bundle of identification papers to their respective owners; he drowns in this forest of hair, in this profusion of average noses and round chins, and finally ends up inviting everybody to recognize themselves.
> >
> > There could be a clever way of replacing passports, and that would be to provide the constabulary with a daguerrotype camera: while the coach is being weighed, all the passengers could be recorded. Each police chief would collect this portrait gallery; so that whenever a recorded nose decided to pull a political prank, one could follow him on his trail.]

But the last word on this panoptism should be left to the *Physiologie des physiologies*. By a final crushing irony, the anonymous author bemoans the fact that these little books, precisely because they satirically celebrate the diversity of contemporary Parisian life, will usher in a phantasmagoria in which everything and everyone will look absolutely the same:

> Hélas! hélas! Maudits soient les physiologies! Savez-vous ce qui arrivera par elles, avant peu? Les hommes, se voyant ainsi d'agueréotypés [*sic*] corps et âme, sans pouvoir se defendre, feront comme les hommes qui veulent arrêter les regards de la foule, il tireront leurs rideaux. Or, une fois les rideaux tirés, mes maîtres, vous aurez beau braquer votre lunette en tous sens, vous ne verrez plus rien; sinon partout le même voile uniformément blanc, qui ne

Figure 23

laissera rien percer de la comédie que se jouera derrière. . . . Une ressemblance accablante passera sur tous les fronts. Un cordonnier déclamera comme un poète. Une fille publique sourira comme une grande dame. Le garde national aura un air martial et marchera au pas comme un soldat. L'épicier même, s'il le peut, aura de l'esprit pour ses chalans. Vous vous frotterez les yeux, Messieurs les physiologistes, et vous ne découvrerez partout que le même type à dessiner. Non pas un type original, saillant, comme vous en heurtiez naguère à chaque pas. Mais un type tranquille et froid comme l'eau dormante d'un bassin de marbre, sans fleurs, —sans herbes, —sans roseaux, —sans crapauds verts.

> [Alas! alas! Damn these physiologies! Do you know what is going to happen because of them in just a little while? Men, seeing themselves thus daguerrotyped body and soul, and unable to defend themselves will do what those men who want to avoid the eyes of the crowd do—they will pull their curtains. Now, once these curtains are pulled, my dear physiologists, you can point your telescope on anything or anyone you want, but you won't see a thing; except, perhaps, the same uniformly white veil, which won't reveal anything of the comedy that is unfolding

behind it. . . . And then everybody will look alike. A cobbler will recite verses like a poet. A prostitute will smile like a lady. The national guard will assume a martial demeanor and will start marching like a soldier. Even the grocer, if he can, will be witty toward his customers. You will rub your eyes, my dear physiologists, and still you will see nothing to draw but the same type, over and over again. And not an original type either, nothing striking, as you were once used to finding at every step. Now you will only find the same banal type, as calm and cold as the stagnant water of a marble pool, with no flowers, with no grass, with no reeds, with no green toads.]

Notes

1. Further background material on the *physiologies* may be found in Andrée Lhéritier, "Les Physiologies," Claude Pichois, "Le Succès des Physiologies," and Antoinette Huon, "Charles Philipon et la Maison Aubert," all in a special number of *Etudes de la Presse 9/7* (1957). A full-scale study of the *physiologies*, more descriptive than analytical, exists in German: Hans-Rüdiger van Biesbrock, *Die Literarische Mode der Physiologien in Frankreich 1840–1842* (Frankfurt: Peter Lang, 1976). One hundred and nineteen *physiologies* exist on microfilm, ed. W. Hawkins (Paris: Service International de Microfilm, 1966). There are reproductions of a number of *physiologies* in *Portraits et caractères du dix-neuvième siècle* (Paris: Le Club Français du Livre, 1960). Unless otherwise indicated, all translations from French and German are my own.

2. Quoted in Lhéritier, "Les Physiologies," p. 1. Gérard de Nerval, reporting from Brussels in 1846 on the Belgian tendency to imitate (or counterfeit) anything French, similarly comments on the "mille et une physiologies, que Dieu maudisse ce mot, qui fondent sur nous commes des avalanches." (*Oeuvres* [Paris: Editions de la Pléiade, 1961], vol. 2, p. 912). Stendhal in turn responded to the fad by rebaptizing his *De l'Amour* of 1822 as *Physiologie de l'Amour* in a March 1842 "Projet de Préface." (*De l'Amour*, ed. H. Martineau [Paris: Garnier, 1959], p. 330).

3. See Biesbrock, *Die Literarische Mode der Physiologien*, pp. 5–47. Graem Tytler, *Physiognomy in the European Novel* (Princeton: Princeton University Press, 1982), traces the impact of Lavater on novelistic portraiture, while Judith Wechsler, *A Human Comedy: Physiognomy and Caricature in 19th Century Paris* (Chicago: University of Chicago Press, 1982) deals with the visual arts.

4. See Biesbrock, pp. 52–60. Also Karlheinz Stierle, "Baudelaire's 'Tableaux parisiens' und die Tradition des *Tableaux de Paris*," *Poetica 6/2* (1974), pp. 285–322.

5. See Albert Prioult, *Balzac avant la Comédie humaine* (Paris: Courville, 1936), pp. 404–30, as well as his "Les Codes littéraires et Balzac," *L'Année Balzacienne* (Paris: Garnier, 1972), pp. 151–71.

6. Charles Baudelaire, "Quelques caricaturistes français," *Oeuvres Complètes* (Paris: Editions de la Pléiade, 1976), vol. 2, p. 559.

7. Wechsler, *A Human Comedy*, p. 36. For a fuller treatment of the evolution of the illustrated book in the early nineteenth century, see Gordon N. Ray, *The Art of the French Illustrated Book 1700–1914* (Ithaca: Cornell University Press, 1982), vol. 2, pp. 300–324.

8. The term "panorama literature" is Walter Benjamin's. See his *Charles Baudelaire, Ein Lyriker im Zeitalter des Hochkapitalismus*, in *Gesammelte Schriften* (Frankfurt: Suhrkamp, 1980), vol. 1, pt. 2, p. 537.

9. Quoted in Lhéritier, "Les physiologies," p. 5.

10. Charles Baudelaire, "De L'Essence du rire," *Oeuvres Complètes*, vol. 2, p. 535.

11. Benjamin, *Charles Baudelaire*, p. 538.

12. Baudelaire, "Quelques caricaturistes français," p. 555.

13. Edouard Maynial, *L'Epoque réaliste* (Paris: Crès, 1931), p. 40.

14. Honoré de Balzac, "Le Rentier," in *Les Français peints par eux-mêmes* (Paris: Curmer, 1840), vol. 3, p. 1.

15. "The Doxa is popular belief, meaning repeated *as if there were nothing to it,*" Roland Barthes, *Roland Barthes* (Paris: Seuil, 1975), p. 126. The rewriting or reclassification of pre-existing discourses that one finds in the *physiologies* is characteristic of all description. See Philippe Hamon, *Introduction à l'analyse du descriptif* (Paris: Hachette, 1981), p. 5. This tendency toward descriptive "méta-classement" may in turn be related to those techniques of citation and reiteration which Ruth Anossy and Elisheva Rosen analyze in *Les Discours du cliché* (Paris: CDU SEDES, 1982).

16. Walter Benjamin, "Paris, Capitale du XIXe siècle," in *Das Passagen-Werk, Gesammelte Schriften* (Frankfurt: Suhrkamp, 1982), vol. 5, pt. 1, pp. 60–61. This 1939 French version of the essay contains a number of important variants. I have therefore preferred it to the German version.

17. Walter Benjamin, "L'oeuvre d'art à l'époque de sa reproduction mécanisée," trans. Pierre Klossowski, in *Gesammelte Schriften*, vol. 1, pt. 2, p. 713.

18. Roland Barthes, "La Grande Famille des hommes," in *Mythologies* (Paris: Seuil, 1970), p. 14.

19. The only *physiologie* to address itself to the industrial proletariat is Emile de la Bédolliere's bland *Les Industriels, métiers et professions en France* (1841). Walter Benjamin cites a somewhat later *Paris inventeur, Physiologie de l'industrie française* (1844), as a typical example of the reassuring stereotype of the "happy worker" (*Charles Baudelaire*, p. 540). While the *physiologies* reflect a specifically Paris-oriented, petit bourgeois ideology, their rival series, *Les Français peints par eux-mêmes*, at least pretended to a more catholic perspective on French society. The first five volumes are devoted to Parisian types, the following three to provincial life. But even here the representation of the lower classes remains obviously problematic: Léon Gozlan's article on "L'Homme du peuple" in volume 3 of the series provides a telling example of the ideological contortions involved when it comes to representing *le peuple* or the proletariat.

20. Benjamin, *Charles Baudelaire*, p. 539.

21. The dim awareness on the part of the bourgeoisie that it is precariously sitting on a political powderkeg emerges briefly in Maurice Alhoy's *Physiologie du Voyageur*. A steamboat passenger reflects on the worker stoking the furnace below: "My life belongs to a worker who might want to parody the late Erostatos. Two shovelfuls of coal at the wrong moment, and we'll blow up. A fit of pride to outdo a competitor, a sudden revulsion for one's social status, a burst of envy against the happy of the earth, a few centileters more of alcohol in the head of this man, and we'll blow up!" (p. 45). The entire section of this *physiologie* dealing with "excursions maritimes" provides a marvelous intertext for the first chapter of Flaubert's *L'Education Sentimentale.*

22. Benjamin, "Paris, Capitale du XIXe siècle," p. 65.

23. Jean Baudrillard, *Pour une critique de l'economie politique du signe* (Paris: Gallimard, 1972), p. 64.

24. Benjamin, "Paris, Capitale du XIXe siècle," p. 71. The sandwichman reappears throughout the *Passagen-Werk*: "Grundsätzlich is die Einfühlung in die Ware Einfühlung in den Tauschenwert selbst. Der Flâneur ist der Virtuose dieser Einfühlung. Er führt den Begriff der Käuflichkeit selbst spazieren. Wie das Warenhaus sein letzter Strich ist, so ist seine letzte Incarnation der Sandwichman" (*Gesammelte Schriften*, vol. 5, pt. 1, p. 562).

25. Baudrillard, *Pour une critique de l'economie politique du signe*, p. 100.

26. Benjamin, "Paris, Capitale du XIXe siècle," pp. 70–71. This passage does not exist in the German version of the essay.

27. On Flaubert and cliché, see Shoshana Felman, *La Folie et la chose littéraire* (Paris: Seuil, 1978), pp. 157–217; and Anne Herschberg-Pierrot, "Problématiques du cliché: Sur Flaubert," *Poétique* 41 (1970), pp. 334–45. Michael Riffaterre has recently discussed the portrait of "La Femme Adultère" in *Les Français peints par eux-mêmes* as an example of the *sociolecte* which informs the *ideolecte* of *Madame Bovary*: "Flaubert's Presuppositions," in *Flaubert and Postmodern-*

ism, ed. Naomi Schor and Henry Majewski (Lincoln: University of Nebraska Press, 1984). Charles Bernheimer's analysis of *Bouvard et Pécuchet* is also relevant here; see his *Flaubert and Kafka* (New Haven: Yale University Press, 1982), pp. 102–38.

28. In the taxonomy of the "Ordre Gendelette" included in Balzac's *Monographie de la presse*, "Le Rienologie" is a subgenus of "Le Publiciste."

29. Benjamin, "Paris, Capitale du XIXe siècle," p. 71.

30. Roland Barthes, *Système de la Mode* (Paris: Seuil, 1967), p. 302.

31. Jean Baudrillard, *Le Système des objets* (Paris: Gallimard, 1968), pp. 120–50. To transform things into objects of collection, Baudrillard observes, is not only to strip them of their use value, but to subtract them from the contingencies of temporality by inserting them into the perfect synchrony of an autarkic system (p. 135). Despite all their topical allusions, the *physiologies* similarly de-historicize and defunctionalize the material they describe. Classified and subdivided into its component species, rearranged into a collection, the social space of the city can therefore be manipulated and dominated as a field of "partial objects," thereby fulfilling the narcissistic fantasy of a world untroubled by the intrusion of otherness, since each of its serial parts is merely the projection of the self. This is why Baudrillard can speak of a collection as "the perfect elision of the presence of the other" (p. 141) or as a solipsistic mirror which lends itself to "a total environment, to a totalization of one's self-image, which is the very miracle of the collection. For we always collect ourselves" (p. 128). For a more historical perspective on collection in the early nineteenth century, see Pierre-Marc de Biasi, "Système et déviances de la collection à l'époque romantique," *Romantisme* 27 (1980), pp. 77–94.

32. Baudrillard observes: "Surveys show that the customers of book series (*10/18, Que sais-je?*), once they have fallen into the groove of a collection, keep on buying books whether their titles interest them or not: mere difference in the series is enough to create a formal interest that replaces the real one. What pushes people to buy is the sheer power of association" (*Le système des objets*, p. 147).

33. Daumier's drawing of the *chiffonier* (described by Huart as "le flâneur prolétaire, le roi du pavé") is part of the intricate intertextual network which informs Baudelaire's "Le Vin des chiffoniers" and his description of the *chiffonier* in "Of Wine and Haschisch": "He catalogs and collects all that the city has disdained, everything it has broken" (*Oeuvres Complètes*, vol. 1, p. 381). Baudelaire goes on to equate the *chiffonier* with the poet, just as the *Physiologie des physiologies* speaks of the *physiologistes* as "literary ragpickers who fill their books as if they were baskets with everything they find in the mud of the streets" (p. 123). *Chiffonier, physiologiste,* poet, and *flâneur* are, as Benjamin pointed out, all figures of the collector. For further background on images of the *chiffonier* in the early nineteenth century, see Luc Badesco, "Le Vin des chiffoniers," *Revue des sciences humaines* (1957), pp. 57–88; and Benjamin, *Charles Baudelaire*, pp. 520ff.

34. See "Descriptif et taxonomie" in Hamon, *Introduction à l'analyse du descriptif*, pp. 54–61. The relation between description, allegory, and phantasmagoria is explored by Michel Beaujour, "Some Paradoxes of Description," *Yale French Studies* 61 (1981), pp. 27–59. Beaujour's essay nicely complements Benjamin.

35. According to Bloch and Wartburg's *Dictionnaire etymologique* (1960), the term *collectioneur* first occurs in French in 1839; over the course of the nineteenth century it will slowly replace the more traditional term, *curieux* (I thank Joel Hoff for this information). Benjamin devotes an entire section of his *Passagen-Werk* to the collector (Konvolut H): he is a figure not only closely cognate to the *flâneur*, but also to the melancholy brooder (*Grübler*) or allegorist (*Gesammelte Schriften*, vol. 5, pt. 1, pp. 269–80).

36. August de Lacroix, "Le Flâneur," *Les Français peint par eux-mêmes*, vol. 3, p. 67.

37. "Le Flâneur," from *Le Livre des Cent-et-un*, vol. 6, p. 101. Quoted by Stierle, "Baudelaire's 'Tableaux parisiens'," p. 292.

38. Lacroix, "Le Flâneur," *Les Français peints par eux-mêmes*, p. 69.

39. Alain Buisine, "Sociomimesis: physiologie du petit-bourgeois," *Romantisme* 15–18 (1977), pp. 44–55.

40. Benjamin, *Charles Baudelaire*, p. 543.

41. Gérard de Nerval, *Oeuvres Complémentaires* (Paris: Minard, 1959), vol. 1, p. 161.

42. Michel Foucault, *Surveiller et punir* (Paris: Gallimard, 1975), p. 215. Foucault's chapter on "Les moyens du bon dressement," which analyzes the ways in which various codes ("code physique du signalement," "code médical des symptômes," etc.) are deployed to examine, document, and textualize the individual, is also relevant to the strategies of social control implicit in the *physiologies*.

Spiritual Insurance: A Strategy for Psychological Survival / *Helena Waddy Lepovitz*

During the eighteenth century, peasants and craftsmen in the Catholic areas of Central Europe began to buy colorful, framed wall-paintings executed on the back of glass by local village craftsmen. These glass-paintings were used primarily for religious purposes and only as they began losing their market to the popular lithograph in the nineteenth century did the secular use of popular framed art gain real momentum. The changing appearance, subject matter, and significance of popular art form part of a story that begins with the hanging of framed glass-paintings to create a cottage shrine and ends with the decorative display of framed chromolithographs in the various rooms of a working-class home.[1]

The glass-paintings hanging from the pole of a hawker or resting in the framework of his pack were designed to appeal to the interests and pocketbooks of a wide range of customers. Yet he was unlikely to be carrying much more than a selection of biblical and doctrinal themes. These might have included New Testament scenes drawing from stories of Jesus's life. The Annunciation, the Nativity, the Flight into Egypt, the Holy Family at work, the Last Supper, Jesus on the Mount of Olives, the Scourged Christ, the Stations of the Cross, the Crucifixion itself, and the Holy Grave were all popular subjects. Such a display would also have included a selection of the many saints augmenting Catholic religious beliefs who appear in glass-paintings bearing attributes that drew attention to their life stories and paintings of the central doctrinal figures of Jesus, Mary, and the Holy Trinity. All such wares reflected the development of a variety of local renditions, not only for each theme but also for all its subcategories. Moreover, the heritage of both medieval and Renaissance iconographical traditions meant that these motifs showed varying degrees of humanistic or hieratic intent.

The style and use of color and decor in glass-paintings varied enormously. Treatment of subject matter was complemented by the choice of border surrounding it and much of the beauty of glass-paintings emerges from the intense color and pleasing design of these borders, sometimes highly elaborate. Juxtaposition of strong colors gave the paintings a brilliance and power that clearly attracted the eye of consumers. Pfarrer Bäumer gives expression to this appeal in a letter written to Mathias Noder of Seehausen in 1816 placing an order for 4,000 paintings. "The crown over Mary's head and the stars, also God the Father's hat and the halo around Jesus's head, also the Holy Ghost must be made with gold rays and the background must be completely white, so that the painting shines more brightly to the eye." Framing was an important selling point, as Pfarrer Bäumer's letter confirms since he specifies not only the color and design of the paintings, but also that they must be framed.[2] Such frames could be simply constructed of plain or colored wood or decorated with floral designs. Identical framing often emphasized the pairing of paintings so common for users in the nineteenth century.

A substantial range in size and price of glass-paintings is proof of the craftsmen's deliberate intention to market their product so that all but the poorest customers could afford them. Comparison with food prices in Bavaria for the early nineteenth century suggests that, for example, a pair of Josef Wüstner of Schönstein's small paintings of saints represented the sacrifice of about a dozen eggs, while a pair of Alois Gege of Seehausen's souls in purgatory paintings cost no more than a large glass of beer.[3] Research by Reinhard Haller into a series of inventories from the Bodenmais area of Lower Bavaria suggests that landed farmers and wealthier crafts-men, particularly innkeepers, millers, and shopkeepers, were important consumers of glass-paintings. Unmarried persons, servants, and retirees owned the fewest paintings, if they had any at all. Poorer households, it seems, had their share of paintings, but on a smaller scale than that of their wealthier neighbors.[4]

These devotional objects were not considered luxury purchases but necessary household items. They contributed to the creation of a household shrine, usually centered above the dining table in one corner of the living room. In this *Herr-gottswinkel* (literally, "Lord God's corner") a crucifix hung directly in the corner, while glass-paintings or paper prints flanked it on either side. J. M. Ritz notes that delimitation of the *Herrgottswinkel* "is connected to the importance and early development of the living room in upper German farmhouses. It is the scene of common meals and of all the communal activities of the household." A picture of the fundamental role played by this family shrine in Southern German Catholic households emerges from Ritz's general research into inventories, as it does from Haller's more specific survey of Bodenmais inventories. Both establish that not only the dining table but also the crucifix were fixtures belonging to the house itself. Haller adds that the paintings too, although normally personal possessions, would sometimes remain with the house when it was sold, while Ritz suggests that all the contents of the *Herrgottswinkel* were left as fixtures.[5] Retirees usually took few or no paintings with them to their rooms. In the case of the widow of Mathias Bergmann, her husband's will stipulated that although she could enjoy the use of the couple's paintings and other devotional objects during her lifetime, they were to revert to the holding after her death. When inventory takers entered the home of a deceased Bodenmais villager, their orientation in listing the household's possessions reflected the customary prominence afforded the *Herrgottswinkel*. Crucifix and paintings always appear first on the list, followed immediately by the dining room table. It is no wonder that so strong an identification of household with household shrine influenced the purchase of glass-paintings by homemakers rather than single persons, while the importance of these symbols to household unity serves to explain the extent of their popular market.[6]

The attraction of glass-paintings over paper prints for Catholic families, as Dr. Netto suggested in 1840, was part of a wish to adorn "their house-altars with a Raphael Madonna or with protective saints in a copy which radiates the brilliant color of an original." This accounts for their success in capturing so large a market during the nineteenth century.[7] Inexpensive, colorful, and aesthetically pleasing objects of art, they found their way by the thousands into houses throughout Central Europe. A skeptic might argue that such a painting's appeal was no more than decorative, that the *Herrgottswinkel* itself was no more than a conventionalized form of household arrangement and decor. Its function would thus be reduced to a social "keeping up with the Joneses," or an echo of familial custom, mixed with personal aesthetic preference. But it is my argument that the function of religious glass-paintings was fundamental to the operation of a Catholic household. There is a great deal of evidence to show that their significance for the members of the household included a frame of reference that extended far beyond limited social implications and economic symbolism.

The anthropologist Robert Redfield's distinction between the "immanent" and "transcendent" functions of art is helpful in identifying the varied uses to which the paintings could be put.[8] Redfield associates immanence with the aesthetic impact of form and certainly the decorative nature of glass-paintings did fill an aesthetic need for the consumer. Yet each glass-painting presents a subject that extends the implications of the image beyond form to substance, beyond immanent or aesthetic enjoyment to transcendent meaning. Redfield reminds us that primitive artists use "a highly formalized, intensely local and very long established style."[9] But the transcendent references of images produced in eighteenth- and nineteenth-century Bavaria were not even necessarily the same as those of very similar images appearing elsewhere in Europe at the same or other periods. Any interpretation of the meanings assigned to such images by the Central European Catholic customers of glass-paintings must take into account the specific cultural context in which those customers made transcendent use of their paintings.

This is an enterprise fraught with practical difficulties due to lack of evidence, but it is also a conceptual problem as a recent article by Stuart Clark in *Past and Present* reminds historians of popular culture.[10] Clark is particularly critical of those historians of French peasantry who, he claims, have failed to avoid the conceptual pitfalls already encountered by anthropologists. They suggest that "preoccupied with surviving in hostile, mysterious surroundings, lost in a world of which they had only imprecise knowledge, simple men became victims of severe, even psychotic anxiety," which their culture then reflected. According to Clark such authors have fallen into the trap of "comparing the limitations of one period or society with the more real achievements of a later" by viewing that society's understanding of the world as "mere approximations of ideal descriptions of things, as if their entire discourse was the product of a conjectural blunder." Clark argues further that

> it is . . . conceptual propriety and not the weight of any evidence which demands that we take for granted the existence of categories in terms of which the world made perfectly good sense to the early modern peasant and he could engage in all manner of practices with perfectly reasonable expectations of success or failure.

Eric Hobsbawm phrases a similar plea in the language of class when he asks that we "see mentality . . . as a problem . . . of the discovery of the internal logical cohesion of systems of thought and behavior which fit in with the way in which people live in society in their particular class and in their particular situation of the class struggle."[11]

However, cultural systems can become outdated as mechanisms for interpreting and dealing with new social conditions. William Bouwsma has argued recently that the "peculiar anxiety" of Europeans in the late Middle Ages and Renaissance periods in contrast to that of the previous two centuries was "a problem of culture and of its capacity to manage and reduce the anxiety of existence." The medieval culture of "boundaries" became increasingly inappropriate to a new social and to a large extent urban reality.

> No objective system of boundaries could now supply either security or effec- tive guidance. When man still clung to the old culture, he seemed to have become, in spite of himself, a trespasser against the order of the universe, a violator of its sacred limits, the reluctant inhabitant of precisely those dan- gerous borderlands—literally no man's land—he had been conditioned to avoid. But his predicament was even worse if this experience had taught him to doubt the very existence of boundaries. He then seemed thrown, dis- oriented, back into the void from which it was the task of culture to rescue him. And this, I suggest, is the immediate explanation for the extraordinary anxiety of this period. It was an inevitable response to the growing inability of an inherited culture to invest experience with meaning.[12]

But the popular culture of this late medieval and early modern period, which was based primarily in rural areas, still drew its strength from the older culture of "boundaries." Relying on premises of supernatural explanation, it provided a com- plete system of definitions and imagery that proved remarkably adaptable when meeting the challenge of social change. It seems reasonable to assert, on the basis of Bouwsma's analysis, that it was not the peasants of early modern Europe who displayed psychotic symptoms in the face of a dimly perceived "real" world, but the members of better educated classes who experienced anxieties as they gradually forged a new culture out of the old. New popular Catholic practices for the man- agement of problems did emerge during the period, such as the concept of offering votive paintings in the shrines of cult images.

But these cultural forms drew from older folk traditions, merely reshaping them to provide new categories of meaning and action. The multiplicity of popular religious practices prescribed to deal with a multiplicity of problems does suggest that such practices served to reduce an anxious concern about the future, and beyond that about death and judgment, into more manageable "fears." For, as Bouwsma argues, "Fear is distinguishable from anxiety by the specificity of its object; and because the object of fear is concrete and may be dealt with by some appropriate action, fear can be reduced or overcome."[13] But there is no particular reason to project the metaphysical dimension of anxiety described by Bouwsma onto the recurrent popular technique for providing specific solutions for specific fears. The old Catholic culture served well enough, and, at least in Southern Germany, it was only very gradually, though more swiftly in the nineteenth century, that belief in various forms of supernatural intervention gave pride of place to new cultural forms of problem solving or explanation.

It is in the context of the particular Bavarian form of Catholic culture that analysis of both the *Herrgottswinkel* and the glass-paintings must be located. As a culturally prescribed religious form belonging to a coherent and comprehensive cultural system, the *Herrgottswinkel*'s place within that system controlled the meanings it conveyed to its users. It would be easy to argue that, operating from within the religious system to which they belonged, the images displayed in the *Herrgottswinkel* were primarily intended to relate to the cultural mechanisms beyond that system, in particular to ways of dealing with specific fears about central household concerns. That was indeed one of their basic functions. But it would be wrong to limit so complex a group of images in this way. Popular Catholic culture during the period made use of religious symbols in so comprehensive a way that it is necessary to find a means of defining not one but many relationships between these religious images and the cultural context to which they belonged.

The primary transcendent meaning of such images should actually be defined as iconic, because of their place in the religious system. Yet their significance reached beyond the iconic to encompass areas of meaning that not only included the resolution of practical concerns but also extended to a range of reference including the spiritual and therefore impractical. Their iconic nature made these images desirable as focal points for a variety of questions and actions: they served as what Victor Turner has called "dominant" symbols, compressing many meanings into one "multi-vocal" image.[14] Moreover each multi-vocal symbol combines referents polarized into two major groupings that Turner labels "orectic" and "normative." Their meaning is at once "grossly physiological, . . . relating to general human experience of an emotional kind," and ethical, relating "to moral norms and principles governing the social structure." Turner's emphasis in defining the orectic power of symbols rests on their ability to "express and mobilize desire."[15] As he argues later in another context,

> ritual is not just a concentration of referents, of messages about values and norms; nor is it simply a set of practical guidelines and a set of symbolic paradigms for everyday action, indicating how spouses should treat each other, how pastoralists should classify and regard cattle, how hunters should behave in different wild habitats. . . . It is also a fusion of the powers believed to be inherent in the persons, objects, relationships, events, and histories represented by ritual symbols. It is a mobilization of energies as well as messages.[16]

Turner's theoretical analysis of ritual imagery permits the kind of flexibility needed to identify the many relationships between image and cultural systems that the *Herrgottswinkel* represents. Working with both the categories he identifies, the normative and the orectic, it is possible to construct a horizontal diagram of an ideal range of referents to which a single image could lead the viewer. But because of the religious nature of the images, a vertical line of significance is needed to complete their potential range of meanings, since they combine supernatural and natural references in a way that quite clearly distinguishes the properties of each. If the category "supernatural" or "miraculous" is to exist, it is surely necessary for a distinct category "natural" to be clearly defined first. Indeed, we need look no further than the treatment of supernatural and natural in the images themselves to find this distinction in operation. To say, as Michael Phayer did recently, that "for Baroque man, who saw his world as an extension of the spirit world, reality was a blur" is patently misleading in the face of clear evidence to the contrary.[17] The horizontal plane of relationship to spiritual and practical meanings must intersect with a vertical plane of supernatural and natural reference to the powers and life histories of the religious figures portrayed (see figure 1).

This kind of model should allow us to fulfill Natalie Zemon Davis's stipulation that "we examine the range of people's relations with the sacred and the supernatural, so as not to fragment those rites, practises, symbols, beliefs and institutions which to villagers or citydwellers constitute a whole."[18] But we must recognize that the multiple reference of each symbol was curtailed by the same cultural context that invested it with such a width of meaning. Normative and orectic levels of significance must be understood within the limits of possibility set by the cultural norms governing them. When a glass-painting uses the expression "baby," for example, we must be careful not to give it normative or orectic significance that the cultural attitudes then prevalent towards babies precluded. Nor should we exclude possible resonances that do not appear in our own responses to the word.

A symbol was not just subject to the limiting controls of its cultural context. The particular way in which it communicated its transcendent meanings to the viewer depended upon its position within the painting and also on the painting's relationship to the *Herrgottswinkel* as a whole. As Turner argues, "the positional meaning of a symbol derives from its relationship to other symbols in a totality, a *Gestalt*, whose elements acquire their significance from the system as a whole."[19] If, as Clifford Geertz claims, "the culture of a people is an ensemble of texts," and the *Herrgottswinkel* is such a text, then the individual paintings are "pages" of that text and so must be analyzed within the context of their entire setting.[20] When a painting contains several symbols, it too must be viewed as a composite of individual elements, and the symbols become, in Geertz's metaphor of text, either "sentences" or "thoughts." Although the larger symbolic or ritual unit of the *Herrgottswinkel* can be seen to break down into ever smaller fragments, it is as much the place of these fragments in the combined image as their individual significance that is important in establishing their specific range of meaning for the household.

The application of our completed model to the dining corner as a whole allows us to see that the *Herrgottswinkel*, itself a religious image, immediately takes on the ambiguities inherent in a fusion of practical and spiritual frames of reference. Because it was removed from the explicitly sacred enclosure of a church and located

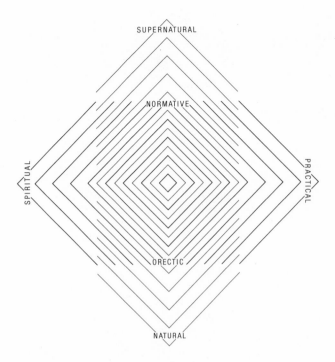

Figure 1.

in the secular context of a home, its range of reference to both areas of concern was emphasized. Drawing on the suggestive combination of physical nourishment and spiritual communion symbolized in church by the altar/table, a combination that in German is stressed by the very word *Abendmahl* or "supper" used to describe the communion service, the dining table became both the focal center and the shrine or altar of the home. The obvious emotive and physiological references of the locus of food consumption in a household for which survival might well have been a major concern thus merged with the normative and didactic functions of spiritual "nourishment" suggested by the communion of believers.

Within this very general context of the *Herrgottswinkel*'s frame of reference our model adds the dimension of supernatural and natural meaning implicit in the use of religious imagery. By reducing the focus of study to the individual symbols composing those images, we can see that the practical significance of their presence in the home was intimately related to another dimension of meaning. The miraculous power provided by the subjects of glass-paintings could be put to effective practical use as a protective force intervening on behalf of the household while it dealt with the problems of daily life. But we can also see how the saints and biblical figures portrayed, who had themselves led natural lives and encountered the normal life experiences now facing household members, could serve as normative models for behavior.

Figure 2. Haus Patronen (Raimundsreuth) (*left*). Photograph courtesy of Fastner Collection, Zwiesel. *Haus Patronen* (Gege) (*right*). Photograph courtesy of the Oberammergau Folk Museum.

One of the most popular forms of glass-painting was copies of an original *Gnadenbild* or cult image that depicted one or several of the most important Christian devotional figures, in particular Mary, Jesus, or the Holy Trinity. Many local renderings of these figures had become associated with popular pilgrimage sites and pilgrims had become accustomed to buying personal copies during their journeys to hang at home in the *Herrgottswinkel*. Glass-painters would frequently reproduce motifs from pilgrimages located no farther away than the surrounding countryside: the collection of patterns at Haus Gege surveyed by Büchner included the "Seehausen Mary, the suffering Mother Mary from Murnau, the scourged Jesus from Wies bei Steingaden, the bountiful Lady from Ettal, the patron of cattle Saint Leonhard from Tölz and Froschhausen, the suffering Mary from Gaisach, the miraculous Cross from Polling, and the black Mary from Absam, Tyrol."[21] Raimundsreuth painters took advantage of the popularity of the local Kreuzberg pilgrimage to reproduce images of the Saint Anna statue venerated there. Many variations on the figure of Mary, Mother of God, were, as the above example shows, included among the most popular *Gnadenbilder*. The whole subject of Mary was such a popular one that it seems to be the most prominent of all the themes portrayed in glass-painting. Haller claims that "no other holy figure has ever appealed to and fascinated ordinary people more than the Mother of God."[22] Lenz Kriss-Rettenbeck does point to the balancing factor of the importance of Jesus in votive paintings and the evidence provided by Johann Baptist Reisbacher of Kollnburg's account book supports this proviso. Of the 205 votive paintings commissioned from Reisbacher for which a motif was indicated, 82 included variations on the theme of Christ's life and passion. Yet 85 of these votive paintings included variations on the Mary motif while 18 included the Holy Trinity.[23] It is because of the central significance of these local Marian cult images in the lives of glass-painting consumers that I have chosen them to represent the *Gnadenbild* category in general.

Pfarrer Bäumer's order for copies of the Holy Trinity *Gnadenbild* clearly incorporated the Mother of God. These images were of the type known as the Crowning of Mary. A Raimundsreuth version of this motif presents the Holy Trinity in one of the two most popular arrangements of the three figures of God, in which the Father and Son sit side by side underneath a centralized and hovering Holy Ghost as dove. (See figure 2 for the vertical arrangement also very popular in glass-painting.) The reason for this choice of configuration becomes obvious when the viewer's attention turns to the also centralized figure of Mary as she stands between and beneath Father and Son, who together hold the crown over her head. The triangular nature of the Trinity is emphasized in the standard iconographical interpretation depicted here by a triangular halo placed around the head of God the Father. Yet the inclusion of Mary in the group causes a quadratic, lozenge-shaped effect to predominate in the final image, balancing or even cancelling the triadic suggestions of the Trinity itself.[24] Eva Hunt, in a fascinating book about Zinacantecan deities, has pointed to the tension between the triadic form of Roman Catholicism and the "problem of fitting a . . . quartet into a trio. . . . In the medieval traditions of European Christianity many breakaway sects developed over the issue of incorporating a fourth personage (usually the Virgin Mary, but sometimes even the devil) into the Trinity."[25] For, in agrarian societies, a quadratic "armature" is indicated by the seasonal nature of peasant life rhythms. Mary provides the necessary squaring factor and her prominence in the iconography of eighteenth- and nineteenth-century Bavaria suggests that she took her place in the minds of local believers alongside the Trinity in a position of special favor and grace, if not of equality, accorded no other holy figure.

Andrew Greeley has recently elaborated on the concept of Mary as "a symbol of the feminine component of the deity. She represents the human insight that the Ultimate is passionately tender, seductively attractive, irresistibly inspiring, and graciously healing."[26] Her inclusion within the configuration of the Trinity does indicate that her presence provides believers with a means of contemplating the role of femininity in the context of God's power. This role is, of course, predicated on Mary's intimate association with the Trinity by virtue of her motherhood of Jesus. Mary's role as mother was often expressed in her depiction as a mother mourning the death of her son, alone in her suffering. The usual pairing of the suffering Mary was with the *Ecce Homo* that caused her state of grief. In addition, the two central figures of the Passion were often united by the Pietà motif in which Jesus lies dead across the lap of his sorrowing mother. But perhaps the most popular thematic development in Bavaria of Mary's motherhood was the myriad of variations of the Madonna and infant Jesus.

Torsten Gebhart has divided the Madonna and Child motifs prominent in popular Catholic practice into two theoretical categories: Mary the Helper and Mary of Loreto.[27] The difference between these two major variations is one of humanistic versus hieratic intent, although the two types could often be blended and hybrid versions were not uncommon. (See figure 3 for examples of the two major types.) On one hand, the adaptations of detail in local presentations of Mary the Helper have never succeeded in disguising the original human scene of the Lucas Cranach painting, which has been rightly called an "idyll of family life."[28] By contrast, any sense of interactive warmth in the mother-child combination is lacking from the Mary of Loreto type. Here the majesty of Mary as Mother of God takes precedence over her human relationship to the baby from whom she derives her special power and prominence. This clear transference of power from the divine child to the mother who gave him birth makes for her successful intercession with her resurrected son on behalf of the human beings for whose salvation he was sacrificed.

Karl Mindera has pointed out that the Mary the Helper motif is related to cultish medieval depictions of Mary, exemplified by the fifteenth-century Madonna revered at Hohenpeissenberg near the Staffelsee, in which Mary hands her child an apple and so "symbolically asks [him] to take on the burden of sins and their consequences." The very title "Helper" given the motif, derived from a cry for help, draws attention away from the playfulness of the scene towards the lovingly protective role of the mother. Mindera argues that the "times of growth and

Figure 3. Mary of Loreto (*left*); Mary the Helper (*right*). Photograph courtesy of the Oberammergau Folk Museum.

expansion of the veneration of Mary the Helper" were just those of "religious difficulties, . . . wars, epidemics, and natural catastrophes. . . . Therefore, the first half of the seventeenth century with the Thirty Years War and the plague of 1634, the decade of battles with the Turks from 1683 until around 1700, the times of the War of the Spanish Succession and the Napoleonic campaigns," as well as the period of the Reformation, were particularly conducive to a rise in the numbers of believers seeking her protection.[29] This need for loving shelter and aid is mirrored in other names given to Marian cult figures, such as Mary of Good Counsel and Mary of Solace. It is also evident in the graphic depiction of the "Heart of Mary," prominently displayed on the Madonna's chest. Both prototypical images of Mary as Mother serve the essential purpose of expressing the protective power and inter-cessory efficacy of the Mother of God.

The importance for consumers of the protective role provided by the many *Gnadenbilder* of Mary, and by the images of numerous other saints, is further confirmed by the repeated depiction of these cult figures in votive paintings. Both pictorially and verbally, such paintings offer evidence for the effectiveness of Mary's intervention on behalf of believers in need. The thankful expression, "Mary has helped" is thus the corollary to the cry for help implied by her invocation. The knowledge that she had proven her ability to stand by victims of disaster in the past strengthened the faith of her cult followers for the future. If, as Turner points out for the Mexican context, "the belief that on several occasions the Remedios and Guadalupe Virgins saved Mexico City from plague, floods, and drought now forms part of the 'meaning' of these images," this was certainly no less true of the faith held by Bavarian Catholics in the many miracles recorded in miracle books and pictorially on the walls of cult shrines all over Southern and Central Europe.[30] A substantial text telling the story of both disaster and rescue often accompanies a votive painting and this leaves no doubt as to the mechanism of supernatural intervention involved.

These paintings give proof of the clear distinction made between natural and supernatural phenomena. In almost all cases, the supernatural power appears in the sky, suspended in clouds, while the natural scene takes place in the familiar, earthly surroundings of the victim. Scenes of disaster, ranging from the swaddled infant mauled by a hog and the farmer's wife's problems with her geese to military disasters, accidents on land, sea, and lake, and a myriad of illnesses, offer a fasci-nating picture of the perils of daily life.[31] The interactive nature of the two principal elements in the painting is often depicted by the use of rays emanating from the cult figure to touch the victim below, thus rendering the necessary aid. For example, an *ex voto* dated 1770 reveals Mary the Helper in the course of assisting a boatman who has fallen over the side of a cargo vessel into the river. As he is being rescued by fellow workers with the help of an oar extended over the side of the boat, the rays sent out by Mary's cloud-borne figure suffuse the scene and the man is already clutching onto the oar that has doubtless saved his life.[32] Such scenes of both natural and supernatural intervention suggest that the supplementary power of the supernatural was requested to bolster what were clearly seen as less than adequate human activities. As Keith Thomas has argued, "It is unquestionably true that it is the technological gap between man's aspirations and his limited control of his environment which gives magical practices their relevance."[33] Whether the attribution of final success in a situation of danger and uncertain outcome is "magical" or not is beside the point here. What is significant is that invocation of a cult figure was a culturally shaped way of both conceptualizing and dealing with a life crisis that worked for the many believers who gave visual proof of their survival. In painting after painting, we either see the victim reaching out to the chosen intercessor or read about the chain of events through which a promise to offer a votive painting came to be made. But the sense of inadequacy perceived and expressed by a victim's commitment of his fate to a supernatural protector should not be taken to confirm the analysis of early modern man as incapable of dealing adequately with his environment. These are disasters that the most sophisticated technological controls known to man have not eradicated from human experience.

The syntax suggested by the use of Marian images as protective devices lays greater emphasis on the viewer than on the child. It seems to me that Jesus, although his role is implicitly central to the proceedings, is relegated to a dependent clause preceding the primary interplay of subject and object in the sentence. My reading of the Madonna's message is as follows: "Because I am the mother of God (Jesus), I, Mary the Mother, will help and protect you (the viewer)." While the past tense invoked by past performance makes an integral contribution to Mary's significance in the eyes of the beholder, the future promise of motherly protection is his focus of attention.

Because it is as a mother that Mary promises to help her believers, her role as a female intercessor can perhaps lead us to a better understanding of male-female power relationships in the Catholic households where the habit of seeking her mediation was a common one. Her activities can be seen both to reflect and to effect social realities by the power of example. But in order to establish the meaning of female mediation of this sort for household members, it is necessary to return to the combinations of paintings displayed in the *Herrgottswinkel*. We have seen Mary paired with the Trinity and with her son both as the Christ of the Passion and as an infant in arms. But we have not yet considered the very popular pairing of Mary with her husband Joseph, both in pendants clearly intended as pairs and in single paintings presenting variations on the theme of the Holy Family. This reference to Mary's natural life raises interesting questions about female power in the household. As a counterpoise to the all-powerful figure of God the Father, whose ultimate right to judge must be mitigated by the supplication of a host of intermediaries, Mary amongst them, the figure of Joseph seems weak and approachable. While God the Father appears in his majesty in depictions of the Trinity, he is never to be seen alone as a source of protection in votive paintings or as a pendant in the *Herrgottswinkel*. The human Joseph, however, was frequently used as a pendant, and his derivation of power from wife and child, sometimes explicitly portrayed by the crown of flowers held by Jesus over his head, undermines the sense of authority that his position as male head of household should lend him.

Thus we have two contradictory images of the male role, and we would be unwise to make a hasty judgment of the patriarchal supremacy derived from the legal, moral, and social power of the *Hausvater* or house father that is suggested by the need to find an intercessor on behalf of his "subject" family members. Mary's power to intercede, expressed in innumerable images, could no doubt both encourage and reflect independence and authority in the wives whose economic status in the household provided essential, at times primary, benefits for the family. The new familial relationships described by Hans Medick in which the husband might be the parent responsible for child care and domestic duties could surely draw strength from images of the Holy Family that resembled the form of their power base, such as that in which Mary spins while Joseph holds the child Jesus on his lap, watching his wife work.[34] Certainly the attractions of family life so often reflected in Renaissance and early modern high art seem no less popular with peasants and craftsmen. Nevertheless the constant resort to mediators does suggest that where patriarchal authority was strongly imposed, the role of the mother could be expected to be that of intercessor, as the one of the weak most likely to be successful in gaining the ear of the oppressor.[35] By way of example, the diary of an English farmer's wife written in the 1790s illustrates the effectiveness of female manipulative powers in the similar context of a farming household. Anne Hughes conveys the sense of her almost motherly attitude to the male foibles of her very respectable husband when she tells us on the first page of her daily notations that "men be verry tiresome sometimes." It soon becomes clear that she and her maid have well-established patterns of dealing with any problems that the head of the household might put in their way. One can imagine the means by which this resourceful woman would have acted as intercessor for the child whose expected appearance ended her activity as diarist.[36]

Despite the possible ambiguity of Marian images as normative guides to the correct apportionment of power within familial relationships, Mary's motherhood was the key to her significance. Although I have interpreted her primary function to be that of intercession on behalf of the viewer, she was repeatedly depicted as the mother of an infant or small child, and thus as the nucleus of a family. In this context, her descent from pre-Christian fertility goddesses left Mary with strong reproductive implications, stressing the important role of the wife in each household as sole bearer of children. So, despite the provisos discussed above, one could speculate that the striking popularity of both Mary the Helper and other variations on the Madonna theme were connected with the concerns about family and household implicit in many glass-painting customers' purchase of other scenes of family life in the holy household. Mary's duties as mother would, therefore, also include the nutritive function explicitly expressed both in elite art as the breast-feeding of the Infant Jesus and in popular art as the motif Mary Breast-feeding.

The didactic force of Mary's reproductive and nutritive significance was not lost on observers and it could be used to emphasize the dignity of motherhood. As Ingeborg Weber-Kellerman points out, "The cult of Mary surrounded the picture of woman and mother with a new ethical dignity that must have acted as prototype for the population in its numerous visual representations."[37] This was the argument of the Catholic philosopher Albert Stöckl (d. 1895). Drawing on "trains of thought that . . . were already to a large extent expressed in the Liturgy of the old Church," he declared that

> Christians compare the mother in the family to the holy Mary, Mother of God, and as they praise the high dignity of Her motherhood, they say to the family mother that she shares in the dignity of this motherhood to some extent, since she bears certainly not Christ himself, but, however, children of Christ and members of his mystical body—the Church.

The practical bite to such high-flown language was surely revealed by the moralist Johann Michael Sailers' injunction that "the healthy, strong mother obeys the call of nature, suckles, nurses her child herself, certainly out of a feeling of love, enjoying a clear conscience and a feeling of composure and with fearless adherence to dietary prescriptions."[38]

The need for such admonitions has been made abundantly clear by both primary and secondary literature on the long-entrenched custom of hand-feeding infants in Southern Germany. Mothers there were slow to heed advice such as that of Sailers and there was strong peer pressure to conform to traditional feeding methods. Indeed the use of artificial feeding was in places

> so firmly ingrained that any exception to it met with social condemnation. [Hugo] Bernheim reports the following example from a district in Oberbayern: "A woman who came from northern Germany and wanted according to the customs of her homeland to nurse her infant herself was openly called swinish and filthy by the local women. Her husband threatened he would no longer eat anything she prepared, if she did not give up this disgusting habit."

This form of feeding has even been suggested to represent at times a resistance to the continual burden of motherhood thrust on Catholic mothers, for it could work as a means of family limitation. It may also have been seen as a symbol of relative affluence. Whatever the reasons, a great many Bavarian infants were not receiving the recommended breast milk at all, not even from wet-nurses. They were subjected to such alternatives as meal, maybe the "thick indigestible meal pap" used near Augsburg and "given in a sweetened form, cooked in milk, to children almost from birth."[39]

It was in Swabia and in the traditional Bavarian lands, not in the northern areas added to Bavaria in the early nineteenth century, that the lowest breast-feeding rates persisted. There seems little doubt that these variations in breast-feeding habits were reflected in infant mortality rates also strikingly different for the northern and southern regions of the Bavarian kingdom. A 1910 survey of infant mortality in Bavaria listed the highest percentage of infant deaths to live births in the five-year periods from 1835–39 to 1900–1904 as 43.3 percent for Upper Bavaria, 42.2 percent for Swabia, 36.9 percent for Lower Bavaria, 36.8 percent for the Upper Pfalz, 34.5 percent for Middle Franconia, 25.3 percent for Lower Franconia, 22.3

percent for Upper Franconia, and 20.5 percent for the Pfalz.[40] The high overall percentage for the entire kingdom caused by these uneven figures meant that while elsewhere in Europe infant mortality was on the decline in the nineteenth century, it was actually on the increase in Bavaria, reaching a peak of 32.7 percent of dead infants to live births between 1862–63 and 1868–69. Bernheim's 1888 study showed that of all European states, only Württemberg had a record worse than Bavaria's in this regard, while France, England, and even Spain registered under 20 percent for observation periods in the 1850s and 1860s.[41] The combination of this persistently high rate of infant deaths with culturally prescribed artificial feeding habits created mothering norms in Southern Bavarian popular culture that were substantially different from those put forward by Sailers and other concerned observers of infant mortality. There were, therefore, two standards of motherhood united in the once again ambiguous cult figures of the Mother of God.

The popular conception of a mother's role is our primary concern here. We are reminded that it concerned not only the care of a live infant but also the duty owed to a dead one. The numerous votive paintings of the dead babies can provide supplementary evidence for a specifically Southern Bavarian interpretation of Mary's relationship to her own baby in the Madonna theme. I have chosen one of these *Totenbilder*, or portraits of the dead, to represent the votive painting category in glass-painting (see figure 4). The absence of a protective supernatural figure in this painting makes it unusual as a votive offering and we cannot pinpoint its destination in a specific cult shrine. Yet the same commitment of human beings to supernatural care noted in other votive paintings is implied by this form of representation. In it, dead family members are depicted as they were last seen in life, but with crosses suspended above their heads. The swaddled infant lying on a cushion in the right foreground of the picture space is, therefore, dead, as may well be the two swaddled figures lying to the extreme right of the group and cut off by the frame. The entire extended family is here, including the old father and mother, now dead, and the two brothers (most likely younger sons) whose involvement in the wars has led to their deaths. The heir, flanked by his parents, has now two women to take care of, as well as a wife and children still living. But his intention in this painting was to fulfill his duty to the dead members of his family. It is not the need of commitment to a cult figure experienced by a living person in danger, but rather the need for eternal peace now experienced by the souls of the dead that is expressed in this kind of appeal. The cry, "O Lord, grant her eternal rest" inscribed on the 1844 votive painting of an Oberandorf goatherd dead from a fall captures the wish of all such offerings.[42]

The tiny figure of the swaddled baby in our *Totenbild* represents a duty to feed, clothe, and protect and a duty to care for an eternal soul. A child such as this one might well have been hand-fed meal and other substitutes for breast milk that so often proved mortally threatening to its health. There is great poignancy in the text of a similar votive painting in which Barbara Haimbmatnerin reports the death of "her beloved child, named Melchardt." For his illness appeared due to the *Frais* or digestive disorder so commonly fatal for infants and so clearly connected to their diet.[43]

Figure 4. Anonymous *Totenbild.* Photograph courtesy of the Oberammergau Folk Museum.

Our infant example, as was sometimes the case with images of the Baby Jesus in cult figures, is wrapped in the swaddling bands universally used to depict infants in votive paintings of this period. This reminds us that it was still a part of many a mother's duties in the eighteenth and nineteenth centuries to swaddle her baby. It was not until well into the nineteenth century, or even later, in some country areas of Southern Bavaria, that this custom died out in Southern Germany. "Everyone saw firm swaddling as indispensable. It was not only to protect the tender nursling, whose limbs were like green branches, from hurts of all kinds, but people thought it would hold straight the back and extremities." For mothers whose duties in the household required long hours of work, the dual role of swaddling as corrective clothing and as protective device must have been significant indeed. It ranks with other such devices, leading-reins and the like, as a precaution taken so that the accidents so frequently described in votive paintings as befalling young children could be prevented.[44]

Whether an infant were born alive or dead, it was necessary for the parents to care for its soul. This duty was considered so important that doctors often complained about the dangers of hurrying babies to a christening service in bad weather. Some of the many votive paintings that depict dead infants may be expressing gratitude for movements made by a stillborn child while at such a christening service. For the official reception of a living infant into the body of the Church would reassure the grieving parents that they had ensured its soul's access to eternal rest.[45] Their final duty in this case was consequently to fulfill the promise made during the crisis to commission and deliver a votive painting to the cult figure whose aid had delivered their child from the danger of dying unbaptized. Lenz Kriss-Rettenbeck has also suggested that the act of committing a dead child to supernatural care included the hope explicitly expressed in a 1775 votive painting from Austria. Father and mother kneel beneath a Pietà with eight dead babies lying between them. They offer up their prayer through the figure of the Mother of God: "Dear God, eight children are with you, so give the ninth to me."[46]

Knowledge of the customary duties and experiences of Southern Bavarian mothers would form a subconscious background to the normative and orectic significance of Mary's motherhood in the minds of Bavarian glass-painting owners. It is interesting to note that such knowledge may also have contributed to limiting the number of images depicting the explicit motif Mary Breast-feeding. The humanistic prototype Mary the Helper apparently provided a sufficiently positive picture of motherly love and protection for most consumers, a picture, moreover, that did not threaten the sensibilities of those hostile to the idea of breast-feeding. So it is not surprising that graphic depictions of the nutritive procedure were limited to the few isolated motifs that do show a mother holding her child to her bare breast. A very early, mid-eighteenth century Raimundsreuth pattern that ended up in the Schönstein workshop of Wüstner deals with this theme and the motif is not uncommon in collections of glass-paintings. Wilhelm Theopold even reproduces a votive painting in which the cult figure is a Mary Breast-feeding that strongly resembles the Raimundsreuth pattern.[47] Yet the vast majority of Marian images do not emphasize this motherly duty. What they certainly do stress is that Jesus was a healthy, living child. However, the implications of death contributed by the knowledge of his Passion lurk behind even the healthy infant form. This combined message of life and death was familiar to Bavarian viewers as the repeatedly painted child Jesus lying on the cross known as the Reclining Child. Greeley stresses the fact that Mary too represents both life and death, as expressed by the Pietà motif in which she receives back in death the body to which she first gave life.[48] For these reasons, it seems certain that any Bavarian owner of Marian cult images would bring an awareness of the frailty of the child in Mary's arms to his or her understanding of the painting.

The uncertainty of life of small Southern Bavarian infants can perhaps be seen as a paradigm for a more general uncertainty about family and household safety experienced by their parents, an uncertainty for which the intervention of super-natural patrons such as Mary provided a reassuring solution. Surviving figures for the year-by-year experience of infant mortality in two glass-painting villages, Uffing and Oberammergau, show that the striking fact about the relationship between births and infant deaths is precisely its very lack of predictability.[49] This kind of uncertainty, undoubtedly perceived by the villagers themselves, required the very strongly supportive patterns of cultural response that Marian worship represented. Ironically, the normative example implicit in the role of Mary as a Southern Bavarian mother was a cause of the very uncertainties it was her primary function to assuage. But for her followers, Mary the nourisher and fertility symbol merged with Mary the intercessor and protectress in a complex dominant symbol of unprecedented power and love.

Images of Mary were by no means the only biblical or doctrinal motifs chosen by glass-painting consumers to hang in their homes. Not only were there also the many variations on the story of Christ's life and Passion, but there was a myriad of saints' portraits to buy singly or in pairs. These saints were popular with local consumers because their patronage of specific interest groups rendered them useful as protective forces supplementing the doctrinal figures of the Holy Trinity, Jesus, and Mary. No saint could offer the all-embracing protection of these powerful religious symbols. But with a variety of well-defined problems went specialists whose expertise could be called upon in a moment of need and whose images were, therefore, a desirable addition to the household shrine. Sometimes such saints would be asked to support a doctrinal figure in its protective duties, and the patron invoked would then stand beside the cult image as they acted together in providing a miraculous solution to the problem at hand. When Mychael Purgmayr of Hohenkirchen, Upper Bavaria, fell beneath a waggon in 1748, for example, he called on both a local Madonna and a Tyrolean saint popular in Upper Bavaria, Saint Notburga. In the votive painting he later commissioned, the two women hover close together above the scene of disaster and the rays extending from the Madonna are augmented by those emanating from Notburga's haloed and cloud-borne figure. At other times the saint would act alone, as Notburga did on behalf of the child with a nasal hemorrhage whose plight is recorded in a 1773 votive

Figure 5. Saint Notburga (probably Tyrol) (*left*). Photograph courtesy of the Bavarian National Museum. Saint Notburga (Raimundsreuth) (*right*). Photograph courtesy of the Fastner Collection, Zwiesel.

painting.[50] It was also possible for a victim to invoke the aid of two or more saints in combination.

The repeated commitment of humans in need to the protection of patron saints confirms that their practical role for household members resembled that of the Mother of God: the specific duties that they could be called upon to perform as protectors were related to their life stories and occupations. Individual saints could influence household concerns both by their supernatural contribution to the solution of problems arising out of the daily lives of the family and by the examples their natural lives provided for dealing with specific issues. Saint Notburga, whose popularity as a local Alpine saint demonstrates the extent to which such saints served the needs of glass-painting customers, exemplifies how the strong interconnection between her life story and her role in the household resulted in pleas for her help.

Notburga was a farm servant; she became the patroness of farmmaids, but her protection was extended to include both farmers and cattle. The Chronicle of the Bavarian pilgrimage site dedicated to Saint Notburga at Weissling recorded over 600 answers to prayers by the saint from 1749–91. Around 200 of these cases involved problems with cattle, while the others dealt with human sufferings. Over 250 times Notburga cured illnesses such as the eye, ear, and foot diseases committed to her care and she aided women in childbirth, a function that surviving votive paintings from the Tyrol also attribute to her. While "whole communities and parishes promised processions to Saint Notburga" in gratitude for her protection, grateful families would bring her such offerings as calves or butter and lard. The gifts that expressed the thanks of healed or protected cult followers could thus reflect the specialization of their patron, although her helping hand clearly reached beyond the narrow confines of farm management.[51]

Wolfgang Pfaundler has mapped out the extent of Notburga's influence, which was greatest in the Tyrol, Southern Austria, and Yugoslavia. Weissling was the only pilgrimage site to be established in Bavaria itself, although the saint could be called upon by Bavarians wishing to bolster the power of the local *Gnadenbild* and her portrait was certainly produced by glass-painters. (See figure 5 for a Raimundsreuth example of Saint Notburga and a comparable one probably painted in the Tyrol.) Eben, where Notburga was buried, became the site of an important pilgrimage to her. Just over the border from Bavaria, that area of the Upper Inn Valley once belonged to Lower Bavaria, so Notburga is considered a Bavarian saint as well. Where she was not popular—in Switzerland and the Vorarlberg—Pfaundler suggests that division of properties excluded the problem of farm servants because resulting landholdings were small enough to be worked by family members alone. In Bavaria, where landholdings were passed on only to one son, the need for servants could be acute, particularly since the high infant mortality may have perpetuated a scarcity of extra hands available at harvest time and also of course for craft occupations.[52] Lutz Berkner has pointed out the relationship between the family life cycle and the need for servants in the peasant households of Central

Europe, while Heinz Haushofer suggests that "economic conjunctures, especially better and worse harvests, but also . . . the ebb and flow of individual fortunes" affected the servants' position as well as their masters'.[53] Scarcity of farm labor and the consequent expense of attracting young men and women to the farm was often a source of complaint in Bavaria. Yet the number of servants in Bavarian employ was considerable throughout our period, particularly in comparison with other parts of Germany. Fifteen percent of the total population were servants in 1771 and over 17 percent of the Upper Bavarian population were servants as late as 1840. Many of these men and women may have been local farmers' children, often even related to the landowner for whom they worked. Berkner has drawn attention to the fact that in the Austrian area he studied, tensions between master and servant were common, as expressed in both local laws and local songs. Similar problems seem to have afflicted Bavarian employers.[54]

Notburga's own story reflected the need for employing servants to take care of the farm animals and to bring in the harvest as well as the tensions that could result when employment of a faithful servant conflicted with the life of charity and devotion to God that such a servant might be expected to lead. She angered her employers on at least two famous occasions, when her duty to God and her fellow men took precedence over her practical duties as servant or harvester. Although she was "an example of industriousness and loyalty, self-sacrificing charity and profound piety," her very charitable nature led to her dismissal from her post as kitchenmaid at Castle Rottenburg. She was forbidden to give extra food from the castle kitchens to local beggars, but she took them instead both her own food and the jug of wine customarily apportioned the Rottenburg servants. Her employers immediately dismissed her and she was obliged to find a new position with a farmer in the nearby village of St. Ruprecht auf dem Eben. When harvest time came, her help was required in the fields and she worked diligently until the sound of church bells informed her that with evening a feast day had officially begun. Notburga wished to stop her reaping forthwith, but her employer asked her to complete her work first. She replied that she would cast her sickle in the air to ascertain God's will in the matter. If it stayed suspended, she was to observe the feast day; if it fell to the ground, she must continue to work. Of course, it stayed in the air and all work in the fields ceased. Notburga was eventually invited back to the castle as housekeeper and encouraged in her charity towards the beggars. She oversaw the Christian education of her employer's children until her death in 1313.[55]

The need for good, loyal servants (and perhaps for considerate, sensible employers) who observed the Christian commandments inherent in the work rhythms and behaviors of traditional Bavarian life was clearly expressed in the story of Saint Notburga. Her story serves to pinpoint the significance of the Christian example provided by her own and other saints' portraits in the *Herrgottswinkels* of Bavarian farmers and craftsmen. They were *Andachtsbilder* or devotional pictures and they were intended to aid the viewer both in prayer and in shaping the pattern of his own behavior. Such paintings had to remind their owners of relevant details in the history of the saint or saints portrayed and of the attributes symbolizing their key significance.

Consequently, in all paintings of her, Notburga is accompanied by the sickle associated with her saintly adherence to the commandments of God. She usually carries a jug as well, reminiscent of the jug of wine she brought to the beggars. The Raimundsreuth version reproduced in figure 5 shows her with both sickle and jug, but the Tyrolean version omits the jug and includes a rosary instead. It seems clear that Notburga could be disassociated from her charitable acts but not from the miracle of the sickle that became her primary form of identification. Indeed, together with their adaptation to the needs of local believers, this kind of selection of attributes was a common popular practice. Only the most significant contributions of the saint were retained or emphasized, and in Notburga's case, her connection to the farming household and its continued prosperity, although within the context of spiritual commitment provided by the sickle story, seems to have concerned her viewers more than her charitable activities. In a schematic painting of the sort provided by the Raimundsreuth example, the emphasis on the saint's figure and her two attributes helps to confirm that many customers made their purchases primarily because of the painting's content. As Herschel Chipp has pointed out, when the main significance of a painting lies in its "sacred meaning, . . . craftsmanship was necessary only to the point where it produced forms that adequately suggested or symbolized the all-important meaning." [56] There are few concessions to the need for embellishment in this painting; it is about as functional an image as one can imagine.

Notburga derived her protective powers from her sainthood and her spiritual example was not unconnected with her ability to render practical assistance to her followers. In a votive painting dated 1818, the cult figure of Mary from Kirchenthal sends down the message to a woman still recumbent on her sickbed: "Your faith has helped you." [57] This reminder of the intimate relationship between sanctity and health serves to emphasize the impossibility of disentangling the various functions of a complex dominant symbol like Notburga. The spiritual example of her noble life of sacrifice, which seems logically to belong on the extreme left of our schematized model as a spiritual, normative, and natural phenomenon, translates into a practical, orectic, and supernatural phenomenon. Her message is an exhortation to the viewer: "If you want my protection, follow my example!" For those of her followers whose lives were patterned after her own high standards of faith and sanctity, health and good fortune were to be their reward on earth, while a place in heaven and eternal rest were to be their final prize in death.

There is one form of glass-painting that illustrates separately the various fragments found inextricably intertwined above. This final glass-painting category, the *Haussegen* or *Haus Patronen* (protectors of the home), provides supporting evidence for my original contention that the glass-paintings hanging in *Herrgottswinkels* were intended to protect the household. The behavioral model that these motifs embodied was an integral part of their protective function. In the two examples of

Bavarian *Haus Patronen* included in figure 2, the protective powers of four saints are combined with those of the Holy Trinity. A cursory examination of the patronage associated with each saint establishes that the coverage provided by the composite image extended well beyond the purely practical problems of the household to include those spiritual and doctrinal issues that were the special concern of the Trinity itself.

At the center of both paintings, the artist has placed the vertically arranged Holy Trinity motif so popular with glass-painting customers, thus providing himself with a solidly doctrinal centerpiece around which to group the four saints who fill the corners of the quadratic picture space. In the lower right-hand corner stands Saint Sebastian, pictured, as was customary, undergoing the martyrdom by arrows that he miraculously survived. His recovery from the wounds inflicted had, by the time of this painting, led to his patronage of the plague and other contagious diseases. His inclusion in our group of saints was, therefore, primarily intended to ensure the health of household members. In the lower left-hand corner, Sebastian is joined by Saint Florian, whose ability to protect the house from fire had made him one of the most popular local saints in the area. He was originally a patron of soldiers, but his martyrdom by drowning had, by the end of the fifteenth century, suggested the possibility that he might make use of the water associated with his death to quench the fires so often threatening Bavarian towns and villages. This adaptation of Florian's patronage to the needs of Bavarians whose fear of fire led them to seek out the most logical protector for their vulnerable, wooden houses exemplifies the way in which particular saints were pressed into service by the people of a specific region. A further example of this practice stands above Saint Florian in both paintings. Saint Leonhard, the very popular patron of livestock, was originally the patron of prisoners, as the iron chains he holds suggest. Gradually, he became the protector of livestock as well, and his chain became the ordinary leading-chain used to guide cattle. Even the religious order to which he was portrayed belonging was changed from Cistercian to Benedictine because the Benedictine's ability to cure animals had been established in the Middle Ages. Leonhard thus contributes his particular ability to protect the livestock, so important in the area, to the composite protective powers of the saintly group.[58]

The motif in the upper right-hand corner explicitly conveys the spiritual message only implicit in those already interpreted. While the Gege *Haus Patronen* includes Saint Ulrich in this corner of the painting, the Raimundsreuth painter has chosen to depict Saint Wolfgang. The interchangeability of this fourth saint was due to his special role in ensuring the faith and sanctity of the household. Both saints had been bishops and popular local patrons, carrying attributes that emphasized the rules and affairs of the Church. Ulrich's fish reminded his viewers that although he had eaten meat as he sat beyond midnight one Thursday evening deep in conversation with another bishop, the offending remains brought by a disloyal servant to the Bavarian Duke changed miraculously into the fish customarily eaten by the faithful on Fridays. Saint Wolfgang's church drew the viewer's attention to his construction of a small church in a remote area near Lake Aber. Wolfgang's assistant in this holy enterprise was, as Moritz von Schwind reminds us in his delightful rendition of the bishop's famous story, the devil. The artist pictures Wolfgang's evil slave laboriously pushing a cart full of stones up the steeply winding path that leads to the construction site, while the figure of the bishop appears in the background, calmly at work on his project. In the verse that accompanies the painting, the artist tells us:

> St. Wolfgang baut ein Kirchlein, der Teufel reisst's ihm immer ein.
> Doch statt den heil'gen Mann zu irren, muss er ihm dienen und Steine führen.
> Ein Bild für jeden braven Mann, den dumme Teufel fechten an.

> [Saint Wolfgang built a little Church, which the Devil kept tearing down again. But the saint became angry and obliged the Devil to serve him and carry stones, setting an example for every honest man to contest the stupid Devil.] [59]

Together, Saints Sebastian, Florian, Leonhard, and Ulrich or Wolfgang acted with the Holy Trinity to protect the household from illness, fire, starvation, and loss of faith. Their combined message as the plural subject of these paintings was, therefore, as simple as Saint Notburga's: "Have faith and we will protect you (the viewer)." By incorporating the explicitly clerical patronage of the bishop and spiritual patronage of the central doctrinal figures into a painting that also so explicitly provided physical protective patronage for the household, the artist has revealed the practical meaning of religious figures for glass-painting consumers. Certainly the presence of the two bishops, Ulrich and Wolfgang, and of the Holy Trinity in the center of the paintings, serves to underline the role played by Church doctrine in the lives of Bavarian Catholics. But it is their practical guarantee of continued faith that best illuminates the way in which faith and health, faith and safety, faith and livelihood were but one and the same thing for the household members whose daily round was conducted under the protective eye of the saints and doctrinal figures looking down at them from the *Herrgottswinkel*.

Lithographers were quick to assess the market in religious art for which both older graphic procedures and the new technique of glass-painting were being used to produce an immense variety of images. When Alois Senefelder invented his planographic printing method at the end of the eighteenth century, he made possible an explosive growth in the distribution of wall-paintings that changed the shape of the popular consumption of graphic art during the course of the nineteenth century. Already in the 1830s, the demand for glass-paintings was so great that five Wolfstein glass-painting families alone were producing 30,000 to 40,000 paintings yearly and Johann Verderber had streamlined his workshop along the lines of a factory assembly line by 1850 in an attempt to keep up with the market. But it clearly required the level of manpower and equipment that were assembled in the city workshops of lithographic printers to satisfy the public's growing appetite for decorative art. The second half of the nineteenth century, therefore, marked the decline of glass-painting and the victory of the chromolithograph.[60]

The close connection between lithography and other graphic procedures, including the printing of books, music, and maps, meant that religious art represented only a percentage of the total production of popular prints envisaged by lithographic firms. Classification of German single-leaf woodcuts produced in the sixteenth and seventeenth centuries has shown that religious subjects accounted for only 34 percent of all titles produced during that earlier period and nineteenth-century printers certainly included the variety of profane themes that they had inherited from their predecessors in their thematic selections. The firm of Gustav Kühn, for example, which in 1870–71 sold 3 million picture sheets known for their "rakish reds, garish blues, thunder greens—printed and for sale at Gustav Kühn's" included all manner of entertaining and instructive subjects together with their devotional pictures. Illustrations of soldiers, fairy tales, battles, and animals; games; puppets; children's theaters; even targets for shooting practice were among the profane motifs that Kühn's distributed to their vast public.[61] Brückner mentions the frequency of traditional themes such as the Four Seasons and hunting scenes in popular graphic pictures and suggests that these themes remained popular in their new form as "lower-middle-class drawing room and bedroom art" later in the nineteenth century.[62]

Despite the obvious popularity of profane motifs, however, many of the lithographic firms serving popular markets in the early days of production before the victory of the chromolithograph in the 1870s did find religious imagery to be a very substantial sales item. Rudolf Schenda writes that, based on a catalog of French graphic sheets registered with the Ministry of the Interior during the 1850s, "there can be no doubt that even in 1860 picture sheets with religious subjects were in greater demand than all other picture sheets put together." The Wentzel firm in Alsace, for example, registered for local colportage "103,000 images in 1858 of which 72,000 were religious, that is 7/10"; it sent many similar prints to Southern German markets. The May factory produced around 1850 "largely images of saints and biblical scenes for the holy corner in the living rooms of Catholic rural inhabitants."[63]

Familiar themes appear in the products of both French and German firms like Wentzel and May. Schenda found Mary listed in 172 separate forms under the title "Notre Dame" or "Our Lady," while other versions of her portrait were listed under a variety of different titles. Christ appeared 200 times as "Jesus" or "Christ" and the usual scenes from his life, such as the Nativity (8), the Flight to Egypt (10), and the Last Supper (10), were also repeatedly produced. About 1,500 different portraits of saints rounded out the picture. The Wentzel firm included the Souls in Purgatory theme so often produced by glass-painters in its selection of religious motifs. In prayer form, it is listed as "A very strong prayer for the poor souls in Purgatory." The Wentzels also elaborated on the theme of the Haus Patronen and several versions of that popular motif still appeared on their diminishing list of religious themes in the early twentieth century. When Christa Pieske cataloged surviving prints from the May factory, she found familiar motifs such as Mary the Helper, still paired with St. Joseph as in so many glass-painting pendants, the Holy

Family, the *Ecce Homo*, again paired with the Sorrowing Mary, the Crowning of Mary, the Holy Trinity, the Hearts of Jesus and Mary, and assorted saints. Thomas Driendl's small devotional pictures remind us that many of the religious motifs printed lithographically must have been *Gnadenbilder*, for Gustav Gugitz found examples of Maria Dreieichen, Maria-Kumitz, Maria-Lanzendorf, Maria-Luschari, Maria-Neustift, Maria-Plain, Maria-Taferl, Maria-Trost bei Graz, and Mariazell, a very popular *Gnadenbild*, among surviving devotional prints produced by his firm.[64] Clearly the profitable market for religious glass-paintings and small devotional pictures had provided newly industrializing manufacturers of lithographs with an inviting and stimulating field for their own productive potential.

From Senefelder onwards, the developers of color lithographic printing were interested in both religious and profane subjects for their experiments. Lithographic production for middle-class consumers that had inherited a strong bias towards such secular themes as landscapes and genre scenes, reproductions of old masters, and book illustrations from the eighteenth-century graphic arts industry. Yet Senefelder himself was almost immediately involved in a project that brought him in touch with the popular taste for religious art. One of his first artistic prints was the picture of Jesus as a child entitled 'Der Liebenswürdigste (the one most worthy of love) that School Inspector Steiner ordered in large numbers for local school children. For at least seven years after he created the original in 1798, Senefelder printed a couple of thousand copies yearly of the print and accompanying text. Steiner also "wished . . . to ornament various schoolbooks with pictures of this kind, and thus, gradually, to replace the miserably drawn species of saints that generally fill the prayer-books of the pious households."[65] Ironically, Senefelder's driving interest in color printing suggests that he may as well have been influenced by the popular taste for color if not by the draughtsmanship of the despised popular prints. For "only in popular, unpretentious art did the taste for colourfulness, or rather gaudiness, remain untouched" in the early nineteenth century.[66] The majority of his work in color, however, did involve secular subjects for it was the procedure by which oil paintings could be successfully copied lithographically rather than the popular market that preoccupied him during these experiments. Already in 1808, he had claimed in his *Pattern Book* that he had found a process that "almost allows one to provide copies of oil paintings." By 1818 he could write that "I have made such progress in color printing that, besides pictures illuminated with colors, I can also produce pictures quite similar to oil paintings, so that nobody can discover that they have been printed, because they possess all the distinguishing points of paintings." Yet he was still intrigued by the challenge to produce a perfect oil print; his rather pathetic attempts to finance his project during the 1820s and 1830s fill many pages of correspondence in the Bavarian governmental archives.[67]

Senefelder's two pupils, whose work in color printing led to the discovery of a three-color process, inherited his interest in reproductive art. But while Engelmann's products revealed his preponderant interest in the secular themes popular with Parisian and middle-class customers, Heinrich Weishaupt's experiments in the Bavarian context reflected more traditional motifs from the *Herrgottswinkel*. His first chromolithograph was an *Ecce Homo* after Hemling and it met with such success that he had printed and sold over 1,500 copies by 1843. The second of his efforts was logically the pendant to the first, a Sorrowing Mary after Kling. The boy Jesus theme already reproduced by Senefelder was also one of his early motifs in chromolithography, together with Raphael's Sistine Madonna and other religious subjects.[68] Even his early attempts at secular chromolithography were reminiscent of the popular Four Seasons theme; Spring and The Reaper appear, apparently intended as a pair in the mounted copies of each print now owned by the German National Museum. Weishaupt followed his early production efforts with a Holy Trinity in 1841 and he made explicit his appreciation of the importance for the popular market of religious motifs when he requested permission in 1842 to reproduce three paintings from the Pinakothek. He wrote that he had used his discovery, which allowed him to make prints "similar to oil paintings," "particularly for religious reproductions" with the "public taste" in mind. Rubens' *Holy Trinity*, Van Dyck's *Rest in Egypt*, and Reni's *Ascension of Mary* were the three paintings that he considered would be suitable as chromolithographs: two of these works still hang in the Old Pinakothek, and their simple color schemes can be clearly seen to be easily adaptable to color printing. But Weishaupt was not the only printer whose understanding of the importance of religious art for popular consumers influenced his search for a cheap color process. Netto's description of the Liepmann procedure includes the remark that such paintings "meant more than decoration" to their owners.[69]

Engelmann, Weishaupt, and Liepmann were faithful disciples of Senefelder in their attempts to create believable replicas of oil paintings. As the century progressed, the hopes of all these early experimenters were fulfilled by the increasing numbers of firms which began to specialize in chromolithographic production, so that by the late nineteenth century, the products pouring off presses in both the European states and America were indeed the oil painting substitutes that they had dreamed of. Of course, the same function had been filled by glass-paintings for at least a century before lithography became the primary means by which the popular taste for wall-paintings was met. So it is not surprising that one can trace the way in which graphic prints were shaped into a product resembling not only the oil paintings that hung in art galleries and the homes of wealthy families but also the glass-paintings that decorated lower-class *Herrgottswinkels*. For if, as Sebastian Heindl wrote in 1843, the middle classes who, "before the discovery of lithography were reduced to only badly painted glass-paintings or woodcuts, especially devoted to the reproduction of religious subjects," now had "copies of good works by Masters" to enjoy in their homes, it was not to be long before the possibility of owning a fancy oil painting was extended to country residents as well. Josef Hetzenecker of Viechtach began selling these expensive yet increasingly popular household items in the 1870s.[70]

Yet the addition of frames, which were stressed in the Munich address book advertisements placed by firms such as the Kitzinger's that began advertising gold-framed prints in the early 1860s, clearly brought the price up sharply, perhaps out of the reach of lower-class customers. Certainly firms producing popular prints made agreements with framing companies in order to make suitable frames available to these customers. But when expensive framing was beyond the means of the lower-class consumer, clever bordering of the print could be provided to give the effect of a frame.[71] Moreover, the colorfulness and brilliance that characterized glass-paintings even more than unglazed oil paintings was an attractive feature of the new prints. Driendl's chromolithographs were admired by the anonymous author of a notice in the *Bamberger Zeitung* of March 27, 1859, for example, because of their "brightness and . . . splendid color" that, together with their "durability," approximated the qualities of real oil paintings.

As their product grew closer to resembling the glass-paintings so popular with country consumers, lithographers were responding to an increasing demand for the secular themes so popular with middle-class consumers earlier in the century. In the 1870 advertisement of the Artistic Institute for Chromolithographs placed in the Munich address book, for example, the firm announced the availability of "portraits, landscapes, genre and animal pieces," as well as religious prints. A great many religious subjects continued to be produced, as such extant examples as the cult figure of Mary with the Rosary owned by Wüstner and Souls in Purgatory chromolithographs distributed in the Bavarian Forest bear witness. But even the popular doctrinal figures and saints were now often transformed into "Salon-Madonnas, Salon-Saints—a complete heaven full of perfumery." This was because the multiple functions served by religious glass-paintings were gradually diffused into separable categories of paintings that more precisely met the particular need for which they were purchased. Religious paintings could be used to decorate and sanctify both bedroom and living area, of course, but secular themes suitable to the individual character of each room in the home could also be used to embellish it in a way acceptable to the social aspirations of the family—"hunting scenes and still-lifes in the dining room, and wine and tavern scenes and patriotic motifs for the smoking room. In the living room was later placed the large landscape chromo-lithograph" for which the sofa arrangement suggested a wide format.[72]

Our four glass-painting examples can be seen to adapt quite readily to these new specifications. Their protective functions were by the end of the nineteenth century largely superseded by the expansion of insurance coverage, well-organized community preparations for combatting the problems of fire, better medical and veterinary assistance, and an expanding welfare state. The didactic messages that the glass-paintings had communicated were expounded in schools and churches, while growing magazine and newspaper production complemented the literacy that compulsory schooling brought in its train. Secular subjects, such as the very popular mother and child genre scenes, the updated versions of Summer, or the landscape once evoked by the harvesting backdrop to Saint Notburga's sickle-bearing figure, could replace religious expressions of these concepts. Moreover, the family photograph surely replaced the *Totenbild* in many homes by the late nineteenth century. Yet the need for protection remained, at least for that precious jewel of the "new" bourgeois family nest, the child. Brückner suggests that the theme of the Guardian

Angel best typifies the new chromolithographs of the period. Where earlier protective figures such as Mary the Mother or the *Haus Patronen* stood guard over the members of rural households placed in their charge, a beautiful, shining, winged female form hovered lovingly over the healthy growing boys and girls whose presence now adorned the homes of that growing public of all classes whose consumption of wall-paintings had supported the chromolithographic revolution.[73]

Notes

1. I would like to thank Professors H. Stuart Hughes and Robert I. Levy for their advice concerning the preparation of this article.

2. Heinrich Büchner, *Hinterglasmalerei in der Böhmerwaldlandschaft und in Sudbayern: Beiträge zur Geschichte einer alten Hauskunst* (Munich: Neuer Filser, 1936), pp. 88–89.

3. *Ibid.*, p. 91; Raimund Schuster, "Hinterglasbilder und Risse aus dem Bayerischen Wald und anschliessendem Böhmerwald," *Der Storchenturm* 3 (1979), pp. 7–8; *Königlich Baierisches Intelligenzblatt für den Regenkreis* 5 (1819), pp. 125–28. See also Helena Waddy Lepovitz, "The Industrialization of Popular Art in Bavaria," *Past and Present* 99 (May 1983), p. 106.

4. Reinhard Haller, "Volkstümliche Hinterglasbilder in Verlassenschafts-inventaren des 18. Jahrhunderts: Aufgezeigt am Beispiel der Hofmark Bodenmais," *Verhandlungen des Historischen Vereins für Niederbayern* 99 (1973), p. 55.

5. Joseph M. Ritz, "Deutsche religiöse Volkskunst: Zu ihren Forschungsaufgaben: III. Hauskunst. (Der Herrgottswinkel)," *Volk und Volkstum* 3 (1939), p. 257; Reinhard Haller, personal communication.

6. Haller, "Volkstümliche Hinterglasbilder in Verlassenschaftsinventaren des 18. Jahrhunderts," p. 55; Haller, personal communication; Verlassenschaftsinventar aus dem Jahre 1754, Kurfürstliche Hofmark Bodenmais, Archiv Dr. Reinhard Haller, 8372 Zwiesel, Deutschland.

7. Dr. F. Netto, *Das Geheimniss des Oelbilder-Drucks, erfunden vom Maler Liepmann in Berlin* (Quedlinburg and Leipzig: Basse, 1840), p. 5.

8. Robert Redfield, "Art and Icon," in *Anthropology and Art: Readings in Cross-cultural Aesthetics*, ed. Charlotte M. Otten (New York: Natural History Press, 1971), pp. 39–65.

9. *Ibid.*, pp. 47–48.

10. Stuart Clark, "French Historians and Early Modern Popular Culture," *Past and Present* 100 (August 1983), pp. 62–99.

11. Eric Hobsbawm, "Comments," *Review* 1/3–4 (1977–78), p. 162.

12. William J. Bouwsma, "Anxiety and the Formation of Early Modern Culture," in *After the Reformation: Essays in Honor of J. H. Hexter*, ed. Barbara C. Malament (Philadelphia: University of Pennsylvania Press, 1980), pp. 216–17, 228, 230.

13. *Ibid.*, pp. 218, 220, 222.

14. Victor Turner, *The Forest of Symbols: Aspects of Ndembu Ritual* (Ithaca and London: Cornell University Press, 1967), p. 50.

15. *Ibid.*, p. 54. This allows us to include in the model what Turner calls the "operational" meaning of symbols, for that is his term covering action associated with them. See Victor Turner, *Image and Pilgrimage in Christian Culture: Anthropological Perspectives* (New York: Columbia University Press, 1978), p. 146.

16. Victor Turner, "Symbols in African Ritual," *Science* 179 (1973), p. 1102.

17. Michael Phayer, *Sexual Liberation and Religion in 19th century Europe* (London, 1977), p. 21.

18. Natalie Zemon Davis, "Some Tasks and Themes in the Study of Popular Religion," in *The*

Pursuit of Holiness in Late Medieval and Renaissance Religion, ed. Charles Trinkaus and Heiko A. Oberman (Leiden: Brill, 1974), p. 312.

19. Turner, *The Forest of Symbols*, p. 51. See also Turner, *Image and Pilgrimage in Christian Culture*, p. 146, in this context.

20. Clifford Geertz, "Deep Play: Notes on the Balinese Cockfight," *Daedalus* 101 (1972), p. 29.

21. Büchner, *Hinterglasmalerei in der Böhmerwaldlandschaft und in Sudbayern*, p. 93.

22. Haller, "Volkstümliche Hinterglasbilder in Verlassenschafts-inventaren des 18. Jahrhunderts," p. 58.

23. Lenz Kriss-Rettenbeck, *Bilder und Zeichen religiöse Volksglaubens* (Munich: Callwey, 1971), p. 57; Siegfried Seidl, "Der volkstümliche Maler Johann Bapt. Reisbacher sen. in Kollnburg bei Viechtach (Bayer. Wald)," *Bayerisches Jahrbuch für Volkskunde* 81 (1980), p. 30.

24. Wolfgang Brückner, Hanswernfried Muth, Hans-Peter Trenschel, "Hinterglasbilder aus Unterfränkischen Sammlungen," *Mainfränkische Hefte* 79 (1983), p. 189.

25. Eva Hunt, *The Transformation of the Hummingbird: Cultural Roots of a Zinacantecan Mythical Poem* (Ithaca and London: Cornell University Press, 1977), pp. 273–74.

26. Andrew M. Greeley, *The Mary Myth: On the Femininity of God* (New York: Seabury, 1977), p. 13.

27. Manfred Brauneck, *Religiöse Volkskunst: Votivgaben, Andachtsbilder, Hinterglas, Rosenkranz, Amulette* (Cologne: Dumont, 1978), pp. 74–76, quoting Torsten Gebhard, "Die Marianischen Gnadenbilder in Bayern. Beobachtungen zur Chronologie und Typologie," in *Kultur und Volk. Festschrift f. Gustav Gugitz*, ed. L. Schmidt (Vienna, 1954), pp. 93–116.

28. Karl Mindera, *Maria Hilf: Ein Beitrag zur religiösen Volkskunde* (Munich: Don Bosco, 1961), p. 12.

29. *Ibid.*, pp. 8, 12, 23; Josef Rosenegger and Edith Bartl, *Wallfahrten im Bayerischen Oberland*, 2d ed. (Freilassing: Pannonia, 1981), p. 6.

30. Turner, *Image and Pilgrimage in Christian Culture*, p. 146.

31. Wilhelm Theopold, *Das Kind in der Votivmalerei* (Munich: Thiemig, 1981), p. 95; Lenz Kriss-Rettenbeck, *Das Votivbild* (Munich, 1958), illustration 127; and in most books on votive paintings.

32. Brauneck, *Religiöse Volkskunst*, illustration 6.

33. Keith Thomas, "An Anthropology of Religion and Magic, II," *Journal of Interdisciplinary History* 6/1 (1975), p. 101.

34. Hans Medick, "The proto-industrial family economy," in *Industrialization before Industrialization: Rural Industry in the Genesis of Capitalism*, by Peter Kriedte, Hans Medick, and Jürgen Schlumbohm, trans. Beate Schempp (Cambridge: Cambridge University Press, 1981), pp. 61–62; B. H. Röttger, "Volkskunst im Bezirk Bogen," *Die ostbairischen Grenzmarken* 18/4 (1929), p. 104.

35. See Bertram Schaffner, *Father Land: A Study of Authoritarianism in the German Family* (New York: Columbia University Press, 1948), p. 31ff., however, for more modern responses to the question, "A mother, who interferes when a father is punishing his son, is . . . ?" "Germans responded in terms of the threatened injury to the father's status or the effects of a possible interruption of an abstract conception of child-training. Seventy percent of the candidates felt that in one way or another she was transgressing an unwritten law."

36. Anne Hughes, *The Diary of a Farmer's Wife, 1796–1797* (Harmondsworth: Penguin, 1981), especially p. 11.

37. Ingeborg Weber-Kellermann, *Die Familie: Geschichte, Geschichten und Bilder* (Frankfurt am Main: Insel, 1976), p. 44.

38. Georg Schreiber, *Mutter und Kind in der Kultur der Kirche: Studien zur Quellenkunde und Geschichte der Karitas, Sozialhygiene und Bevölkerungspolitik* (Freiburg im Breisgau: Herder, 1918), pp. 121–22.

39. John Knodel and Etienne Van de Walle, "Breast feeding, Fertility and Infant Mortality: An Analysis of some Early German Data," *Population Studies* 21/2 (1967), pp. 119–20, including the quotation from Hugo Bernheim, "Die Intensitäts-Schwankungen der Sterblichkeit in Bayern und

Sachsen und deren Factoren," *Zeitschrift für Hygiene* 4 (1888), p. 577; W. Robert Lee, *Population Growth, Economic Development and Social Change in Bavaria, 1750–1850* (New York: Arno, 1977), pp. 69–70, 73.

40. Knodel and Van de Walle, "Breast feeding, Fertility and Infant Mortality," p. 119, including a map of the differential; Alfred Groth and Martin Hahn, "Die Säuglingsverhältnisse in Bayern," *Zeitschrift des Königlich Bayerischen Statistischen Landesamts* 42 (1910), p. 88.

41. Lee, *Population Growth, Economic Development and Social Change in Bavaria*, p. 63; Bernheim, "Die Intensitäts-Schwankungen der Sterblichkeit in Bayern und Sachsen und deren Factoren," p. 544.

42. Lenz Kriss-Rettenbeck, *Ex Voto: Zeichen, Bild und Abbild im christlichen Votivbrauchtum* (Zurich: Atlantis, 1972), p. 206ff.; Bayerisches Nationalmuseum, K. 41.

43. Kriss-Rettenbeck, *Ex Voto*, p. 206; Lee, *Population Growth, Economic Development and Social Change in Bavaria*, p. 71.

44. Reinhard Haller, personal communication; Christa Pieske, *Das freudige Ereignis und der jungen Kindlein Aufzucht* (Munich: Bruckmann, 1981), p. 53; Ingeborg Weber-Kellermann, *Die Kindheit: Kleidung und Wohnen, Arbeit und Spiel: Eine Kulturgeschichte* (Frankfurt am Main: Insel, 1979), pp. 42–43.

45. Theopold, *Das Kind in der Votivmalerei*, p. 38; Almut Amereller, *Votiv-Bilder: Volkskunst als Dokument menschlicher Hilfsbedürftigkeit, dargestellt am Beispiel der Votiv-Bilder des Klosters Andechs* (Munich: Heinz-Moos, 1965), p. 19.

46. Kriss-Rettenbeck, *Ex Voto*, p. 207.

47. Raimund Schuster, *Risse zu Hinterglas-bildern aus dem 18. und 19. Jahrhundert* (Rosenheim: Rosenheimer, 1978), pp. 20–21; Raimund Schuster, personal communication; Wilhelm Theopold, *Votivmalerei und Medizin: Kulturgeschichte und Heilkunst im Spiegel der Votivmalerei* (Munich: Thiemig, 1978), p. 76.

48. Greeley, *The Mary Myth*, p. 185ff.

49. Staatsarchiv für Oberbayern, AR 1173/30, 1174/31, 1174/35, LRA 131474.

50. Edgar Harvolk, *Votivtafeln aus Bayern und Österreich aus dem Museum für Deutsche Volkskunde* (Berlin: Gebr. Mann, 1977), p. 21; Wilhelm Theopold, *Hab ein kostbar Gut erfleht: Ein Essay über Votivmalerei* (Munich: Thiemig, 1977), pp. 40–41.

51. Klaus Beitl, *Votivbilder: Zeugnisse einer alten Volkskunst* (Munich: Hugendubel, 1982), illustrations 22 and 23; Otto Aubry, *St. Notburga-Buchlein zum 200 jährigen Jubiläum der Wallfahrtskapelle in Weissling* (Pfaffenhofen-Am: Prechter, 1952), pp. 3–5.

52. Aubry, *St. Notburga-Buchlein*, pp. 2, 6; Wolfgang von Pfaundler, *Sankt Notburga, Eine Heilige aus Tirol: Eine Bildgeschichte in drei Teilen* (Vienna, Munich: Herold, 1962), pp. 178–79.

53. Lutz K. Berkner, "The Stem Family and the Developmental Cycle of the Peasant Household: An Eighteenth-Century Austrian Example," *American Historical Review* 77/2 (April 1972), p. 413; Heinz Haushofer, "Ländliche Dienstboten in Altbayern," *Zeitschrift für Agrargeschichte und Agrarsoziologie* 23/1 (April 1975), pp. 48–49.

54. Walter Hartinger, "Zur Bevölkerungs- und Sozialstruktur von Oberpfalz und Niederbayern in Vorindustrieller Zeit," *Zeitschrift für bayerische Landesgeschichte* 39/3 (1976), p. 800; Lee, *Population Growth, Economic Development, and Social Change in Bavaria*, pp. 156–59; Haushofer, "Ländliche Dienstboten in Altbayern," p. 48; Berkner, "The Stem Family and the Developmental Cycle of the Peasant Household," p. 418.

55. Beitl, *Votivbilder*, illustration 22; Aubry, *St. Notburga-Buchlein*, pp. 7ff.

56. Herschel B. Chipp, "Formal and Symbolic Factors in the Art Styles of Primitive Cultures," in *Art and Aesthetics in Primitive Societies*, ed. Carol F. Jopling (New York: Dutton, 1971), p. 165.

57. Theopold, *Votivmalerei und Medizin*, p. 32.

58. Bayerischen Versicherungskammer, *St. Florian: Schutzpatron in Feuersnot* (Munich, 1977), p. 21; Günther Kapfhammer, *St. Leonhard zu ehren* (Rosenheimer, n.d.), p. 33, quoting Romuald Bauerreiss, no reference, 34.

59. Rudolf Zinnhobler, *Der Heilige Wolfgang: Leben, Legende, Kult* (Linz, 1975), pp. 43ff. and illustration 157.

60. See the general argument in Lepovitz, "The Industrialization of Popular Art in Bavaria," pp. 88–122.

61. Dorothy Alexander and Walter L. Strauss, *The German Single-Leaf Woodcut, 1600–1700*, vol. 1 (New York: Abaris, 1977), p. 20; Westphalisches Landesmuseum für Kunst und Kulturgeschichte, *Bilderbogen des 18. und 19. Jahrhunderts* (Münster, 1976), p. 5; Wilhelm Weber, *A History of Lithography* (London, 1964), p. 76; Wolfgang Brückner, *Populäre Druckgraphik Europas: Deutschland* (Munich, 1969), p. 224.

62. Wolfgang Brückner, *Hinterglasmalerei* (Munich and Würzburg, 1976), p. 93.

63. Rudolf Schenda, "Ein französischer Bilderbogenkatalog aus dem Jahre 1860," *Schweizerisches Archiv für Volkskunde* 62/1/2 (1966), p. 52; Dominique Lerch, "Imagerie profane, Imagerie religieuse sous le second Empire, dans le Bas-Rhin: L'imagerie Wentzel de Wissembourg," *Archives de l'Eglise d'Alsace*, new ser., 22 (1975), p. 335; Wolfgang Brückner, *Die Bilderfabrik* (Frankfurt am Main: Historisches Museum, 1973), p. 44.

64. Schende, "Ein französischer Bilderbogenkatalog aus dem Jahre 1860," p. 53; Lerck, "Imagerie profane, Imagerie religieuse sous le second Empire, dans le Bas-Rhin," p. 220; Adolf Spamer, "Weissenburg im Elsass als Bilderbogenstadt," in *Beiträge zur Geistes- und Kulturgeschichte der Oberrheinlande: Franz Schultz zum 60. Geburtstag gewidmet*, ed. Hermann Gumbel (Frankfurt am Main, 1938), p. 230; Christa Pieske, "Katalog der lithographischen Anstalt Eduard Gustav May," *Anzeiger des Germanischen Nationalmuseums* (1967), pp. 134ff.; Gustav Gugitz, *Das kleine Andachtsbild in den Österreichischen Gnadenstätten in Darstellung, Verbreitung und Brauchtum nebst einer Ikonographie* (Vienna: Hollinek, 1950), pp. 109–11, 113.

65. Franz Maria Ferchl, "Uebersicht der einzig bestehenden, vollständigen Incunabeln-Sammlung der Lithographie," *Oberbayersiches Archiv* 17/2 (1856), pp. 144–45; Alois Senefelder, *The Invention of Lithography*, trans. J. W. Muller (New York: Fuchs and Lang, 1911), p. 22.

66. Felix H. Man, *Artists' Lithographs: A World History from Senefelder to the Present Day* (London, 1970), p. 52; Wilhelm Weber, *A History of Lithography* (London, 1964), p. 79.

67. R. Arnim Winkler, *Die Frühzeit der deutschen Lithographie* (Munich: Prestel, 1975), p. 438; Senefelder, *The Invention of Lithography*, p. 89.

68. Heinrich Weishaupt, *Verzeichniss der lithographischen Incunabeln-Sammlung* (Munich, 1884), p. 40; Sebastian Haindl, "Ueber den lithographischen Farbendruck in München," *Kunst- und Gewerbe-Blatt* 29/3 (March 1843), p. 218.

69. The Holy Trinity is in the Staatliche Graphische Sammlung in Munich; Hauptstaatsarchiv, Bavaria, M. Inn 30104 includes Weishaupt's letter of September 15, 1842.

70. Haindl, "Ueber den lithographischen Farbendruck in München," p. 213; Josef Hetzenecker, *Einschreibe-Buch 1867–1884/5*, in the possession of the Grötz family in Viechtach.

71. Christa Pieske, *Bürgerliches Wandbild, 1840–1920: Populäre Druckgraphik aus Deutschland, Frankreich und England* (Göttingen: Goltze, 1975), p. 6.

72. Schuster collection, Zwiesel; Reinhard Haller, personal communication; Adolf Spamer, *Das kleine Andachtsbild vom XIV. bis XX. Jahrhundert* (Munich, 1930), p. 267; Pieske, *Bürgerliches Wandbild*, pp. 7–8.

73. Brückner, *Die Bilderfabrik*, p. 78.

Contributors

Marc Blanchard teaches French and Comparative Literature at the University of California, Davis. He has published widely on the semiotics of literature and culture. His books include *Description, Sign, Self, Desire: Critical Theory in the Work of Semiotics*, *La Révolution et les Mots: Saint-Juste et Cie*, and *In Search of the City: Engels, Baudelaire, Rimbaud*.

Harold Bloom is Sterling Professor of the Humanities at Yale University. His books include *The Anxiety of Influence* and *Agon*. Forthcoming are *Poetics of Influence: New and Selected Criticism*, edited by John Hollander, and *Freud: Transference and Anxiety*.

John Dolis has published on Hawthorne, Shaw, Hegel and Heidegger. The recipient of a fellowship from the National Endowment for the Humanities to Yale University and a Fulbright Professorship in American Literature at the University of Turin, Italy, he is currently teaching English at the University of Kansas. He has just completed a book on Hawthorne and has begun one on Thoreau.

Helena Waddy Lepovitz is completing her dissertation entitled "The Industrialization of Popular Art" at the University of California, San Diego. She has published in *Past and Present* and is currently working on two articles on the European avant-garde and on the fin-de-siècle in collaboration with Dana Rodman Tiffany.

Eugène Nicole, Associate Professor of French at New York University, has just completed a book on the semiotics of proper names in the French novel. Also a Proust scholar, he is currently doing research on the genesis of *The Remembrance of Things Past* in connection with the forthcoming Pléiade edition. His articles on Proust, literary linguistics, and poetics have appeared in *Poétique*, *Etudes Proustiennes*, *Lingua e Stile*, *PTL*, and *Semiotica*.

Dennis Porter is Chairman of the Department of French and Italian at the University of Massachusetts, Amherst. He is the author of *The Pursuit of Crime* (Yale, 1981) and of numerous articles on the nineteenth- and twentieth-century novel and aspects of mass culture. He is currently at work on a comparative study of travel literature.

Mark Poster is Professor of History at the University of California, Irvine. He is the author of *Existential Marxism in Postwar France* and is currently working on a book entitled *Foucault's Historical Materialism*.

Sarah Sanderlin is employed by New York University and has an M. Litt. in Early Irish History from Dublin University (Trinity College). She has contributed articles and reviews in that field. She is currently re-editing the *Annals of Clonmacnois*, editing a Middle English poem, and preparing several articles on late medieval English literature.

Richard Sieburth teaches French and Comparative Literature at New York University. He has published *Instigations: Ezra Pound and Remy de Gourment* (Harvard, 1978) and *Friedrich Holderlin: Hymns and Fragments* (Princeton, 1984).

Paul Smith is Assistant Professor in English at Miami University in Ohio and author of *Pound Revised* as well as of articles and translations published in *SubStance*, *Enclitic*, *Parachute*, *Dalhousie Review*, *Woman's Studies*, and *20th Century Studies*. He is currently working on a study of subjectivity in contemporary radical discourse and on a book about the representation of women in the 1920s cinema.

Mark Taylor is Professor of Religion at Williams College. His books include *Kierkegaard's Pseudonymous Authorship: A Study of Time and the Self*, *Journeys to Selfhood: Hegel and Kierkegaard*, *Religion and the Human Image*, *Deconstructing Theology*, and the forthcoming *Erring: A Postmodern A/Theology*. As general editor of the Florida State University Press series on Kierkegaard and postmodernism, he is preparing a volume with Jacques Derrida and others to be titled *Rewriting Kierkegaard*.